LEROY COLLINS LEON COUNTY PUBLIC LIBRARY

3 1260 00931 6731

DATE DUE

SEP.09.1999		
SEP.25.1998		
OCT.19.1999		
FEB.15.2000		
MAY 06.2000		
MAY 31.2000		
JUL.07.2000		
8/15		

8/99

X

A

by Cliff Jacobson

The Globe Pequot Press

Old Saybrook, Connecticut

The Globe Pequot Press assumes no liability for accidents happening to, or injuries by, readers who engage in the activities described in this book.

Copyright © 1987 by Cliff Jacobson
Copyright © 1998 by The Globe Pequot Press

All rights reserved. No part of this book may be reproduced or transmitted in any form by any means, electronic or mechanical, including photocopying and recording, or by any information storage and retrieval system, except as may be expressly permitted by the 1976 Copyright Act or by the publisher. Requests for permission should be made in writing to The Globe Pequot Press, P.O. Box 833, Old Saybrook, Connecticut 06475.

Cover design: Adam Schwartzman
Illustration credits: Cliff Moen and Mary Ballachino

Library of Congress Cataloging-in-Publication Data
Jacobson, Cliff
    Camping's top secrets: a lexicon of camping tips only the experts know/ by Cliff Jacobson.— 2nd ed.
    Rev. ed. of: Camping secrets, c1987.
    Includes index.
    ISBN 0-7627-0391-1
    1. Camping. 2. Hiking. I. Jacobson, Cliff. Camping secrets. II. Title.
GV191.7.J33   1998   98-8548
796.54—dc21   CIP

Manufactured in the United States of America
Second Edition/First Printing

Contents

LeRoy Collins
Leon County Public Library
300 W. Park Avenue
Tallahassee, FL 32301

796.54 Jac
00931 6731   08-03-99   NEB
Jacobson, Cliff.

Camping's top secrets :
a lexicon of camping

ADB

A

anchor / 1
animals (bears and other beasts) / 1
axe (use and safety) / 8

B

baking / 15
bannock / 17
binoculars / 19
boots / 20
bottles / 26
bugs/Susie bug net / 28

C

camera / 34
canteen / 35
car-top carriers (canoe racks) / 37
canoe and boat rigging tips/make a splash cover / 40
children—tips for camping with kids / 46
clothing / 49
compass / 52
contact cement / 54
cooking and food ideas / 54
cord/cord locks / 69
cozies / 70

D

dental floss / 72
diapers and diaper pins / 72
duct tape / 73

E

ethics in the wilderness / 73

F

fire-making procedures / 77
first aid for the common ailments / 83
flashlights and camp lighting devices / 92

G

GPS (Global Positioning System) / 94

H

hand cream and lip balm / 95
honey—good medicine for wounds / 96
hypothermia / 96

K

knives—selection, sharpening, sheathing / 98
knots and hitches/lashings / 105

L

lightning / 111
lyme disease / 113

M

maps and map tricks / 115
monofilament fishing line / 122

N

Nalgene™ bottle trick / 122
netted bags / 122

P

packs and packing methods / 123
pillow / 126

R

rain gear / 127
ropes/rope tricks / 131

S

saw (folding) / 137
shovel / 137
shower / 137
skis (cross-country) / 138
sleeping bags / 138
sleeping pads/air mattresses/sleeping systems / 144
snow glasses / 146
snowshoes / 147
snow shelters / 147
sleeping on snow / 155
soaps / 156
sponge / 156
stool (camp) / 157
stoves / 157
stuff sacks / 161
survival shelters / 161
survival kit / 164

T

tablecloth / 166
tarps (rainflies) / 167
tents—selection/care/storm-proofing / 179
tent site: how to cope with a bad one / 199
tents: classic tents you can make / 200
towels / 206

U

ultraviolet protection / 207

W

wanigans / 208
water treatment / 209
weather forecasting / 214

Y

yard goods and repair materials / 217

Appendix A:

A glossary of common camping terms / 225

Appendix B:

Sources of recommended products / 236

Index / 240

Dedication

To Biff Kummer, Kurt Warnke and Herb Hill—three crazy guys who love canoeing wild rivers as much as I do. Your wholehearted support and cheery smiles saved the day when we "walked" down Manitoba's Caribou River; when we discovered the "field of dreams" on the South Seal River; and when we nosed our canoes into the icy ocean of Hudson Bay on that windy, "iffy" morning.

Neither rain nor bugs nor a too-tight schedule can ever spoil your day. Every crew should be so lucky as to have friends like you on their next canoe trip.

Credits

I wish to express thanks to the following people for their support and encouragement:

My friend, Dr. Tom Schwinghamer, for his practical tips on wilderness medicine; and to my wife, Sue Harings, who has an endless supply of good ideas. Thanks also to my publisher, Tom Todd, who believes that the American public still values "skills" more than "things." I also wish to thank my friends, Dr. Bill Forgey, Mike Rapatz, Dan Cooke, Bob Dannert and Charlie Wilson for some of the tips in these pages. And, to everyone, everywhere who gives their time and knowledge to the Boy Scout movement. I earned my Eagle badge in 1956 and I continue to cherish the accomplishment.

Acknowledgments

In my book, *Canoeing Wild Rivers* (ICS Books, 1989), I said, "Canoeing the wild rivers of the far north makes one understand why primitive man felt so close to God." I am not a religious man, but I have brushed with death often enough in the bush to appreciate the caring spirits who guide my actions. I have spent nearly a lifetime canoeing remote rivers in northern Canada and neither I, nor anyone in my charge, has ever suffered a serious illness or injury. I believe that I owe much of my "good luck" to a kindly spirit who watches my back and helps me make wise decisions. I often feel the presence of my "river angel," and wish to say thanks.

What! Another Camping Book?

Camping out has changed considerably since the good old days of pine bough beds, bonfires and fresh-cut trail shelters. No longer is it ethical to shape the land to suit our whims. There are just too few wild places and too many of us!

As a result, a whole new style of camping has evolved—one geared to the high-tech lightweight equipment of today. Forty pound canvas tents have been thoughtfully replaced by equally spacious nylon models of one-fourth the weight. Camp stoves have taken over where fires once ruled, and a deluge of new fabrics—polypropylene, polyester pile, orlon acrylics and Gore-Tex, have challenged traditional fibers. Packsacks, hiking boots, rain gear—everything has become lighter, more compact and reliable. Surprisingly good outdoor gear can now be purchased at big city discount stores—testimony to the growing interest in camping out.

Amidst the generally welcome improvements in gear, the one thing that has not changed at all is "knowledge" of the sport. The wise old scoutmaster who could sniff a coming storm and rig a tight camp in a driving rain, has all but been replaced by the well-meaning leader who atones the night in his pick-up camper . . . or more likely, doesn't camp at all. Everyone, it seems, has plenty of gear to cope with the elements, but precious few know how to use it. If misery loves company, you'll find plenty of it in the backcountry. Just watch the campers roll home (or to the nearest motel) at the first sign of rain. The notion that bad weather spells bad times afield is so firmly entrenched in the minds of modern man that it is probably pointless for me to argue "the truth" in the pages of this book. Nonetheless, I shall try.

This book is not intended to take the place of a "sport-specific" text on backpacking, canoeing, family camping or the like. Rather, it details hundreds of ideas and procedures which are never found in traditional camping texts—ideas that will make your next campout safer and more enjoyable. Everything has been alphabetized and indexed for your convenience, and space-consuming anecdotes have been eliminated to make room for the obscure but important things you really need to know.

Some of you may recognize procedures from my books *Canoeing Wild Rivers,* and *Canoeing & Camping, Beyond the Basics.* These are repeated here for the benefit of those who don't canoe. After all, the rules of backcountry comfort are the same whether you travel by foot, ski, canoe or truck camper. Foul weather can make you just as miserable in a state park campground as on a remote canoe trail.

Here's wishing you warm winds, fair weather and bug-free days, and enough good camping skills to cope with the worst of times on the best of terms.

About this New Edition

When I wrote the first edition of *Camping Secrets*, I thought it would never need updating. After all, building a wet weather fire, rigging a storm-proof camp, sharpening a knife, and cooking outdoors is much the same today as decades ago. What has changed, of course, is the equipment. New technology, like the GPS, waterproof/breathable fabrics that are reliable in any weather, synthetic fibers which approach the light weight and warmth of down, etc., allow modern campers to stretch the envelope far beyond what the old timers could have imagined.

My views also continue to change. Each new outdoor experience tests old ways and asks new questions—I am always looking for an easier and faster way to accomplish old tasks. Some recent innovations include the use of fitted "cozies" on cooking pots to shorten cooking times and keep foods hot (see page 70); a lightweight universal handle system that fits any pot or pan; and the wonderful Susie bugnet, designed by my wife, Sue Harings (page 33), under which you can eat, relax and do camp chores in an insect-free environment. There's also the fully screened tundra tarp (page 176), which I developed with the help of Cooke Custom Sewing in Lino Lakes, Minnesota, and some slick new ways to modify and rig rain tarps. You'll find lots of wonderful new tips in *Camping's Top Secrets!*

But the new technology has brought some disappointments: Outdoor clothing and footwear have become more stylish and less adapted to use in the serious outdoors. Tents have become more exotic and difficult to pitch, and less weatherproof than old designs. Have we forsaken old ways that work for fashionable new styles that don't?

I encourage everyone who loves camping to read *Camping and Woodcraft*, by Horace Kephart, which was published in 1917; and *Woodcraft and Camping*, by "Nessmuk" (George Washington Sears) which appeared in 1920. These books are long out-of-print but may still be obtained through inter-library loan. The theme in both is that the old timers were not bungling idiots who slashed and trashed the backcountry. They *knew* it took a long time to build a bough bed or a snug shelter so they devised surprisingly good (and ecological) alternatives. For example, Kephart carried a one-pound mattress tick; Cal Rutstrum—author of *The New Way of the Wilderness* (a *must* read!)—had a down-filled air mattress and a "convertible A-tent." And every woodsman felt that a light tarp was essential for rain—something modern voyageurs are just beginning to admit. If you asked a turn-of-the-century woodsman for advice, he'd be more apt to tell you about the method than the gear. Now, as every modern camper knows, the emphasis is on "things" not "skills."

At a recent seminar, a man wryly suggested that my camping ideas were old hat. "You've just taken the good ideas of Nessmuk, Kephart and Rutstrum and updated 'em with new technology," he said. "Shhh," I replied. "Promise me you won't tell a soul!"

Cliff Jacobson

Anchor

Here's a slick way to make a light, portable anchor for fishing in a canoe. All you need is a basketball net and carabiner (an aluminum link used by mountaineers—available at most camp shops). Tie off the net bottom with cord. Fill the net with rocks then gather the net perimeter and clip it together with the carabiner. Attach a rope to the "biner" and you're set for action.

You can also make an anchor out of the nylon "mesh" bags you buy at camping shops. However, few of these bags are as tough as a basketball net.

Animals

Bears and other beasts

Background: Each year, thousands of campers lose food and equipment to persistent critters. The common advice is to protect foodstuffs by one of these three methods:

1. Store food inside your car.
2. Place food in a "critter-proof" container.
3. Suspend food from a tree limb at least 15 feet off the ground.

Store food inside your car

This is acceptable even in grizzly country providing you take care to seal *all* car windows *tightly*. Bears (especially grizzlies) will insert their claws through the tiniest openings in windows and doors and rip out the glass or metal to get at food. Today's hardtop cars make it relatively easy for a determined bruin to steal food. For this reason, a car trunk is safer than the passenger compartment.

Use a critter-proof container

A plastic or metal ice chest will deter ravaging raccoons and ground squirrels. Squirrels have very sharp teeth and will bore right through a nylon packsack.

A thick-walled, PVC plastic pipe with threaded end caps makes a reliable "food safe" from bears. There are some commercial bear-proof containers which are heavy, bulky and expensive. If you want to know the current technology, check with the managers of national parks like Yellowstone and Glacier, which have a large population of bears.

Hang your food in a tree

Expert campers usually *do not* store their food in trees to protect it from bears. Instead, they seal their food tightly in plastic to eliminate odors, then they remove the food from the immediate camp area. Setting food packs *outside* the campsite perimeter is usually enough to foil hungry bruins and other animals. The rationale for this procedure is based on the fact that bears are creatures of habit—they quickly learn that camps, packs and tin cans contain food. In each campsite there is seldom more than one or two trees with limbs high enough to deter a bruin. Bears aren't stupid; they learn the location of these trees and make daily rounds to secure whatever is suspended from them. When they find something (anything!) hanging from "their" tree, they'll get it down, one way or another. All black bears (even fat old sows) can climb to some degree. And cubs climb like monkeys. If momma can't get your food, the kids will! Polar bears and most grizzlies don't climb.

Recommendation: Double bag (in plastic) all foodstuffs, especially meats. If possible, ask your grocer to vacuum seal smelly foods. Or, buy your own vacuum-sealing machine. Set food packs on low ground (to minimize the travel of odors) well away from the confines of campsites and trails. As an added precaution, separate food packs by 50 feet or more. Do not, as commonly advised, put food packs in trees!

If you're camping in grizzly or polar bear country, locate your kitchen at least 50 yards *downwind* of your tents. Naturally, cooking areas must be scrupulously clean—free of the last "Rice Krispy." Nonetheless, human odor is stronger than most food smells: Don't be surprised if the bear smells you before he smells your food!

Raccoons and squirrels

A plastic or metal ice chest will protect foodstuffs from ravaging raccoons and ground squirrels, but there is no acceptable portable container that will reliably discourage bears. Ground squirrels and raccoons have very sharp teeth and will bore right through a fabric packsack. Best recommendation is to store food in vehicle trunks or on the ground outside campsite areas. Caching food from high trees is a good idea only in infrequented wilderness. Even then it's a waste unless you'll be separated from your food supply for long periods of time.

Bear encounters:

Here's the recommended procedure in the event you meet face to face with . . .

Black bears

Blackies are timid and will ordinarily run away at the first smell of you. Bears don't see very well; what most people interpret as a "charge" is usually nothing more than simple curiosity. Screaming, blowing whistles and other noise-making will usually send a wild bear running, but an experienced camp bear will remain totally oblivious to the racket. Best procedure is to hold your ground, spread your arms wide (so you look bigger), talk authoritatively and back off slowly. *Do not run!*

The danger signs are "woofing" and "clacking." If the bear goes *"woof, woof, woof"* and you hear loud hiccuping sounds with the clacking of teeth, the situation is deteriorating. The bear's mad and unpredictable. If there's a tree handy, climb it now. If you can beat a path to safer ground, go for it. But remember, your safe haven better be close because you can't outrun the bear by far! If you are attacked, fight like mad! Do not play dead with a black bear! Use all your might—and whatever tools (knife, axe, rock, log) you can find—to fend off the bear!

Grizzlies

Grizzlies have been clocked at 45 miles per hour on flat terrain. No way can you outrun one. Again, these are shy animals; they will usually run away from you. Grizzlies are king of the hill in their domain; it's doubtful you can bluff them. I was once charged by three grizzlies on the open tundra of Canada and I can vouch for the effectiveness of this procedure:

1. Talk in a moderate, non-threatening tone to the bear as you slowly back away. *Do not* make eye contact! Let the bear know that you made a mistake and are trying to skeedadle.
2. If the bear runs toward you, interpret this as curiosity, not a charge. Remember, bears don't see very well, and they can't smell you if you're downwind.
3. When the bear is within 50 feet, drop to the ground, *face down, nose in the dirt,* and clasp your hands tightly behind your head. Spread your legs wide so the bear can't turn you over easily. **Note:** Until recently, the recommended method was to assume a tight fetal position, hands behind the head. I did this, and it worked for me. Discouraging bears is not an exact science!

New research by Stephen Herrero, author of *Bear Attacks* (Lyons & Burford, 1985), suggests that the "face down" plan is best. Herrero found that the face is where most serious injury occurs. If the bear bites and claws you, try to remain quiet and passive. If the bear tries to flip you over, do a complete roll and maintain the face down position. You will probably survive the attack.

In case you're wondering, "my" bear came within a dozen feet, checked me out, then high-tailed it over the next hill. "Your" bear will likely do the same.

What if you see a bear who doesn't see you? Simply leave the area, as quickly and as quietly as possible. It's best if you don't advertise your presence.

Polar Bears

Good luck! These are fast on the flats and they can swim 4 or 5 miles per hour for hours on end in ice water. They will, on rare occasions, eat human flesh. They have been

known to stalk humans! Nonetheless, most polar bears will do their best to steer clear of you. It's best you do likewise. You cannot intimidate or outrun these animals. And, in their habitat, there is usually no place to hide. You are at their mercy!

Some final "protective" thoughts

1. Bears don't like large numbers of people. Two people are more likely to be attacked than six. If a bear comes into your camp, huddle together and spread your arms wide, so as to make a large presence. *Do not* throw rocks at the bear, as advised in the Boundary Waters Canoe Area training film, "Leave No Trace—A Wilderness Ethic." I did this once, years ago and the bear nearly had me for dinner. Regrettably, space does not permit details.

2. You are safer to sleep inside a tent than on open ground, especially in grizzly country. Evidently, the big bears mistake a human in a sleeping bag for their natural food.

3. Women who are menstruating may be at greater risk from bear attacks, though there is no clear evidence to support this. Stephen Herrero addresses this topic in detail in his highly acclaimed book, *Bear Attacks*. Bear-wary travelers will want to read it!

4. Pepper spray (sometimes called "bear mace") contains 10 percent oleo capsican—the flaming ingredient in red pepper. If properly used, it will stop nearly all bears all the time. Herrero observed that even a dangerous mother with cubs will run away from the spray more than 80 percent of the time. Herrero *did not* find a single case where spraying a bear with pepper enraged it and made it more aggressive.

   The large, one pound can sprays up to 30 feet; pocket-sized models go half as far and deliver less pepper. Get the *largest* can you can find! A belt holster wuth a fast release is essential. "Bear mace" won't do you any good if it's locked away in your pack or dangling from a belt clip you can't quickly unsnap.

By the way, mace and pepper spray are illegal in Canada, but *Animal Protection Devices* are not! If the cayenne-based product has a picture of a bear on the label and is clearly labeled "for use on animals," it is legal in Canada, though you may have to explain this to some customs officials. "Bear mace" is available at many outdoor stores and western U.S. national park shops. I rely on a one pound can of Counter Assault® (there's a bear on the label!). It's available from *Caldwell Enterprises, 1335 West 11th, Port Angeles, WA 98363, (360) 457–3009.* Pepper Power®, another popular brand, can be obtained from *UDAP Industries, 13160 Yonder Road, Bozeman, MT 59715, (800) 232–7941.*

My wife Susie accidentally triggered a split second burst of Counter Assault® in her mother's kitchen. Her dad was sleeping upstairs. Seconds later he was coughing and his eyes were watering. The home had to be evacuated for two hours! The product works!

Obvious tip: Do not trigger the pepper spray if the wind is blowing in your face!

P.S. "Bear mace" works even better on human attackers than on bears! This said, be aware that pepper spray is not 100 percent reliable. Studies suggest that it may not work against enraged animals or seriously starved ones that are determined to eat your food (or you!). And it may not discourage a drug-enraged human attacker who is bent on destruction.

A final note: Desk-bound environmentalists would have you believe that all wild animals are harmless, while Rambo-survivalists will suggest otherwise. Facts indicate that you are more at risk when crossing a four lane highway than in a face-to-face encounter with a bear. Nonetheless, some critters, like some people, are plainly crazy and quite unpredictable. So beware of the small percentage of bears who don't share your live-and-let-live philosophy. Don't over-react to bear encounters; just follow the recommended guidelines. And be aware that you are much safer in seldom traveled wilderness than in heavily used national parks where bears are used to the sight of people and the taste of their garbage.

Axe

Background: The trend today is against the use of axes in the backcountry. The argument is that they are more often used to deface green trees and injure people than to produce firewood. In truth, it is not the tool that is dangerous, it is the person who wields it. Outdoor experts value a good sharp axe. They know it is much simpler to produce fire after a week long rain if a splitting tool of some sort is available.

What size axe? Old time camping books suggest use of the full-length to three-quarter size axe under the guise these are safer than the short hand axe (hatchet). Hogwash! A properly used hand axe is the safest of all edged tools; it is lighter and more compact than a large axe, and when used in conjunction with a folding saw, it will produce all the camp wood you need with surprisingly little effort.

Here are the rules for safe, efficient use of the hand axe:

1. Saw wood to be split into 12-inch lengths (see section on Saws).
2. Use the hand axe as a *splitting wedge*. Do not chop with it! The folding saw performs all cutting functions.
3. Set the axe head lightly into the end grain of the wood (Figure A-1). One person holds the tool

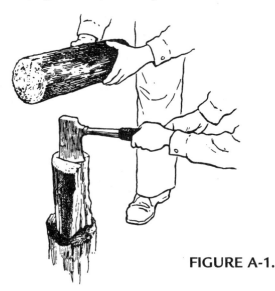

FIGURE A-1.

while a friend pounds it through with a chunk of log. All-steel hand axes are better for this than those with wooden handles as they are less apt to break. When splitting very thick logs (over 6 inches), take multiple splittings off the edges.

Safety concerns: Hold the axe solidly with both hands. Allow the log hammer to do all the work.

4. *To produce kindling:* Kindling splits easiest from the end grain, a process that's made simpler and safer if you use a stick of wood to hold the upright in place (Figure A-2).

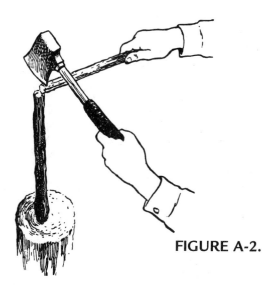

FIGURE A-2.

Sharpening: You'll need a flat mill file and a soft Arkansas or diamond stone. Use special cutting oil, WD-40, or kerosene to lubricate the Arkansas stone and to keep steel particles in suspension. Lube the diamond stone with water.

Procedure

Drive two pegs into the ground about 4 inches apart, or use a peg and log chunk, as illustrated (Figure A-3). File perpendicular to the edge. A file guard (tin can lid with hole punched in center) placed over the rat-tail handle is recommended to prevent cut fingers.

FIGURE A-3.

When a rough working edge has been obtained with the file, switch to the stone(s). For greatest safety, hold the axe blade in the palm of one hand and use a circular motion of the stone. Use plenty of oil and wipe both stone and axe edge frequently to remove filings. If you want a fine, razor-sharp edge, stone the blade perpendicular to the edge as is recommended for sharpening the knife (see *Knives, sharpening,* page 103).

Care of the axe: Axes are forged from relatively soft carbon steel so they must be kept clean, dry, and rust-free. A small amount of gasoline or naphtha (Coleman fuel) will remove pitch and wood stains. Keep axe heads oiled or greased when not in use. Best rust preventative is RIG (Rust Inhibiting Grease) Universal, available from sport and gun shops. Edged tools coated with RIG may be stored for years without rusting.

Blueing the head: Most axes have painted heads to minimize rust. For ease of maintenance and beauty, grind off the paint, buff the head, and apply cold gun blue to the bright metal. The axe head will develop a mildly rust-resistant blue-black sheen, which is instantly restored by dabbing on more blue gun (available at most hardware/sports shops).

Sheathing the axe: Sheaths which come with edged tools are usually too thin and flimsy for practical field service. Make your own as follows:

1. Obtain two pieces of ⅛-inch-thick sole leather from a leather company or your shoemaker.
2. Soak the leather in warm water until it is soft, then cut two matching pieces as shown in Figure A-4.
3. Contact cement (I suggest Weldwood Contact Cement) a ¼-inch-wide strip of leather all around the edge. Then rivet on a buckle or Velcro security strap and contact cement the sheath halves together. Rivet the edges of the sheath for greatest security, or have your shoe repair man sew it for you. Two-piece hammer drive rivets can be purchased from every leather supply store. Hand axes are never carried on the belt so no belt loop is necessary.

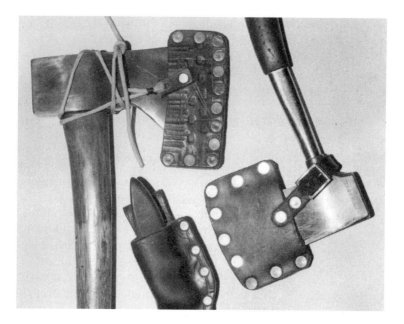

FIGURE A-4. The heavy sole leather sheaths shown here require less than one hour of time to make. Leather and rivets can be purchased by mail from several leather companies. Photo by Mark Lindbeck

Making a permanently bonded head: Camping books traditionally suggest that you occasionally soak the heads of wood-handled axes in water or oil to expand the handle eye so the head won't come loose. The "water treatment" is dreadfully temporary; oil works only marginally better. Here's a permanent solution:

1. Use a very blunt screwdriver or edge of a flat file as a wedge to drive the factory installed wooden wedge tightly into the handle eye. You should be able to sink the factory wedge a full ¼ to ⅓ inch below the level of the steel axe head.
2. Drive a small steel wedge solidly into the heart of the sunken wooden wedge. The steel wedge will not go in all the way but its head must be below the level of the steel axe head.
3. Fill the void (trench) with slow cure or five-minute epoxy. You now have a permanently bonded head which will never come loose.

The case for the big axe!

For serious woodshed splitting, you can make a case for a full-sized axe with a 3½-pound head and 32–36 inch handle—but only if you don't have a splitting maul! Given the excellent saws and splitting mauls we have today, the big axe has pretty much outlived its usefulness.

If you want something lighter and smaller, but with nearly as much power as a full-sized axe, consider the Hudsons Bay three-quarter axe (Figure A-5). And for serious go-light trips in the rain belt, a "hatchet-sized" splitting maul can't be beat. For example, each year in late October, friends and I make an annual trek to the Boundary Waters Canoe Area in our solo canoes. At this late date, we're tempting freeze-up and it's usually raining or snowing.

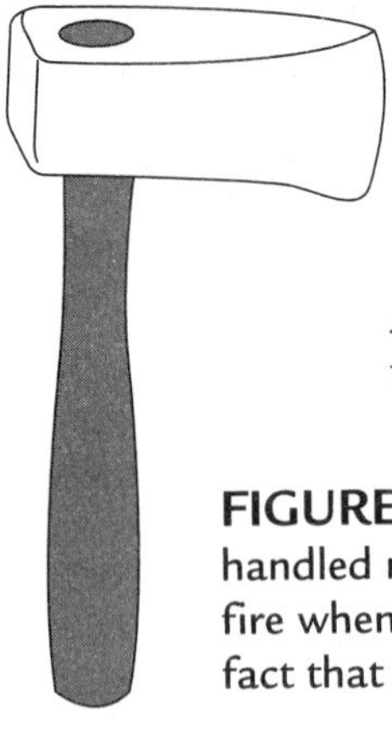

FIGURE A-5. A sharp saw and a powerful, short-handled maul are unbeatable for maintaining a cheery fire when rains come to stay. Equally important is the fact that a maul is much safer than any axe.

But no matter; our 5 pound splitting maul quickly gets to the dry heart of rain-drenched logs.

A large-frame bucksaw is far superior to *any* axe for cutting wood. But, if you lose your saw or break the blade you should know how to use an axe. Here's a safe, efficient way to "chop" dead, downed wood with a full-sized axe.

Procedure

1. Face the downed log and grasp the axe firmly at the pommel of the handle with one hand, and place the other hand just behind the head. Lift the axe to hip level high then start your swing. The handle should slide through your "bit" hand (hand closest to the blade) as the blade comes down.
2. Chop three times on one side, then *reverse hand positions* and chop three times on the other side (Figure A-6). This should release the chip, the width of which should roughly equal the diameter of the log. Note that if you don't change hands when you reverse the blade angle, the bit will fly across your body—a situation which is dangerous and inefficient.

Chop first on one side   and then on the other

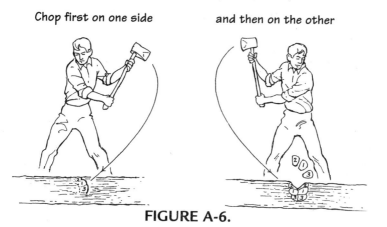

FIGURE A-6.

3. When you've cut halfway through the log, rotate it 180° so the axe blade won't break through to the ground where it can nick and dull.

Splitting

Do not set logs upright on the ground to split them—the axe may bury into the ground and strike a rock. Instead, chop out a level "splitting" platform and split the upright log from the end grain. Some camping texts suggest that for safety's sake, you should split logs from the side not the end. I disagree. If you can't hit the center of an upright log with an axe, you need practice or a more accurate friend!

Always chop limbs from the *underside*, as illustrated in Figure A-7.

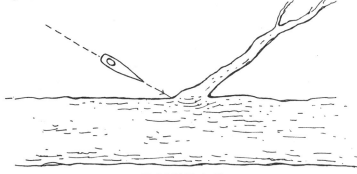

FIGURE A-7.

Where to Store Your Axe

Keep your axe sheathed, and in a pack when it's not being used. Never leave an axe stuck in a log—someone could trip over it! Better to place the axe on its side, blade tucked under a heavy log or rock, as illustrated in Figure A-8.

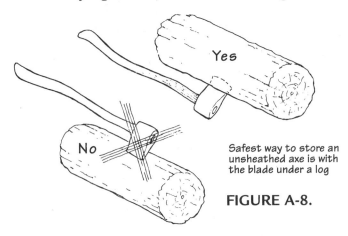

Yes

No

Safest way to store an unsheathed axe is with the blade under a log

FIGURE A-8.

Baking

Background: Reflector ovens and double-pan Dutch ovens are traditional for backcountry baking. However, both require a good hot fire or glowing coals. Modern campers rely almost exclusively on stoves for all their cooking so the oven should reflect this change in style. Here are some *untraditional* baking ideas:

The Jello-mold oven: You'll need a wide ring aluminum Jello mold and a cover of some sort (Figure B-1).

1. Grease the mold and put your batter into the outside ring. Decrease the suggested amount of water by up to 25 percent for faster baking.
2. Bring the stove to its normal operating temperature, then reduce the heat to the lowest possible blue-flame setting. Center the Jello mold over the burner head, top it with a high cover (necessary to allow sufficient room for the bake good to rise) and relax. Cooking times are nearly identical to those suggested in the baking directions.

FIGURE B-1. The Jello mold.

3. Cool the mold by setting it in a shallow pan of water for a few moments, then pop out your entree.

Tips

1. Wind reduces the efficiency of the Jello mold, so use a good wind shield around your stove.
2. Large-burner stoves like the Coleman Peak 1 and

double-burner models may burn the edges of the bake stuff. An electric stove burner shield—available for a few dollars at most supermarkets—will eliminate this problem. Simply place the shield under the Jello mold. The air space between the shield and mold bottom will prevent burning. The large size burner shield will fit large ring Jello molds perfectly.

Other uses of the Jello mold

Your Jello mold may also be used as a steamer to rehydrate dried fruits and vegetables. Here's how:

1. Place dried fruit or beans in the Jello mold ring with about two tablespoons of water.
2. Fill a stainless steel cup with water and set it on the chimney of the mold.
3. Cover the mold and cup and turn the stove to medium-high. Boiling water from the Sierra cup will vaporize and steam your fruit or vegetables to tenderness in a fraction the time of simple soaking. It's the steam that does the trick!

You can also fire the Jello mold with a small (2⅝ ounce) can of Sterno or a small tin can filled with rubbing alcohol. Don't use the large size cans of Sterno; they put out too much heat. To ensure ample draft, use a pair of ½-inch diameter sticks to prop the ring above the Sterno. You must ventilate the high cover with a match stick or the Sterno (or alcohol) will go out.

You may also use the Jello mold as a "pot support" on your stove. To heat a single cup of water on your trail stove, set a water-filled Sierra cup into the Jello mold chimney. A cover will speed heating and save stove fuel.

Triple-pan method of baking on your stove: Use this method if you don't have a Jello mold. You'll need two nesting skillets, a high cover and a half dozen small nails or stones.

1. Evenly scatter some nails or stones onto the surface of the large (bottom) frying pan. *Don't* use stones from a lake shore or river bank; the heat of baking could cause them to explode from the

trapped moisture! Small sticks or tiny balls, rolled from aluminum foil may be used in place of nails or stones.

2. Place your bake stuff into the small frying pan and set it on top of the nails (the two pans must be separated by nails or stones to prevent burning).

3. Cover the unit and place it on your stove. Use the lowest possible blue-flame setting.

Warning: Don't use this method with a thin aluminum skillet on the bottom; you'll burn a hole right through it!

FIGURE B-2.

Bannock

Bannock is bread which is traditionally baked before an open fire in a large straight-sided skillet. Bannock is fast and easy to make—no need for special ovens, aluminum foil, pot covers or baking thermometers. Just grease the skillet, press in the dough, fry lightly for a minute or three, then prop the pan before a cheery blaze as illustrated in Figure B-3. No wondering "when it's done"— the beauty of bannock is that you watch it bake!

Ingredients: In the old days, sourdough was the preferred ingredient; now most campers use commercial mixes which are handier but less tasty. Here's my favorite "made-from-scratch" recipe, along with a scrumptious sourdough version:

Easy Scratch Bannock

Mix 2 cups of flour, 3 rounded teaspoons of baking powder, 1 heaping tablespoon of non-fat dry milk, and 1 teaspoon of salt.

To this, add 5 tablespoons of liquid margarine or canola oil and enough cold water to make a stiff dough. Work the dough just enough to mix the ingredients. If you knead too long, the bannock will be tough.

Now, mix in 2 tablespoons of honey and/or a few spoonfuls of blueberry jam. Sprinkle cinnamon and sugar and/or brown sugar on top. Creatively lace the surface of the bannock with liquid margarine (optional). Bake as directed below. Mmmm, good—and enough calories for a half-day hike!

Baking the bannock: Gently fry the bannock on *very low* heat (on a mix of hot ashes and coals) until it is firm—about 3–5 min-

FIGURE B-3.

utes. If you prop the bannock before the bottom is solid, the dough may slide out of the pan!

Prop the pan at a 45° degree angle to the flames and relax. In about twenty minutes the bread will start turning golden brown. The bannock is done when a wood sliver comes out clean.

Tips: Don't make the batter too thick—½ inch is about right. Use a frying pan with relatively straight sides so the dough won't slide out when propped before the fire; avoid thin aluminum skillets, which may warp, and Teflon-coated ones, which may flake from the heat.

Serious Sourdough Bannock

Put about 2 cups of flour, 1 tablespoon sugar, and one-half cake of yeast into a plastic bucket with a *loose-fitting* lid. Add enough warm water to make a pancake-like batter. Let the mixture sit at room temperature about three days until it "sours."

Making the bannock: Remove about 1 cup of well-stirred

liquid and place it in a mixing bowl. To keep the unused mix from over-souring, replace the batter you take with fresh flour and water.

Add about ¼ teaspoon baking soda (the secret is in the soda—don't add too much!). Mix thoroughly. A chemical change will occur and the mixture will bubble up into a meringue-like fluff. Add a dash of salt, about a tablespoon of sugar to taste (don't add too much!), a little melted shortening and enough flour to make a stiff dough. Make a stiff "working" dough for bread or rolls; thin it out for pancakes. Options are endless.

You can keep sourdough almost forever if you keep diluting it with fresh flour and water. The mix will over-sour (possibly "explode"—or at best, ooze out of your bucket) if you don't "use it and dilute it" on a regular basis. Refrigerating the working mix stops the chemical reaction. Sourdough can be dried and stored and used to start a new mix.

Tips:

1. Don't store sourdough in an aluminum pot: A chemical reaction will occur that will adversely affect the flavor. Stainless steel and stoneware are okay.
2. Butter or margarine has better flavor than cooking oil.
3. The most convenient way to carry sourdough on the trail is to mix half a cup of starter with flour until you get a soft ball. Roll the ball in more flour and store it in a plastic bag half filled with flour. This should keep a week or more.[1]

Binoculars

Binoculars are worth bringing along on wilderness canoe trips. They enable you to quickly locate portage trails and campsites on complex lakes and they are a wonderful tool

---

[1] I am indebted to Scott Power for this useful tip, which I discovered in his delightful book, *Cooking The Sourdough Way* (ICS Books, 1994). When Scott graduated from high school, he and a friend over-wintered in Dr. Bill Forgey's log cabin near Hudson Bay. Scott—a superb wilderness chef—developed a wealth of scrumptious sourdough recipes which you'll want to try.

for checking rapids. A monocular is not good enough; you need "two-eye" depth perception for interpreting river dangers.

Boots

Background: Camping footwear is in revolution. Where, a decade ago, a heavy 4-pound pair of boots with lugged soles were the norm, today's hiker chooses the lightest, most flexible footwear he/she can find. The trend began when we quit thumbing our noses at primitive peoples—Indians and Eskimos—who routinely traveled the most difficult terrain while wearing moccasins, sandals, and no shoes at all. The *coup de grace* was quietly administered when American and British mountaineers were out-footed by sandal-wearing Sherpas who casually carried loads far in excess of those toted by well-heeled climbers. Specialized lightweight running shoes set the trend; featherweight hiking boots logically followed suit.

Which boots are for you? There are boots of all leather, leather and nylon, pure (synthetic) rubber, or leather/rubber combinations, like the L.L. Bean Maine hunting shoe. There's also a diversity of unique winter wear. Here are the differences:

Combination leather / nylon boots are light, supple, comfortable, and most popular. They require almost no break-in. The best models are suitable for the most strenuous off-trail applications, with the exception of rock-climbing or boulder hiking. Unfortunately, most of these "combo" boots cannot be re-soled when they wear out—a factor to consider if you'll subject them to heavy use.

Supple, all-leather boots which can be re-soled (check 'em out, most can't!) are the sturdiest, most reliable, and probably the best buy. All-leather boots will outlast leather/fabric combos by decades.

Gore-Tex liners: Some of the best boots (especially leather/fabric ones) come with liners of breathable, waterproof Gore-Tex. Though Gore-Tex liners perform admirably over the short haul, they may not be reliable in the long run. If the Gore-Tex liner in a fabric foot fails, you're doomed to wet feet—an instant displeasure the moment you walk through dew-moistened grass. Traditional all-leather boots can be made acceptably water resistant by a judicious application of wax or grease, but fabric ones cannot.

Despite convincing advertising, Gore-Tex boots have not proven reliable enough for day-in/day-out use in wet country. And neither has any brand of all-leather boots. If you want truly waterproof footwear, follow the lead of lobster fishermen and Alaskan guides, and select all-rubber boots. For occasional wet weather—stepping in and out of water— the vote goes to the leather/rubber Maine Hunting Shoe offered by L.L. Bean *(L.L. Bean, Inc., Freeport, Maine 04033),* which incidentally comes in women's and children's sizes.

Knee-high Tingley™ rubber overshoes (Figure B-4A) are the choice of many wilderness canoeists who must alternately paddle, portage and wade in cold water. Tingley's are very flexible; they roll to fist size and their soft non-aggressive rubber soles won't slip on wet rocks. These boots are actually better for "rock-hopping" than most wet shoes that are built for the purpose. Lightweight Tingley boots are sold in stores that service construction workers and other outdoor professionals. They are very inexpensive.

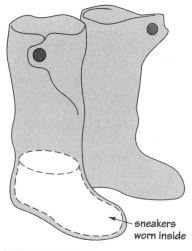

Wear wool socks inside canvas sneakers, and Tingley's over the sneakers, and you're set for an Arctic canoe expedition or a sloppy walk through a swamp. For

FIGURE B-4A. Tingley Rubber Overshoes

transitional cold in near-freezing, sloppy conditions, substitute wool felt snowmobile boot liners for the running shoes. Be sure to wear warm insoles inside (or under) the felt boot liners!

To break in new boots:

1. *The traditional method:* Wear boots an hour or two each day until they fit properly. This painful procedure takes about a week.

2. *The preferred method:* Fill each new boot level full
of lukewarm tap water. Allow the water to soak in
for about fifteen seconds then pour it out. Now put
on the boots (with the correct socks, of course) and
walk them dry—takes about three hours and results in about 50 percent break-in. Wear the boots
around the house for about an hour each day for a
week following the "water treatment" and they'll
be sufficiently broken in for hiking.

Care of boots:

Sponge dirt and grime off leather boots with saddle soap
and water. Work up a good lather then remove the suds
with a damp sponge. Gentle sponging with plain soap and
water is the best way to clean the fabric panels on
leather/fabric boots.

Allow boots to dry thoroughly, away from heat, then
apply an oil-based preservative like "Mink Oil" (with or
without silicone) to oil-tanned leather. Apply a wax-based
compound like "Snow Seal" to chrome-tanned leather.
Waxes do a much better job of waterproofing than oils and
greases. Fortunately, waxes are compatible with oils and
greases, if used sparingly. You can improve the weather resistance of oil-tanned boots considerably by topping the
base oil (which should be well absorbed into the leather
pores) with waxed-based compounds.

To apply boot grease or wax: Melt the preservative
(leave the tin in hot sunlight for a few minutes) and apply
it to lightly warmed leather with your bare hands. Rub in
thoroughly and allow boots to "sun–bathe" until excess
preservative is absorbed. Repeat application of the product
until no excess remains on the leather. A dry rag may be
used to remove excess grease which remains after the second application.

To dry wet boots: Never put boots too near a fire (if you
can't hold your hand near the flame for thirty seconds, it's
too hot for your boots!) or in an oven to dry them. You can
speed the drying of wet boots by stuffing them with fire-
warmed pebbles placed inside socks.

Always carry some boot wax in a 35 mm film can on all
your outings. Apply it frequently in wet weather.

Removing mold from boots and leather gear: Boots and

leather goods stored in damp areas (basements) are sure to mold. Best way to remove mold is with a 25 percent solution of vinegar, household ammonia, or oxygen bleach which will go deep into the pores of the leather and kill fungal hyphae. Thoroughly rinse "mold-treated" leather with clear water and allow it to dry before you apply preservatives. Sunlight kills fungus too, so give your leather goods a frequent airing outdoors.

To improve the warmth of boots: Install warm insoles! Three-eighths to one-half inch thick wool felt "snowmobile boot" insoles (80% wool/20% polyester) are probably the best all-around choice, but closed-cell neoprene or EVA (ethyl-vinyl-acetate) insoles are less compressible and warmer. However, closed-cell foam insoles may be too hot under some conditions. You should have at least two pairs of insoles for your winter boots. Change insoles every day.

Oversocks: If your boots are too small to accept warm insoles, try wearing thick wool socks over them. Of course, the sock bottoms will quickly wear through, but what is left will add considerable warmth. Specialized oversocks are commonly worn over ski boots by cross-country skiers. Oversocks can be purchased at most ski shops.

Winter boots

Military surplus rubber "Mickey Mouse" boots are among the warmest mass-produced boots you can buy. However, they are very uncomfortable for walking. Pure white "bunny" boots—another surplus item—which are made from wool felt, are wonderfully warm and are great for hiking. Wear rubbers or Tingley boots over them in wet snow.

Canadian "Sorels," or fabric top snowmobile boots, are the preferred choice for one day use but become damp after a good workout. The felt liners in these boots *must* be changed daily or frostbite may result.

Mukluks are very roomy knee-high moccasins which are designed for snow. They have a canvas or soft leather outer shell and a wool or synthetic liner which is usually removable. Traditional Native American-style mukluks, like those made in Ely, Minnesota, by Patti Steger Holmberg, are *by far* the warmest, most comfortable and breathtakingly beautiful winter footwear you can buy. World famous Arctic explorer Will Steger swears by Steger mukluks as do most dog-sled racers and snowshoers. There are more than a dozen styles of Steger mukluks and moccasins. *Contact: Steger Mukluks, 125 North Central, Ely, MN 55731, or call (800) MUKLUKS.*

Professional mushers also like Dan Cooke's hand-sewn Cordura nylon mukluks, which are insulated with 200 gram Thinsulate and have a ½-inch thick closed-cell foam insole sewn into the bottom for extra warmth. Styles range from serious "Polar Mukluks," which have been used by top finishers in the Iditarod dog sled race, to the unusual "Telemarker," which is designed to fit over stiff telemark ski boots. Cooke also offers "mukmates"—a double-layer polar fleece mukluk liner that has a non-slip sole on the bottom. *Address: Cooke Custom Sewing, 7290 Stagecoach Trail, Lino Lakes, MN 55014-1988, (651) 784–8777.*

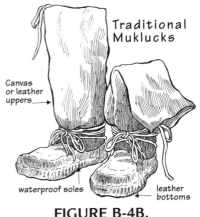

FIGURE B-4B.

Footwraps

The late Gil Phillips, known by the Boy Scouts as the "foam man," perfected the use of low cost open-cell polyurethane foam for clothing, sleeping bags, and footwear. Gil and his Scouts relied on foam "everything" for their sub-zero encampments. Gil's proven system is recommended by the Boy Scouts of America and is described in detail in the *B.S.A. Fieldbook* and *OKPIK Handbook,* which are available from Boy Scout suppliers. Here's the basic plan:

You'll need a loose-fitting canvas or nylon mukluk (military surplus models are sometimes available) and two circular pieces of soft, one-inch thick open-cell polyurethane foam, like that used for pillow padding.

Fold the foam in half, then quarter it, as illustrated in Figure B-5. Pull aside an outside foam layer and put your foot inside with the "single foam layer" at your heel. Wrap the double layers of foam right and left around your foot

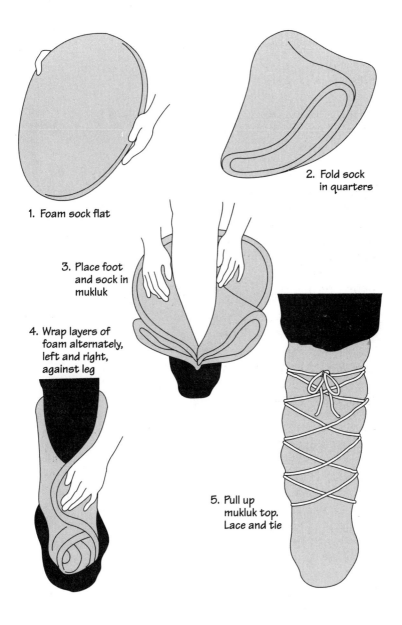

1. Foam sock flat

2. Fold sock in quarters

3. Place foot and sock in mukluk

4. Wrap layers of foam alternately, left and right, against leg

5. Pull up mukluk top. Lace and tie

FIGURE B-5.

and insert both your "foot and foam" into the mukluk. On long trips, dry and re-fold the foam liner every few days. Foam footwraps are incredibly warm, even without socks!

In summary:

1. For relatively dry three-season use, traditional lightweight all-leather boots are best. Combination leather/fabric boots tend to be less waterproof, but lighter, more comfortable and cooler.
2. For mixed (wet/dry) conditions, leather top/rubber bottom shoe-packs like the traditional L.L. Bean Maine Hunting Shoes work best. "Bean Boots" are the most popular boots in the world. Millions of pairs have been sold . . . and re-soled. These are by far the best boots for typical fall hiking and hunting in the wetland states.
3. Tingley™ rubber boots worn over sneakers are good for cold weather canoeing where you have to hop from rock to rock. Tingley's fit more loosely than pull-on rubber boots—they may come off your feet if you wear them in sticky muck.
4. Mickey Mouse boots are best for standing around. Sorels or fabric-topped snowmobile boots work well if liners are changed daily.
5. White bunny boots or felt-lined canvas mukluks (with warm insoles) are the best cold weather combination for dry snow.
6. Foam footwraps really work, even in severe weather. *The Boy Scout Fieldbook* and *OKPIK Handbook* show how to make them.

Bottles

Polyethylene bottles and plastic food tubes

Background: Various sizes and shapes of polyethylene bottles are commonly used by campers to store liquid and semi-liquid foods like jam, peanut butter, pancake syrup and cooking oil. Most of the plastic containers on supermarket shelves are too flimsy for strenuous camping trips; you need thick-walled tough containers for serious backwoods use.

By far, the most reliable containers for foodstuffs are those made by the Nalgene Company. Nalgene® bottles were originally designed for packaging chemicals, so you know they're bomb-proof. Nalgene® containers are positively leak-proof and deservedly expensive. All the best camping stores carry them.

Free bottles (Figure B-6): Hospitals and clinics throw out plastic "sterile water for irrigation" bottles after a single use. These marginally flexible bottles range in size from 0.5 liters to 1.5 liters and have raised ml graduations on one side. Sterile water bottles are deceivingly strong (they won't break if run over by a car!) and won't hold odors like other containers which are made from more porous plastics. They have a gasketed screw-cap on top and a folding plastic "lanyard" ring (to hang them upside down) on the bottom. They come filled with sterile water so they're more germ-free than any container you can buy. The downside is that they have a standard-size opening and thus are thus harder to fill than wide-mouth bottles. I use the smaller sizes for

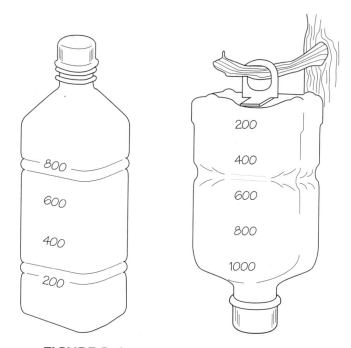

FIGURE B-6. Sterile water for irrigation bottles

water and the larger ones for cooking oil, honey, tomato powder and ground coffee. Ask your doctor to save some of these marvelous plastic bottles for you!

The most reliable supermarket bottle I've found is the "Golden Griddle" pancake syrup container which features a "pop-lock" (the top pops up to open) top. Pop-tops of any type are unreliable. Either replace them with metal screwcaps (available at wine stores) or melt the tops shut in the flame of a gas stove.

Plastic food containers will retain odors after use. A thorough washing won't help much, but a mixture of baking soda and water will. Allow the soda-water solution to remain in the bottles for two weeks and odors will all but disappear.

Plastic food tubes, which are available at camping stores, resemble large toothpaste tubes. They are commonly used to hold jam, peanut butter and other "semi-liquids." The tubes are filled from the open back end and are sealed with a marginally effective plastic clip. To use a food tube, unscrew the cap and squeeze the container (like a toothpaste tube). The idea sounds great but the product is unreliable, especially when the tubes are filled more than two-thirds full. Expert campers don't trust food tubes. I suggest you don't either!

Bugs

Biting Insects: flies, no-see-ums, and ticks
Colors: Dark colors, especially navy blue and black, attract insects. Powder blue, yellow, mist-green, white, and other light colors have a neutral or mild repelling effect. Avoid dark blue rain suits (the most popular color)! Contrary to popular belief, *red* does not repel black flies (almost nothing really repels them!). Red is a fairly neutral color which neither repels nor attracts insects.

Know Your Enemies!
Mosquitoes
They like to bite at dawn and dusk and just before or after a rain. They seem to like navy blue colors more than other insects. Air-Force-blue wool pants and shirts are an

abomination in the woods and are nearly impossible to wear on buggy days. Mosquitoes are mild-mannered compared to flies. Most repellents will keep them away.

Horse flies and deer flies

Horse flies and deer flies are much larger than house flies. They're most active at mid-day when the sun is up. They zoom in fast and take a quick bite which may become infected if you don't clean it fast. Flies can bite through thin "liner" socks but not through thick wool ones.

Black flies

In the northern states and Canada, black flies, which are about the size of rice grains, are the most dreaded pests. They're most active in the calm of dawn and dusk and they breed in fast water—a reason why canoeists don't like to camp by rapids and falls. Big winds and temperatures below 40° degrees Fahrenheit usually keep them away. Black flies have tiny mouths so you may not feel their bite— but they leave a bloody wound which is easily infected and may swell to golf ball size. The good news is that the worst-biting species hatch in spring and only have one generation. Adults live six to eight weeks. Most black flies are gone by late June in the northern states and southern Canada. In the high Arctic they hang around till the first fall frost.

Black flies prefer the constricted areas around wrists, ankles, behind the ear, etc., and they hone in on eyes, ears and nostrils. Only the most powerful—nearly pure DEET— repellents will discourage them—and then, not much. Closely woven clothing, neck-to-toe long-johns, head nets, bug jackets, and full "body armor"—like the Susie bug net, described on page 33—are the best way to keep them at bay. Tuck your trousers into your boots or "blouse" them over the top with military blousing bands or elastic cords. Velcro tabs on shirt cuffs will seal your armor completely. If you don't want to get bitten in black fly country, stay home! Nothing else really works.

Biting Midges (No-see-ums)

They're called "no-see-ums" because they're so tiny they can fly through the holes in conventional mosquito netting. Their bite feels like the jab of a sharp needle. The pain goes away fast but the wound itches for some time. The tiny holes in "no-see-um" netting are hard to see through and they restrict ventilation. Tents that have no-see-um nets become intolerably hot on bright sunny days—when no-see-ums are about. Standard wide-mesh mosquito netting will keep no-see-ums at bay if you spray the net with repellent.

Ticks

Watch out for the Ixodes or "deer" ticks which carry Lyme disease (see Lyme Disease, page 113), and the lone star tick which is the host for Rocky Mountain spotted fever.

Removing an embedded tick:

Ticks must be on your body for a long time in order to bite. If you remove them within six hours, you're probably safe. A vigorous shower will remove most ticks before they dig in.

Don't pour gasoline, alcohol, or other chemicals over an embedded tick, and don't cover one with Vaseline or heat one with a match or cigarette: This could cause the tick to disgorge the contents of its stomach into you!

Do carefully scoop under the tick's body and slowly pull it from your skin. A blunt tweezer works okay if you're careful, but the new Sawyer Tick Plier™ (Figure B-7) is foolproof. Dr. Bill Forgey, author of *Wilderness Medicine,* recommends the Sawyer Extractor™ (it looks like a sy-

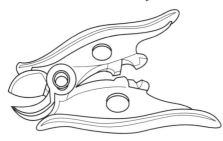

Sawyer Tick Plier™

FIGURE B-7.

ringe, but produces a strong vacuum) to draw out tick saliva and other venoms. *Sawyer, Inc, (800) 940–4464.*

Finally, wash the affected area with soap and water and apply an antiseptic and band-aid.

Your best hope is bug dope!

The most effective repellents contain DEET—a chemical that contains N,N-diethyl-m-toluamide. Generally, the more DEET a repellent has, the longer it works. However, too much DEET may burn sensitive skin and dissolve plastics—eye glasses, Swiss Army knife handles and plastic-coated fabrics. Once, a bottle of DEET leaked through a friend's trouser pocket. The repellent dissolved a huge swatch of his polypropylene underwear in a most embarrassing place!

No one knows for sure how much DEET is needed to keep bugs away. Everyone's body chemistry is different. However, my own experience in the Canadian bush suggests that 25 percent DEET, *in a mixture with other ingredients,* will keep away most insects. The remainder of the repellent should be a soothing lotion or alcohol. Lotion is kinder to your skin and it evaporates more slowly than alcohol, so the repellent lasts much longer. Save pure DEET as a last resort for Arctic rivers where black flies number in the billions and the lesser repellents you've tried don't work.

Caution: Children should *never* use pure DEET—it will burn their sensitive skin!

Build a Skin-Barrier with Sunblock

Kurt Avery, president of Sawyer Products, Inc., suggests you rub sunblock deep into your skin, wait ten minutes, then apply the repellent. The sun block keeps your body from absorbing too much of the repellent. If possible, select one of the new "bonding base" sunblocks which penetrate deep into your skin. "Film base" sunblocks—like the kind available everywhere—cover just the surface of your skin.

Headnets and bug jackets

Headnets are essential for early season trips in the northern states and Canada. Non-military styles that don't have a hoop around the face are best because they roll to fist size and fit in your pocket. You can make a headnet in a few minutes. Just sew up a wide rectangle of mosquito net, large enough to fit over your head and wide-brimmed hat. Make the net long enough to drape lazily on your shoulders. *Don't* sew an elastic band into the hem. Spray the hem with repellent and even black flies will be confused. Spray the entire net if no-see-ums are about. Headnets are best constructed of dark-colored standard mesh mosquito net, both for good visibility and ventilation. It's difficult to see through milk-colored no-see-um net. If you can't find a dark-colored headnet, buy a light-colored one and darken the eye panel with black magic marker or spray paint.

Bug jackets: The "Shoe-Bug" jacket—available at most bait and tackle shops—offers state-of-the-art protection against all manner of biting insects. The jacket consists of a net fabric which you soak with pure DEET (which is allowed to dry). The repellent discourages insects and the cool mesh keeps them away from your body. It's the most effective anti-bug system available. There are also some non-DEET impregnated jackets which are made from tightly woven cotton or no-see-um netting. These work as well as the "Shoe-Bug" models but are much hotter to wear.

Some final tips

1. Bugs will avoid your face if you saturate a cowboy neckerchief with repellent and tie it loosely around your neck. Spray the underside of your hat brim too!
2. Ben Gay™ and Skin-So-Soft™ are reasonably good emergency insect repellents, though they don't last long. Neither product works well against black flies.
3. Some of the most effective first-aid products for bug bites contain aloe, a plant-derived ingredient that has been around for thousands of years. Aloe soothes inflammation, inhibits swelling and keeps skin moist. It also soothes burns and kills bacteria and fungi. To be effective, aloe should make up at least 80 percent of the product's formula.
4. If you have very sensitive skin and are concerned

about using a DEET-based repellent, try a product that has citronella as an active ingredient. Citronella will repel "gentle insects" like mosquitoes, but it's not tough enough for black flies.

5. Liquid or cream repellents are much more potent (a better buy) than sprays.
6. Household ammonia and water will cut the sting of mosquito bites. For bee, wasp, and hornet stings, apply a wet salt pack and allow it to dry. The salt will draw the pain away quickly.

Susie bug net

First, you apply DEET to all exposed skin. As more insects gather, you add a headnet, then a DEET-impregnated bug jacket. Ultimately, you rant and swear, then in disgust retire to your insect-proof tent. Meanwhile, friends nearby enjoy a bug-free after-dinner brandy and a glorious sunset inside their "Susie bug net"—a personal-sized bug armor designed by my wife, Sue Harings:

Materials needed: A piece of mosquito netting 60–72 inches wide and 8 feet long, plus enough ⅛-inch diameter shock cord to span the hem. Don't use no-see-um net: It's not strong enough and you can't see through it.

Procedure: Fold the netting lengthwise to produce a rectangular sheet which measures about 8 feet by 6 feet. Sew up the two long sides, hem the bottom and install the bungee cord in the hem. The finished net will weigh less than a pound and compress to football size.

FIGURE B-8. Susie Bug Net

Here are some uses for your Susie bug net:

1. Eat inside it; there's room for two.
2. Sleep out under the stars. The net covers you from head to toe. Cinch the bungee cord

tightly around the foot of your sleeping bag.

3. Use as a "porta-potty" when bugs are bad.
4. Bathe in it! Amble to the beach as a ghostly apparition in your Susie bug net. Wear your life vest and you'll float confidently inside your bug armor.
5. Lay the net over breads, cheese and lunch meats to keep flies away.
6. Rig a tripod inside and you have a tiny bug-proof teepee in which to wash dishes, cook and make repairs.

Roll and stuff your Susie bug net under a pack flap so it will be available at meals and river rest stops.

Note: The Susie bug net is now being manufactured by *Cooke Custom Sewing, Inc., 7290 Stagecoach Trail, Lino Lakes, MN 55014-1988. Phone (651) 784–8777, fax 784–4158.*

Camera

Waterproof protection: The most waterproof camera container yet devised is the World War II amphibious assault gas mask bag—a no-longer-available surplus item. The original gas mask bags were constructed of heavy rubber covered with 10 ounce canvas duck. Modern commercial copies which are made of heavy vinyl aren't as rugged or waterproof.

Cascade Designs (originator of the Therm-a-Rest® sleeping pad) SEALLINE™ brand "dry bags" are very reliable if you take time to seal them right and don't over-fill them. I rely on a clear vinyl "See Bag" to protect my GPS from the elements. The inexpensive "See Bag" was reliable, even when my canoe capsized in a chilly rapid on the Burnside River, N.W.T, Canada. *Cascade Designs, Inc., (800) 531–9531.*

Thirty- and fifty-caliber steel ammunition boxes are still commonly used by boaters to protect cameras from water. Check the rubber seals on these boxes; they frequently *are not* watertight! The seals are easy to replace, if you can find them!

The plastic Pelican box is by far the most reliable (and expensive!) waterproof container you can buy. Pelican boxes come in an array of shapes, sizes and colors. Every good camping store has them.

If you're shooting a number of rolls of film and want to keep the order straight, try this: Write the number of each roll (1, 2, 3 etc.) on a slip of paper when you load the film into the camera. Photograph the number on the paper. This will identify the order in which the rolls were shot.

Canteen

Only cheechakos and bona fide cowboys use traditional canteens these days. Expert campers rely on poly bottles to carry thirst quenchers. Plastic bottles are cheaper, lighter and easier to pack than metal canteens.

Some backpackers and paddlers prefer the convenience of a self-contained hydration system, like the popular Camelbak®, which you wear on your back (it has pack straps). Water is held inside a plastic bladder that is protected by a tough nylon cover. Water is delivered via a plastic tube that has a sophisticated no-leak mouth-piece. Hydration systems are great for people on the go, especially those who must have their hands free.

Plastic baby bottles make good canteens, and they fit nicely into the side pockets of small hiking packs. Five hundred ml and 1000 ml "Sterile Water For Irrigation" bottles (see *Bottles*) make the best canteens of all!

Fill your canteen four-fifths full of water and freeze it to assure a supply of cold water during the next day's hike.

A glass vacuum bottle, sans cup, makes a surprisingly good canteen. Modern vacuum bottles are quite strong and lightweight; they assure a cold (or hot) drink throughout the day.

The traditional bota, or wine bladder, remains popular with skiers. It also makes a fine, easy-to-carry canteen for

Web handle
for hanging

↖ Sew nylon webbing all
around wine bladder

FIGURE C-1.

summer hiking.

Here's a good way to warm up your sleeping bag on a cold night: Pour boiling water into your canteen, roll the canteen in a towel or shirt, and take this "hot water bottle" to bed.

Do not put carbonated beverages or alcohol into an aluminum canteen. These products will react with the aluminum!

The tough mylar bag (bladder), which lines wine boxes, makes a great "giant" canteen. Sew tough nylon around the bladder so you can hang the unit from a tree and dispense liquid through the efficient rubber faucet-like spout. *Note:* The rubber spouts are easy to remove if you grasp the lip with a thumbnail and pull. No amount of twisting and forcing will break it loose.

Here's how to make a collapsible nylon water bucket:

1. Cut a 3-foot diameter circle of waterproof nylon (taffeta or rip-stop).
2. Gather the circular edge of the material to form a bag, and sew the pleated mouth, leaving an approximate 3-inch opening.
3. Sew seam binding all around the mouth of the bag. Sew a handle of nylon webbing across the mouth.

This water bag (which I call a "spider") is very compact. It will stand freely if you don't over-fill it. *Tip:* Attach a stout 10-foot rope to the handle of the spider so you can toss it into the water from a river bank. Water will stay inside when you drag the spider up the bank (Figure C-1A).

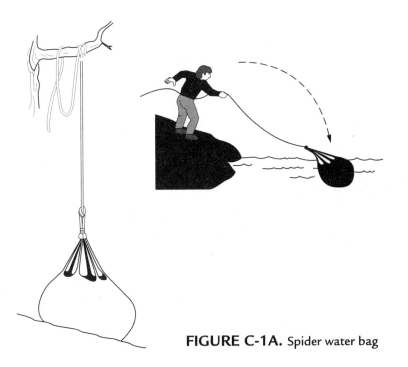

FIGURE C-1A. Spider water bag

Car-Top Carriers (canoe racks)

Canoeists still mourn the passing of rain-gutters, which accepted all manners of clamp-on devices. No current system is as secure as racks that bolt directly to the drip eaves of the car. My '86 Chevy van and my wife's '80 Saab both have rain gutters—and like most canoeists, we plan to keep these cars forever. I'm convinced that the world's first closed cars had rain gutters because they were designed by canoeists for canoeists!

Regrettably, the days of the wonderful generic racks that attach to a car's drip eaves are over. With the exception of full-sized vans and a few SUVs, all of today's vehicles have airplane-style doors which require specially fitted brackets. Thule and Yakima lead the way in gutterless designs and offer racks to fit nearly every car model.

Caution: The load brackets which come with gutterless carriers are built to fit the roof-lines of specific vehicles. Do not jury-rig them to fit cars for which they are not designed!

Even if you don't plan to buy a second canoe, you may need to shuttle a friend's, so be sure to order double-length (80 inches) cross-bars—the factory standard 48-inch carrier is too short to carry paired canoes. Be sure your car top carrier has locking bars to prevent theft. Even then, many paddlers prefer to remove their expensive racks and store them inside their cars when they're on the river.

Never set canoes on hard, unpadded carriers—the gunnels are sure to be damaged. Here's how to protect your canoe, your car and your peace-of-mind:

1. Sew or duct-tape scrap carpeting around the cross-bars. This ancient low-tech method is still the best way to protect fine woodwork. Most "show" canoes ride on old-fashioned carpeted racks. Carpeting tells the canoe world you care about your canoe!

2. Yakima, Quick 'n Easy, and a few other companies use tubular aluminum conduit (Yakima covers theirs with plastic) cross-bars. Some canoeists armor the conduit with rubber heater hose—it slides on easily if you lubricate the rubber with brake fluid.

3. You can bolt L-shaped plastic "gunnel brackets" (an optional accessory) to the cross-bars. The brackets provide a wide, protective bearing surface for the canoe's gunnels and prevent the craft from shifting in wind—a safety advantage. If your canoe has wooden rails, you may want to glue closed-cell foam or scrap carpeting to the hard plastic faces of the brackets.

Watch out that you don't hit your head on the ends of oversize canoe racks when you get in and out of your car. To "cushion the occasional blow," some canoeists replace the plastic caps on the ends of the crossbars with thick rubber "furniture tips." Others tie short pieces of brightly colored surveying ribbon to the bar ends so they'll be more visible in dim light. One friend has impaled tennis balls on the ends of his canoe rack; another has tied small bells to the cross-bars. The bells jingle in the slightest breeze—a reminder to "be careful."

Tie-down Procedures

Separately tie down each canoe you carry! Do it right and the canoe(s) will remain rock-solid even at illegal speeds. Here are the rules for safe travel:

1. Run *two* strong ropes or straps over the belly of the canoe and secure each to its respective cross-bar. Do not string one long rope from cross-bar to cross-bar—it could loosen at highway speeds and the canoe could come off the car!
2. Attach *two* lines to the bow and stern of *each* canoe you carry. Secure each line *separately* to an eye-bolt set in the car's bumper. Or, use plastic-encased (wrap 'em with tape) S-hooks if you don't want to drill holes in bumpers. Locate S-hooks in notches so they won't slide along the bumper.
3. Don't use rubber tie-downs or elastic shock-cords to secure canoes to cars! There should be a law against using these stretchy devices!

Straps or ropes? Many paddlers prefer heavy-duty straps to ropes for car-topping canoes. Straps are fast and easy to adjust and they stay tight in any weather. But, straps may be stolen if you leave them on the car-top carrier while you're off paddling. Ropes are a low theft item and can be left tied to the roof rack for a quick tie-down and get away after the trip. *Caution:* Don't toss straps over the roof of your vehicle when you load your canoe—the metal buckles may take a chunk out of the canoe or car! Straps are best passed to a friend or—if they're long enough—"walked" around the car. Ropes are safe to throw. Straps are more reliable than ropes only if you don't know how to tie the right knots! Most serious canoeists I know prefer ropes to straps. Exceptions: when carrying a single canoe on a small, narrow car, or a bunch of canoes on a trailer.

Concerns for Carrying Fragile and Paired Canoes

You can break the back of a fragile canoe if you secure its ends too tightly. For this reason, many canoeists prefer to tie only the bow. Racers *never* tie down the tail of their ultra-light canoes!

Whenever you carry two canoes side-by-side on an overhead rack, always pad the inside of one of the canoes so the finish won't be galled if the two crafts shift sideways and touch.

Finally, if you carry two canoes on a double rack, place the lightest and most fragile canoe on the passenger side of the carrier. This will allow the sturdier and more rigidly tied craft on the driver's side to take the abuse of high winds generated by passing trucks.

Canoe And Boat Rigging Tips

(See my books, *Canoeing Wild Rivers* and *Canoeing & Camping, Beyond The Basics*, for a wealth of detailed canoeing and canoe rigging tips.)

Compass: For ease in navigating complex lakes, secure a wrist compass around the aft canoe thwart. This will enable you to simultaneously paddle and follow a plotted course.

Custom improvements: Thread loops of fabric shock-cord through holes drilled in the canoe's thwarts and deck plates. End lines (painters) stored under the shock-cord loops will stay put in a capsize and on portages. Oddities may be secured under the thwart cords.

Fiberglass and Royalex canoes should have lining holes or rings installed at cutwater, not high on the deck as is the common practice. See Figure C-2.

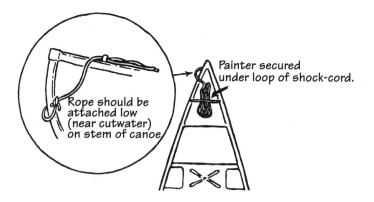

FIGURE C-2. End lines, shocks cords, and lining holes.

A two-quart plastic water pitcher tied to a canoe thwart makes a handy bailer and is useful for mixing powdered drinks in camp.

Canoe Pockets You Can Portage

Where to store small items like eyeglasses, suntan lotion, and repellent is always a problem on canoe trips. Of course, you can store these small items in pack sacks, but getting to them is a hassle. So, why not install pockets in your canoe?

An early pioneer of canoe pockets was Verlen Kruger, whose 7,000-mile canoe trip from Montreal to the Bering Sea made canoeing history in 1971. Verlen simply attached plastic bicycle baskets to his canoe thwarts. The baskets provided a convenient—though not capsize-proof—place to store small items.

Thwart bags are the modern alternative to bicycle baskets. Most clip or Velcro to a canoe thwart. Unfortunately, few thwart bag makers have given much thought as to what to do with these bags when it's time to portage.

GRADE VI, Inc. was among the first to address the problem of portaging thwart bags. They attached plastic buckles to their "fanny" packs so they could be strapped to a canoe thwart. You can turn any small pack into a "portage-able" thwart bag by sewing on buckles or Velcro tabs.

You can make your own "canoe pockets" or buy commercial models from: *Cooke Custom Sewing, 7290 Stagecoach Trail, Lino Lakes, MN 55014-1988; Granite Gear, Inc., P.O. Box 278, Two Harbors, MN 55616; GRADE VI, P.O. Box 8, Urbana, IL 61803.*

Varnish caned canoe seats before use. The varnish will eliminate sag and considerably prolong the life of the cane.

Drill holes in canoe and boat seats so they won't pool water when it rains.

Glue (contact cement) EVA (ethyl-vinyl-acetate) foam to the surface of canoe and boat seats to increase comfort and warmth. The foam will also add flotation to the craft.

The only emergency repair kit you really need for a canoe or boat is a roll of 2-inch wide silver duct tape. Duct tape sticks to anything. Use it for emergency repairs on all your camping gear.

Paint decks on aluminum canoes flat black to reduce glare.

For kneeling comfort when paddling, glue foam knee pads into your canoe. Best foam for this purpose is EVA (ethyl-vinyl-acetate), available at camping stores. Weldwood contact cement is the most reliable adhesive and will work on any surface.

Tying canoes on cars: Best hitch for this is the *power-cinch.* See *Knots,* page 105.

Yoke: A yoke is essential if you plan to carry your canoe alone for even short distances. A curved hardwood yoke, with overstuffed foam-filled shoulder pads, is the most comfortable combination. Commercial yokes cost upwards of $40.00 and are seldom very good. You can make a much better yoke than you can buy.

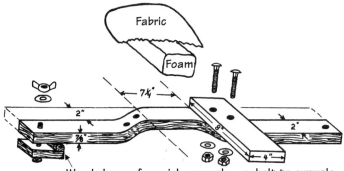

Wood clamps for quick removal. . . or bolt to gunwale

FIGURE C-3. A homemade yoke with drainage holes will take the sting out of a long carry.

Make your yoke from white ash (preferred) and finish to the dimensions illustrated. The completed yoke should have some flex which will take the sting out of a rigorous carry. Use open-cell polyurethane foam (pillow padding) for the shoulder pads. Naugahyde or other heavy plastic upholstery material is the best covering fabric. Attach the yoke to the balance point of the canoe (some prefer a slightly tail-heavy arrangement) with bolts or wood clamps. The clamp and wing nut set-up is best if you plan to carry a third person in the canoe. You can easily remove the yoke to provide more room for your passenger.

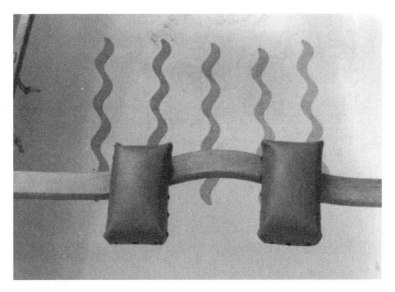

FIGURE C-4. A curved hardwood yoke with overstuffed foam-filled shoulder pads is the most comfortable device for carrying a canoe.

Make a Belly Cover for Your Canoe

If you've ever paddled a canoe in icy wind-whipped rain, fought the waves of a big lake, or edged down huge rapids, you know the value of a canoe cover. My book, *Canoeing Wild Rivers,* has detailed plans for making the "Jacobson 3-piece" tandem cover, the "Jacobson 2-piece" solo cover, and the "Split-Center Arctic" model designed by Bob O'Hara. Commercial versions of these covers are available from *Cooke Custom Sewing, 7290 Stagecoach Trail, Lino Lakes, MN 55014-1988, (651) 784–8777.* Dan Cooke supplies a no-shrink Mylar template which ensures a perfect fit on any canoe.

You don't need a full splash cover unless you're a white-water fanatic or are canoeing the Canadian north. The one piece "expandable belly" described below provides enough protection for all but the most severe conditions. If you can sew a straight stitch you can make a "belly cover" in about three hours.

The belly section described below weighs about a pound

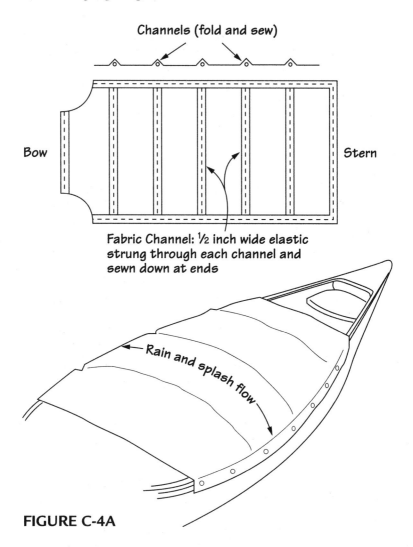

Channels (fold and sew)

Bow

Stern

Fabric Channel: ½ inch wide elastic strung through each channel and sewn down at ends

Rain and splash flow

FIGURE C-4A

and stuffs to football size. You can use it as a small sail or tablecloth, or as a rain cover for packs and firewood.

Materials:

1. Pattern: None! The canoe is your pattern.
2. Snaps: Twenty-four brass snaps. Check 'em with a magnet to be sure they're not plated steel.

3. Waterproof nylon: 2.5 ounces per square yard is strong enough for friendly waterways; 4–6 ounce stuff is best for the Arctic barrens.
4. One-inch wide seam tape or nylon webbing—about 20 feet.
5. Extras: 2-inch wide Velcro, 1-inch wide pajama elastic.

Procedure:

1. Pop rivet snaps through the hull, 2 inches below the rails, 8 inches apart. Begin the snap line at the rear edge of the front seat and end it at the back thwart. Use an aluminum back-up washer behind each rivet. You'll need about twelve snaps for each side of the canoe.
2. Cut a 60-inch wide piece of fabric that reaches from the front edge of the bow seat to the rear thwart. Hem all sides then sew seam tape to the inside hem. Next, fold over and sew the "water deflector channels," illustrated in Figure C-4A. Thread pajama elastic through the channels and rear hem. Tighten the elastic slightly, then sew down the ends.
3. Set snaps through the hem to match those on the canoe (slide #2). Nylon stretches when wet and shrinks when dry, so don't pull the material too tightly!

You can modify the belly to accept a passenger by installing a quick-release skirt in the center.

Gel-coat repair and maintenance tricks

It's doubtful that you'll ever have to repair major damage to a well-built fiberglass or Kevlar canoe or boat. However, you may need to mend chipped gel coat on the bottom—easy, if you *don't* follow the manufacturer's directions. The recommended procedure calls for filling the break with color-matched liquid gel coat, then sanding and polishing to blend the repair.

Nothing could be more difficult or frustrating. Catalyzed liquid gel coat is runny; you must prop the boat at an awkward angle to "level the flow," then build a well of masking tape to contain the resin. Then you have to nurse the slowly hardening liquid with a flat stick to keep it from overflowing the well.

Here's an easier way:

1. Remove the shards of damaged gel coat.
2. Mask the work area, then catalyze polyester or gray auto-body putty (use extra MEKP to produce a "hot" mix) and work it into the break to overflowing. The putty is thick and won't run so there's no need to prop the canoe or build a tape well. *Caution:* MEKP is toxic and can cause blindness. Wear safety goggles and rubber gloves! And mix everything in a well-ventilated area.
3. When the putty is firm (about five minutes), slice off the excess with your jack knife. Allow the remainder to cure for another half hour then sand it level with progressive grits of sandpaper. Finish to silky smoothness with wet 400-grit sandpaper.
4. Spray paint the patch with matching auto acrylic. When the paint has dried, buff it out with a mixture of paste wax and pumice. Or, use a commercial fiberglass boat wax (it contains pumice) which you can get at any marina.

Your patch is now complete. The whole process takes about an hour.

To Keep Gel Coat Looking like New

Occasionally use a commercial hull cleaner (I've had good results with *Star brite*) to remove scum lines and stains from fiberglass and Kevlar gel-coat. Paste wax will brighten and protect the hull. Canoe retailers often wipe on a coat of Lemon Pledge™ before they display their fiberglass canoes and boats in the store.

Children (Tips for camping with kids)

Rain gear

Best rain gear for young children is an inexpensive plastic poncho, a coated nylon windbreaker, and a sou'wester style hat. Trim the poncho to fit with scissors. Waterproof the stitching of the coated jacket with seam sealant (every camp shop has it). Be sure to glue the seams on the sou'wester hat too.

Rationale: The youngster wears the coated wind shell under the poncho—it keeps arms dry and provides a secondary "drip" layer in prolonged rain. The sou'wester hat is worn over the poncho hood and is tied beneath the chin. Together, these garments provide serviceable and very inexpensive protection from rain.

Emergency rain gear for kids (or adults) may be fashioned from a large leaf-and-lawn size garbage bag. Cut head and arm holes, provide a sou'wester hat, and you'll stay reasonably dry.

Wet weather foot gear: Running shoes and galoshes, or any rubber boots sized large enough to fit over the sneakers, are all you need. When rains quit, the boots are removed and freedom of foot is instantly restored.

Camp clothing

Cotton clothing (except underwear) should be *avoided* except in the predictable heat of mid-July. Woolens may be too scratchy for some youngsters, so the logical solution is orlon acrylics. Acrylic sweaters, gloves and hats dry quickly after a wetting and retain their insulating properties when damp or soiled. Acrylic garments are also quite inexpensive; they are ideal for spring canoe and boat trips, for adults as well as kids.

Hats: Kids need three hats on a camping trip—a brimmed cap for sun, a warm stocking cap (wool or acrylic) for chilly days, and the traditional sou'wester for rain.

Sleeping gear: Kids do not need air mattresses or foam pads for comfort. Their young bones will happily conform to the most uneven ground!

You must provide a foam pad (not an air mattress—these conduct cold!) if down sleeping bags are used. Body weight compresses the underside of a down bag to near-zero thickness and chilling will result unless insulation is provided. The typical polyester (Polarguard, Quallofil or Hollofil) sleeping bag provides sufficient insulation below so that, except in very cold weather, mattresses may be omitted.

Sleeping bags are unnecessary for typical summer camping. One or two light wool or fluffy acrylic blankets,

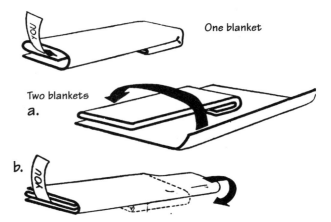

One blanket

Two blankets
a.

b.

FIGURE C-5. For summer use, blankets work as well as a sleeping bag. Here's how to fold them for maximum warmth.

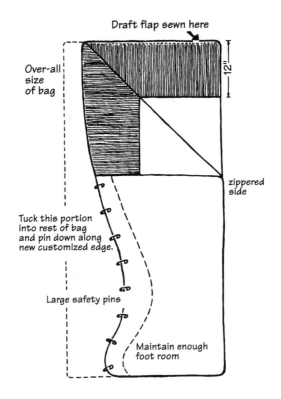

Draft flap sewn here

Over-all size of bag

12"

zippered side

Tuck this portion into rest of bag and pin down along new customized edge.

Large safety pins

Maintain enough foot room

FIGURE C-6. Customizing a sleeping bag for children.

folded as illustrated (Figure C-5), will provide plenty of warmth in temperatures to 45 degrees.

Increasing the warmth of a sleeping bag: The warmth of a sleeping bag is partly related to the amount of space the body has to heat. By reducing dead air space, you'll increase warmth. Figure C-6 shows an easy way to reduce the dimensions, and add warmth, to the typical station-wagon sized sleeping bag. A flannel "draft collar" sewn to the top of a sleeping bag will increase warmth considerably.

Insects (see *Bugs*, page 28). A headnet *and* a Susie bugnet is a wise investment if you'll be camping in buggy country. Choose mild, cream-based repellents rather than more powerful chemicals which may "burn" sensitive young skin.

Toys: Kids will want to bring a favorite doll or teddy bear. Be sure to provide a "rain coat" (plastic bag) for the toy, so it won't be ruined in foul weather.

Clothing

How to tell the real thing from designer wear!

Background: With today's "outdoor look," you'd think it would be easy to locate suitable clothing for backcountry camping. Hardly! Only a handful of manufacturers currently offer attire that is truly functional. The vast majority of clothing makers are simply producing stylish garments which parrot the outdoor look. Here's how to tell designer campwear from the real thing.

Fit: Outdoor clothing should be cut large enough to permit unrestricted movement of arms and legs, even when extra clothing is worn beneath. Shirt and jacket sleeves should be generously sized, even to the point of billowing.

Designer outdoor wear is almost always restrictive in the arms and chest and is usually cut on the short side. This style looks flattering but is an abomination in the wilds. *A rule of thumb:* Properly sized wind and rain gear should have sleeves which are twice the diameter of your arms!

Hoods: Designer hoods are slim, trim, and stow away into collars. "Wilderness" hoods are large enough to fit over a brimmed hat. Hood zippers continue to the nose. This "continuous zipper" design naturally precludes a stow away feature, essential to the designer look.

Designer wear also features more pockets than you can possibly use, suggesting utility and driving up tailoring costs. Really now, when was the last time you used more than two pockets in your parka or rain jacket? Least expensive and most versatile trousers for camping are military surplus chinos and fatigues. For cold weather use, surplus wool trousers are the norm. Trouser legs should hang straight (no cuffs) so they won't trap the environment as you walk through it.

The U.S. Army field jacket, available at every surplus store, makes a fine four-season parka, and is in fact identical to commercial "mountain parkas" which cost much more money.

Sew Velcro tabs to the hem of each trouser leg so you can seal off this area from black flies and mosquitoes.

Before you leave on a lengthy camping trip, have your cotton/polyester garments drycleaned and "waterproofed" at any drycleaning establishment. Drycleaners apply Scotchguard (or similar compound) which slightly stiffens the fabric but makes it quite water resistant (not waterproof). You can do the job yourself with an aerosol can of Scotchguard or Thompson's Sport Seal, but the result will be quite inferior to that of a professional drycleaner. The cost will be about the same.

Despite the ballyhoo over new synthetic fabrics like polypropylene, pile, and chemically treated polyesters, good wool performs about as well in cold, damp weather. In practice, the human body is less sensitive than the machines used to prove manufacturers' claims of superiority. Buy what you can afford but don't be swept off your feet by exotic claims for space-age fabrics. Only cotton in pure form is unsuitable for serious camping.

Blue jeans are a particularly bad choice and have accounted for several deaths due to hypothermia. Even in the heat of summer, there are better choices than pure cotton.

Tip: Pack a small nylon sack inside your clothes bag or pack. This "dirty laundry bag" will keep dirty clothing separate from clean items.

Care and Cleaning of Clothing
Woolens may be drycleaned or washed by hand or machine (gentle cycle only). Best method is to hand-wash—three-

minute soak in a mild detergent (Woolite, Ivory Snow, or any mild dish washing detergent), then hand-rinse and spin-dry in a machine.

Spun-dry woolens are best dried on wooden hangers, out of direct sunlight.

To alter the fit of wool garments: Everyone knows that woolens shrink when exposed to hot water and rough handling. However, shrunken garments can also be restored to a semblance of their original shape by re-washing, stretching, and slow drying. These unique characteristics of wool will enable you to get a custom fit from military surplus and garage sale items.

For example, the sleeves on most shirts are too long for me so I shrink them by washing them (just the sleeves) in very hot water. The shirt is then spun dry in a hot clothes dryer. Careful monitoring of the drying process produces the exact sleeve length I want. When sleeves have shrunk, they'll hold their size for the lifetime of the garment. This procedure is not unique. For years, lobster fishermen have "boiled" their wool mittens to make them warmer and more resistant to wind. This is the same principle used in the manufacture of world famous Dachstein mittens and sweaters. Wool hats, gloves—anything—can be made more wind- and waterproof by "boiling."

Polypropylene garments cannot be drycleaned. The solvent will dissolve the plastic fibers. Hand or machine wash in cold water and air dry. Polypropylene melts at very low temperatures, so don't ever place these garments in a hot clothes dryer or too near a fire.

Polypropylene accumulates body oils and smells quite ripe after a few days afield. Embedded grime also reduces the thermal efficiency of the fibers, so wash these garments frequently. Because of their tendency to retain odors, hunters are switching from polypropylene underwear back to conventional fabrics. Deer can probably smell a sweaty polypro undershirt a mile away when the wind is right!

I've tried all brands of long johns and my personal choice is Thermax®. This non-allergenic Dupont™ material insulates well, even when wet. It "breathes" in hot weather, feels luxurious against the skin, and it doesn't smell—even when it goes unwashed for days. My wife, Sue Harings, is more conscious of odors than I and she insisted that I recommend

Thermax® and its relative Thermastat® by name. Sue says that most of her lady friends also prefer these "sweet-smelling" (whew!) fabrics. *Cabela's Inc., (800) 237–4444*, has a large selection of male, female and unisex styles.

Gore-Tex® must be washed frequently to maintain waterproofness. Ivory Snow was the recommended soap for early Gore-Tex garments; now any good powdered detergent can be used. Wash in cold water and rinse thoroughly—you must get *all* the detergent out! Better yet, use one of the efficient, complete-rinsing Gore-Tex cleansers sold at camping shops. Air or tumble-dry Gore-Tex products at low heat. Do not dryclean Gore-Tex items; you'll destroy them beyond repair!

Coated fabrics (rain gear) must never be drycleaned or machine washed. Hand wash them in warm water with any good detergent. Rinse and air dry.

Be sure coated fabrics are bone dry before you store them away. The stitching and nylon won't rot but the polyurethane coatings will. Certain microorganisms attack polyurethane coatings, which will cause separation (peeling) of the chemical from the fabric.

Compass

Background: The most practical and reliable field compass is the Silva system orienteering type. This compass features a built-in protractor which allows you to compute bearings without orienting the map to north, and a liquid-dampened needle which stops in three seconds. Detailed instructions come with all orienteering compasses. However, you should know how to determine declination.

Declination is the angular difference between geographic or true north and the direction the compass needle points. As you can see from the standard declination diagram below (Figure C-7), the difference can be quite large, especially if you live in the far east or west. Precise declination information (to the nearest fraction of a degree) is given in the legend of all topographic maps.

To adjust your compass for declination, apply the rhyme: ***Declination east, compass least, or declination west, compass best.***

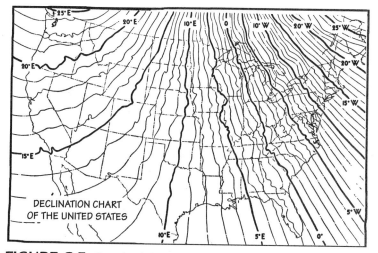

FIGURE C-7. Standard declination diagram.

Example: You are traveling in California where the declination, as given in the diagram (and your topo map sheet), is 16 degrees east. You have computed a *true* map heading to an objective, using the protractor function of your orienteering compass. Your true map heading is due east, or 90 degrees. Adjust this figure for declination by applying the "east is least" (subtract) rhyme: Simply subtract 16 degrees from 90 degrees and travel on a magnetic heading of 74 degrees.

Conversely, the declination would be added (west is best) to your map bearing if you lived in New York, east of the zero (agonic) declination line.

Note: It makes no difference in which cardinal direction you are traveling on your map sheet. The declination in your area holds constant for the entire map sheet (usually), and there is seldom more than a few degrees of difference from one area of a state to another. Once you have determined your area declination you need only remember the rhyme to apply it to any true direction computed from your map.

One degree of compass error equals approximately 92 feet per mile of ground error, so you must consider declination when traveling in regions substantially distant from the agonic line.

A detailed discussion of the compass and navigational

techniques will be found in my book, *The Basic Essentials of Map & Compass.*

Your watch as a compass: You'll need a conventional dial watch for this procedure. Hold the watch level and rotate it until the hour hand points to the sun. Halfway between the hour hand and the "12" on the watch dial is due South. This procedure is reasonably accurate providing your watch is correctly set for the right time zone . . . and you are north of the equator.

Your compass as a watch: The sun will be at these approximate bearings at these approximate times:

East	6 A.M.
Southeast	9 A.M.
South	12 noon
Southwest	3 P.M.
West	6 P.M.

Contact Cement

Best adhesive to use for gluing fabrics and/or porous items. Useful applications include patching holes in canvas tents and bags, gluing foam knee pads into canoes, repairing holes and tears in nylon fabrics, etc. Weldwood contact cement, in my experience, is the most reliable.

Cooking And Food Ideas (see *Baking*)

Cookware

Prepackaged "Trail King" cooksets are a waste of money. Pot sizes are usually awkward and the frying pans are awful. Experienced campers usually assemble their own cookware, buying only those items which they need.

Pots may be aluminum, stainless steel or porcelain-lined steel. The concern that cooking in aluminum may cause Alzheimer's disease has not been proven, and is hardly a concern considering the minimal use received by most camp cookware. Choose low-sided broad pots rather than high narrow ones. A low center-of-gravity is important if you're cooking on a less than rock-stable trail stove. For a crew of eight, you'll need three nesting pots, the largest of which is 24 cups.

You'll find much better cookware at kitchen supply and discount stores than at camping shops. What works at home works afield providing it has a tight-fitting cover and is sized to nest with the rest of your pots and pans. Wire bail handles are necessary only if you do all your cooking on an open fire. One long pot handle or two protruding metal "ears" per pot are adequate if you have insulated pot holders, gloves, bandannas or pliers.

Engrave lines on the *inside* of the pot sides at 2-cup intervals and scratch the total capacity (e.g. 16 cups) just below the rim. This will eliminate guesswork and the need for measuring cups at meal time.

Skillets: The "camping" skillets I've seen are either too thin, too small, or the handles are weak or awkward to use. I prefer to purchase a high grade Teflon™ lined skillet (10 or 12 inch diameter) at my local discount store and cut off the Bakelite™ handle with a hack saw. Then, I make a "universal-style," quickly removable handle from 0.187-inch diameter spring wire (see Figure C-7A). I use a vise, strong pliers and hammer to bend the wire to shape. The mounting bracket on the skillet is made from hardware store aluminum flat stock. Two brass bolts secure the bracket to the pan.

I also outfit my large "spaghetti" pot with a rigid wire handle (Figure C-7A), so I'll have better control when I drain liquid. When a pan wears out, I unbolt the bracket and transfer it to a new pan—no need to make a new one.

Store your cookset in a nylon bag.

Tea kettle: A tea kettle heats faster and is less tippy than a coffee pot and you can pour with one hand. An 8-cup kettle is about right for four; a 20-cup model is better for groups of eight or more. Tea pots are ordinarily left on the fire as a major supply of boiling water, so consider an oversize (20 cup) kettle, even for small groups. A large tea pot will speed heating of dishwater and save stove fuel.

On a long hike, you may want to stop for tea—so always pack your tea kettle (in a fabric bag) at the top of your pack where you can get it quickly.

Utensils: Experienced campers carry only an insulated plastic cup (it keeps things hotter/colder than metal cups), metal spoon, and a sturdy plastic bowl. The individual belt or pocket knife performs all cutting chores. Forks—useful

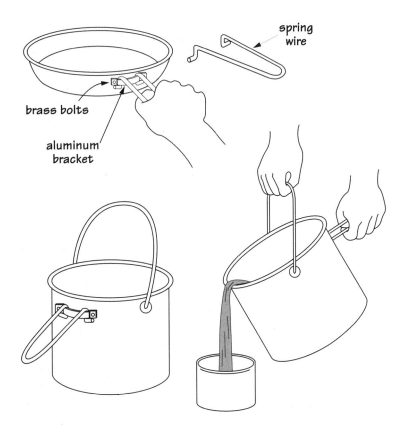

spring
wire

brass bolts

aluminum
bracket

FIGURE C-7A.

for vehicle camping—are a luxury. It's best to have identical, colored nesting bowls. Keep bowls in a fabric bag, stored inside your smallest cook pot. To prevent the spread of illness, each person should always use the same bowl.

You'll need these cooking utensils:

a) pancake turner (wood is best; plastic burns!)
b) rubber spatula for scraping uneaten food from pots and bowls
c) aluminum pliers or "pot grabber" (I prefer the official Boy Scout model)

d) wooden stirring spoon
e) small wire whip for reconstituting instant mixes
f) salt, pepper and other spices are best stored in 35 mm plastic film cans
g) small sheath knife or French folding "picnic" knife (an extra knife is always welcome in the kitchen)

Tip: Be sure your cup has a plastic snap-on lid that will keep coffee hot and heat-seeking insects out. *Make a leash for your lid*: Drill a small hole through an edge of the mug lid and tie a piece of heavy fishing line through the hole. Tie the other end of the line to the mug handle.

A fabric utensil roll (Figure C-8) is used to store tools and spices. Set snaps or Velcro tabs at the top (as illustrated) so you can hang the roll from a tight line, out-of contact with wet ground. If you string a tight rope under your rain tarp (see *Tarps*, page 167) and hang your utensil roll from it, everything will remain dry in the rain.

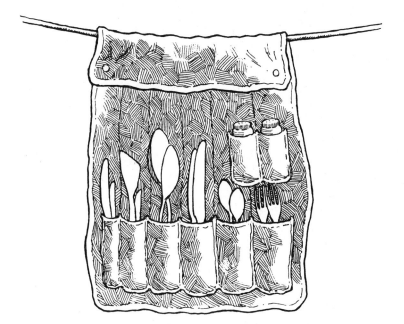

FIGURE C-8. Fabric Utensil roll

Commercial utensil rolls, patterned after my design, may be purchased from *Duluth Tent & Awning Co., 1610 W. Superior Street, Duluth, MN 55816-0024, (800) 777-4439,* and *Cooke Custom Sewing, 7290 Stagecoach Trail, Lino Lakes, MN 55014-1988, (651) 784-8777.*

Pots that are used on open fires get quite black outside. Some experts suggest that you coat the exposed surfaces with liquid soap or shaving cream so the carbon black will clean easily. The result is an awful mess for the dish washing crew. I leave pots black (they cook faster and more evenly) and keep them inside a plastic-lined nylon sack between uses.

Drying dishes: Pack a half dozen sheets of paper toweling for each meal. The toweling is convenient for drying cookware, cleaning the stove, etc.

For a gourmet treat, drop chunks of raw fish into boiling soup and cook for a maximum of five minutes. Sounds terrible but tastes superb and is the logical solution to preparing fish when vegetable oil or stove fuel is in short supply.

Making popcorn: If you're tired of trying to season popcorn in a pot that's too small, try this: Carry some large grocery sacks on your next campout. As you complete each batch of popcorn, pour it into the paper bag (don't use a plastic bag—hot popcorn will melt right through it). Season the popcorn and shake the bag to mix. When the popcorn's gone, burn the bag . . . or fold and store it in a plastic bag for future use.

Making biscuits and cakes: Mix batter in a plastic Ziploc bag. Add the water, knead the bag with your hands until the consistency of the mix is correct, then punch a hole in the bag bottom and force the gooey mess into your awaiting oven. Burn the plastic bag. No mess or fuss.

Quick 'n easy trail suppers can be prepared by adding any or all of these items to boiling soup mix: instant rice, dry noodles, elbow macaroni, Bisquick dumplings (use a plastic bag to mix), or potato buds.

Pasta for lunch: Bagels (a traditionally Jewish food) are ideal trail bread. Buy the frozen kind, which will keep nicely for about a week after thawing. Pile bagels high with sausage, cheese, peanut butter and jelly for a nutritious lunch. Bagels are tasty, tough, and they pack well.

Pita (Mediterranean pocket bread) is another alternative to trail crackers. Pita contains preservatives (bagels do not) and will remain fresh and tasty for at least two weeks in typical summer weather. One pita bread per person is substantial lunch fare, when combined with the usual noontime extras.

Cheese in soup? You bet! Sprinkle dried Parmesan cheese on soup for a gourmet treat. Chunks of cheese (any kind) add spark, flavor, and calories to trail spaghetti and chili.

Peanut butter on pancakes? Sounds awful but tastes divine. The peanut butter melts into the hotcakes and provides a rich taste.

To make good tasting boiled camp coffee: Bring water to a boil, then remove the pot from heat. Add one tablespoon of ground coffee per cup, plus an extra tablespoon for the pot. Stir coffee into the water, put on a lid, and set the pot aside for five minutes to allow the grounds to settle. Do not boil pot-brewed camp coffee; you'll destroy the delicate flavor and introduce a muddy metallic taste.

For classy coffee, add cinnamon or almond extract and you'll draw raves from everyone. A quarter teaspoon of almond extract or powdered cinnamon per eight cups of coffee is about right.

To make delicious camp mocha, use one packet of hot chocolate mix per cup. Fill cup with fresh-brewed coffee and top with some mini-marshmallows. Teenagers love this drink!

Hot pancakes for a big crew: Mix pancake syrup and margarine or butter in a small pot and heat to near boiling. This will assure pancakes are really hot when they are prepared in advance for a large group.

A Thermos bottle is a practical accessory, even on strenuous hiking trips. Boiling water poured into a vacuum bottle that is not used for beverages may provide the nucleus for hot dishwater later. Saves running the stove (using precious gas) to heat dishwater.

Pre-packaging saves time! Pre-pack everything you need to prepare a given meal, in a Zip-loc plastic bag. Everything should be pre-measured and mixed so that you don't have to fuss with this on the trail. For added simplicity, I traditionally pack my plastic bagged breakfasts in green nylon bags, my lunches in blue, and my suppers in red. This saves considerable pack-groping at meal times and provides abrasion resistance for the tear-prone Zip-locs inside. Adhesive tape labels identify the specific contents of each nylon bag.

A Few Last Tips:

1. Place fresh vegetables, crackers, cookies and other breakables in your tea kettle to keep them from being crushed on a strenuous backpacking or canoe trip.
2. A stainless steel Sierra cup is a lousy drinking cup but it is a great ladle for soup and stew.
3. An empty cardboard milk carton makes a handy "safe" for crushable foods like cookies and eggs. Use the wax-coated milk carton to mix powdered soft drinks and as an emergency fire-starter on a rainy day.
4. Dried foods are generally pretty bland unless they're heavily spiced. I carry oregano, garlic powder, seasoned salt, black pepper, cayenne, thyme and cumin inside small film containers which are kept in a nylon "spice bag."
5. Farm fresh eggs will keep for weeks without refrigeration! Small-and medium-sized eggs have thicker shells than large eggs, so they're less apt to break on a hiking or canoe trip. You can check the freshness of eggs by floating them in a bowl of water. The *deeper* they sink, the fresher they are. Discard any eggs which "float to the top."

Some breakfast favorites

Bacon/Cheese McPita/McTortilla

Option 1: Fry and set aside two thin slices of Canadian bacon, per person. Scramble or fry one egg per person and set it aside. Now, lightly fry an open face Mediterranean pocket bread (pita) or tortilla in a teaspoon of cooking oil. When the bottom of the pita or tortilla is brown (20 seconds), flip the bread over and lay thinly sliced cheese on top. Pile on the bacon and egg, add a dash of your favorite salsa (optional), and immediately, toss a dash of cold water into the sizzling skillet. Cover and steam for fifteen seconds then serve immediately. In one minute you'll have a wholesome, delicious sandwich.

Option 2: Same as above, but omit the egg.

Option 3: Cut pita bread in half and fill the pockets with any fresh thin-sliced or grated cheese. Generously sprinkle garlic powder and oregano (optional) over the cheese. Fry each pita half in a well-oiled, covered skillet for about twenty seconds. As soon as you flip the pita, add a dash of cold water—and cover—to "steam the cheese."

Tortillas are less filling than pitas but they have a more delicate, toasty flavor. Cook each tortilla flat in a well-oiled skillet for about ten seconds, then flip it over and add cheese and garlic powder to the toasted side. Immediately roll the tortilla into a burrito shape, add cold water to steam, then cover and simmer for twenty seconds.

Cinnamon Tortillas, Stewed Fruit, and Canadian Bacon

Make a tortilla burrito as described above, but substitute margarine, cinnamon and white or brown sugar for the cheese and garlic. Tastes just like a cinnamon roll!

Boiled dehydrated apples and brown sugar, with a side of Canadian bacon round out this perfect meal.

Note: Freshly baked pita bread and tortillas will keep at least two weeks without refrigeration if they are well-sealed when you leave home.

Swift suppers

Here are some things to consider as you plan your suppers.

1. Most freeze-dried and dehydrated entrees consist of three parts—pasta or rice, freeze-dried chicken, beef or shrimp, and spices. Remember this, and you can mix and match a variety of foods to suit your tastes.
2. The meat is the most expensive part of any dried meal. One-quarter pound of freeze-dried hamburger (essential to make spaghetti, stroganoff or chili) costs three times as much as a Big Mac! Chicken and shrimp are even more pricey.

However, you can easily dry these meats yourself in an inexpensive home dehydrator. *For example, here's how to dehydrate hamburger:*

1. Fry the hamburger, drain the grease, then pour boiling water through the meat to remove as much fat as possible.
2. Line each dehydrator tray with three sheets of absorbent paper toweling and spread the hamburger out on the trays. Allow no more than 1 pound (¼-inch thickness) of hamburger per tray.
3. Turn the dehydrator to high (140° F.) and wait twenty-four hours. Vacuum seal (best) the dried hamburger or double-bag it in Zip-loc™ bags. Use a drinking straw to remove as much air as possible from the Zip-loc™ bags. Vacuum-sealed, dehydrated hamburger will keep about a year at room temperature; carefully Zip-locked meat should last a month. As a safety precaution, keep dehydrated meats frozen until just before your camping trip. Use dehydrated hamburger in spaghetti, chili, soups, and stews.

Hamburger/Cheese Vegetable Soup
Add 1 pound (about ¾ cup) of dried hamburger to instant vegetable soup. Toss in a heavy handful of wide egg noodles or instant rice, and add some dried mushrooms and a few slices of cheese. A dash of red pepper and garlic powder complete the recipe.

Spaghetti and Chili
To prepare spaghetti, you'll need dehydrated hamburger, pasta, spices and tomato paste. Chili requires dehydrated beans which are easily made by drying canned beans: Dump the canned beans (after pouring off the liquid) on the dehydrator tray and turn the heat to high. The beans will be dried and ready to pack in about eight hours.
To make spaghetti sauce, line the dehydrator trays with

Several excellent vacuum sealing machines are available. I've had good luck with a powerful home unit called the FOODSAVER. It's available from Nationwide Marketing, Inc. 1550 Bryant Street., Suite 850, San Francisco, CA 94103, (800) 777-5452.

plastic cling wrap and spread any commercial sauce evenly on the trays. In twelve hours you'll have a thin, rubbery mass that resembles a fruit roll up. Peel the dried sauce off the plastic wrap, roll it up and freeze it. Later, break chunks into a plastic poly bottle. Add water to the chunks to rehydrate the sauce.

If you don't want to mess with this foolishness, order tomato powder at your local co-op. Add a little water to the powder and you'll have paste; add more water for sauce or soup.

Pita Pizza (This is everyone's favorite meal!)
Ingredients: One or two pieces of pita bread per person, dried tomato powder, fresh mozzarella cheese (hard, fresh cheese keeps nearly a month if it's vacuum sealed), oregano, garlic powder, salt, cayenne pepper. Any or all of the following: dried pepperoni, summer sausage, hard salami, Canadian bacon, fresh onion, green pepper, dried or canned mushrooms . . .

Procedure:

1. Slice and fry the meat and drain off the grease on paper toweling. Thickly dice the vegetables and mushrooms, fry them in light oil, then drain off the grease and set them aside.
2. To make the pizza sauce, pour ½ cup of tomato powder into a bowl and add water to make a thick paste. Sprinkle on oregano, garlic, salt and cayenne.
3. Fry an open-faced pita at low heat in a well-oiled, covered skillet. When the bottom of the pita is brown (about 20 seconds), flip over the pita and thickly spread on tomato sauce, cheese, meat and vegetables to taste. Immediately add a dash of water (to steam-melt the cheese) and cover the pan. Allow the pizza to cook at very low heat for half a minute, or until the cheese has melted.

Add Fresh Vegetables to Your "One-pot" Meals!
Fresh onions, tomatoes and green peppers will keep about five days on a camping trip, if they are "properly" packed.

Place onions in a cotton or paper bag. Stow the bag inside a rigid container.

Here's how to prepare green peppers and tomatoes:

1. Wash the vegetables, then float them in a sink full of drinking water that has been treated with about ⅛ cup (the amount isn't critical) of chlorine bleach. Allow the vegetables to soak for several minutes in the treated water before you dry and pack them away. The bleach will kill the surface bacteria which promotes spoilage. A similar procedure is used in some of America's finest restaurants to keep vegetables fresh.

   Tip: Wash in fresh water only the portion of vegetable you need. Do not wash the entire vegetable! Doing so will introduce water-borne bacteria which may accelerate spoilage.

2. Separately wrap each vegetable in clean paper toweling. Pack the towel-wrapped veggies in a paper or cotton sack and set the sack inside a tea kettle or other crush-proof container. Do not wrap vegetables in non-porous plastic!

Two Slick Tips

1. As mentioned, a dash of cold water in a hot, covered skillet will quickly steam-cook foods. You can also use this method to restore the freshness of week old bagels, pita bread and tortillas. Simply "steam grill" the bread in a covered skillet for a few seconds.

2. If you insist on carrying loaves of bread, here's an old woodsman's trick that guarantees perfect toast: Distribute a heavy pinch of table salt on the surface of a hot, dry (no grease!) skillet. Set a slice of bread on the salt. Do not cover! When the bottom of the bread is toasted to a golden brown, flip the bread over and toast the other side. The salt won't burn or stick to the bread or skillet.

How to prepare freeze-dried foods so they always taste good!

Background: Freeze-dried foods are fickle. Prepare 'em according to directions one day and they're great. Repeat the procedure another time and . . . *ugh!*

Take heart. Here's a foolproof cooking method that works regardless of the weather, the Zodiac, or a cranky stove.

Step One

Read the cooking directions but don't take them too seriously. What works at home on the range often fails on a flat rock in a nor'wester.

Step Two

Separate the component parts of the food. Generally, there are two parts—a meat portion, and a noodle, rice or vegetable portion. Sometimes a third "spice packet" is included. (See Note #1 at the end of this procedure for the specifics of preparing cook-in-the-bag meals.)

Typical directions say: *Add contents of all packets to X cups of boiling water. Reduce heat, simmer 15–20 minutes or until noodles* (or whatever) *are tender.*

Step Three

Put 20 percent *more* water in your cooking pot than the directions call for, and add the meat portion only to the cold water. Bring the water to a boil and add a healthy dash of "All-Spice" (suggested recipe below):

Mix approximately equal amounts of the following spices:

Oregano
Onion powder
Marjoram
Thyme
Seasoned salt and pepper mixtures (I buy a commercial blend).

Step Four

When the water is at a rolling boil, add contents of the spice packet (if there is one). Reduce heat to slow boil and let spices and meat stew together for a full five minutes. If there is no spice packet allow meat to stew for five minutes before you proceed to step five.

Step Five

Add contents of noodle, rice or vegetable packet to the boiling water. Reduce heat, cover, simmer and stir occasionally for the amount of time indicated in the package directions.

Step Six

Eat and enjoy. All portions of the meal are thoroughly cooked and the taste has been fully developed.

Notes: Why some meals fail

1. *You haven't cooked the meat long enough.* Half-cooked reconstituted meat spoils the whole stew. Except in very warm weather, "cook-in-the-bag" foods just don't get done. It's best to place the cooking bag in a covered pot of near boiling water for ten minutes. Add about 10 percent more water to the cooking bag than the directions call for.
2. *You burned the pasta!* This is easy to do on a one-burner trail stove, especially if you plop the contents of all food packets into the boiling water simultaneously. If your stove's turned high, you may burn the meal quicker than you can say "turn the heat down, Jack!"
3. *Insufficient water.* Remember, you can always boil out too much water, but there's not much you can do with a stew that's so thick it's burned and glued to the pot bottom.
4. *Not enough spices.* Don't underestimate the value of spices when preparing freeze-dried foods. Most quick-cook products are unacceptably bland unless they're well spiced. The suggested "All-Spice" works wonders on everything from spaghetti to shrimp-creole.
5. *Spoilage:* Dehydrated foods come packed in plastic and have a shelf life of about one year. This is because plastic is not a complete water barrier. Freeze-dried foods come packaged in aluminum foil, which is an absolute vapor barrier. Consequently, these products have an unlimited shelf life.

    This should tell you something about end-of-season food sales. Don't buy dehydrated foods in September if you plan to use them the following

July. Your autumn "bargain" may turn out to be summer indigestion.

It's important to realize that many products contain both freeze-dried and dehydrated components (for example, spaghetti with freeze-dried meatballs). While the foil-wrapped meatballs won't spoil, the plastic wrapped spaghetti and spices might. Only foods which are completely sealed in foil are immune to spoilage. Unfortunately, you almost never see these products offered at sale prices.

6. *Introduction of bacteria and/or water vapor during repackaging.* Don't handle dried foods or expose them to air any longer than necessary when you repackage them. This will reduce the chance of bacteria and water vapor getting into the food.

Tip: Slice meat and cheese with a knife that's been dipped in boiling water for a full minute. This will also reduce transfer of bacteria into the food.

Blacken your pot bottoms: Some campers meticulously scrub and brighten their cooking pots after use, but fire-blackened pots heat faster and more evenly. Aluma-black, a chemical used to blacken aluminum gun sights and mounts, works wonders on pot bottoms. Just daub the chemical on the pot, allow it to dry, and a rich blue-black color will result. Aluma-black is available from most gun shops. It is quite inexpensive. The product may also be used to darken the decks and rails of aluminum canoes and fishing boats.

Cold weather cooking tips

Stoves used on snow must be set on a support of some sort or they'll melt the snow beneath and quietly sink out of sight. Fires built in snow must also have a suitable support.

Don't set stoves on pieces of closed-cell foam (so the fuel tank will retain heat . . . and pressure) as is recommended by some authorities. A hot stove will melt the foam and stick solidly to it.

Pot covers are essential for winter cooking. Open pots lose too much heat; in sub-zero temperatures, water may not reach boiling unless it is placed in a covered pot.

Snow provides a natural windscreen. Dig in your stove

so it's completely protected from the wind. Sub-zero temps and a good wind will lengthen cooking times considerably.

Insulate your water bottles so they won't freeze: Carry water bottles in an inside parka pocket so they won't freeze. In camp, store them upside down in the snow. The frozen interface will then be at the bottom and you'll be able to pour the liquid from the capped end. Snow is a marvelous insulator: Water bottles stored overnight this way will be "pourable" come morning.

Light for the kitchen: Winter nights come early; often there is insufficient light to cook by. Traditional flashlights lose power in cold weather and are awkward to hold. Select instead a powerful headlamp (one that will accept alkaline D-size batteries). Keep the battery pack inside your parka when the light is used.

Securing drinking water in winter may require that you bore through the ice of a frozen lake. For this, an ice chisel is better than the traditional cumbersome auger. Fit a short length of threaded pipe to the tail of the chisel so you can screw on a pole to provide weight when chopping. Don't use a hand axe for chiseling; it is awkward and dangerous.

How to wash dishes in sub-freezing temperatures: Heavy rubber gloves will protect hands from the wet chilling effects of cold. Dish water should be near boiling. A copper sponge or 3M nylon pad is all you need to remove food particles from pots and bowls. Detergents aren't necessary as there is no bacterial growth in sub-freezing temperatures. In fact, dishes need not be washed at all. Some authorities recommend that you clean dishes with snow—a particularly inefficient practice. Boiling water and rubber gloves work much better!

Foods that don't work well in winter: Frozen cheese looks and tastes like candle tallow. Peanut butter and jelly are sure to be frozen; there is no way to keep these items thawed unless you carry them in your pockets.

Gasoline is dangerous in cold weather! Gasoline, naphtha (Coleman fuel), and kerosene freeze at very low temperatures. If these fuels contact exposed skin in sub-zero temperatures, instant frostbite will result. Always wear rubber gloves when fueling stoves in cold weather. (See *Stoves*, page 157, for a thorough discussion of safety and troubleshooting procedures.)

Cord (see *Rope,* for knots and hitches)

Best camp utility cord is ⅛-inch diameter nylon parachute cord. Nylon cord should be "hot cut" (use a butane lighter) rather than sliced, so its core and sheath won't separate.

Singe (melt) the ends of nylon and polypropylene cord and rope to prevent them from unraveling. Nobody "whips" ropes anymore.

Nylon cord locks, available at all camps shops, are handy for securing the chute-cord thongs of nylon sacks. A less expensive solution that works as well is to purchase nylon hose clamps from scientific supply houses. You can buy a dozen rubber hose (tubing) clamps for the price of one "cord lock."

You don't need cord locks to secure the thongs of nylon stuff sacks if you learn the simple knot illustrated in Figure C-9.

Cord Locks

Cord locks are small, spring-loaded nylon clamps used to secure the cords of sleeping bags, parka hoods and stuff sacks. Every camping shop carries a good supply of them for the do-it-yourselfer who wants to add versatility to his/her camping outfit.

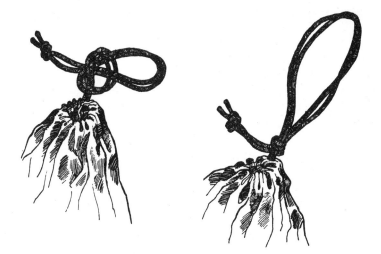

FIGURE C-9. Secure your stuff sack with a quick-release loop.

Now comes the hard part—threading the pair of ⅛-inch diameter nylon parachute cords through the tiny cord lock hole. One cord goes through easily; the second dies a slow death in mid-push. Ultimately frustration reigns and the "good idea" is disgustedly thrown into a drawer for use later. Here's an easy way to thread the paired cords through the cord lock hole: Place the tips of the cords side by side, one tip ⅛ inch below the other. Then tape the two tightly together with masking tape, adhesive, duct tape . . . whatever. Press open the cord lock button, and *voilá*, the cords go through instantly—simple and fast. No other way works as well. Most other ways don't work at all!

Cozies

It's a cold, blustery day and you're anxious for a hot meal. You boil water on your gasoline stove, then place spaghetti noodles in your largest pot, taking care to stir constantly so they won't burn. You know that if you stop stirring and cover the pot, the pasta will boil faster. However, it may also burn and stick to the pot bottom. But, if you continue to stir the uncovered food, heat will escape into the air and the spaghetti will take much longer to cook. What to do?

1. Bring the water to a rolling boil and add the uncooked spaghetti. Turn down the heat to medium and stir until all the noodles are absorbed into the water.
2. Turn off the stove. Cover the pot and set it on a closed-cell foam pad.
3. Immediately cover the pot with an insulated tea cozy or a sweater or jackets (not nylon—it melts!). Pile additional clothes on top to keep the heat in.
4. Entertain yourself for twenty minutes while the spaghetti "slow cooks" in its own heat. "Cozy cooking" saves time, stove fuel, and a burned pot bottom! Use this procedure whenever you make rice, soup or hot cereal.

Tip: Make insulated cozies to fit all your pots. I prefer a two-piece model (top hat and pot band) like the one illus-

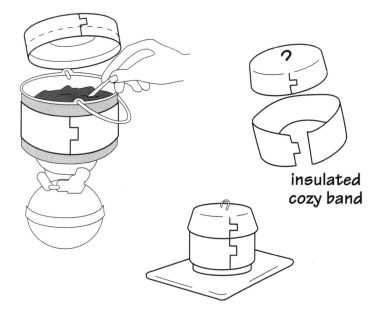

insulated
cozy band

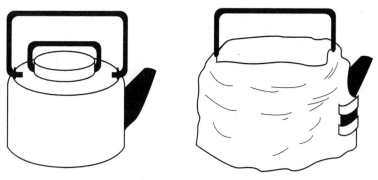

FIGURE C-10.

trated in Figure C-10, because it's more versatile and energy efficient than a one-piece model. The encircling band keeps the pot from losing heat to a cold wind when you remove the cover to stir your food. This saves considerable cooking time and fuel on cold, blustery days. Fitted cozies are essential for winter camping and camping trips above the tree-line, and whenever you must cook a lot of food for a large group. A "skillet-cover cozy" keeps heat in when you steam-cook pita pizza, bagels and tortilla burritos.

I also make a fitted cozy for my tea kettle. The spout pokes through a slit that's controlled by a Velcro tab. Fresh coffee will stay hot for about an hour in a cozy-covered kettle if you place the kettle on an insulated foam pad or fabric pot holder.

Cozy fabrics: Nylon or acrylics catch fire and/or melt! Cotton and wool works well. Insulated ironing board material is satisfactory. An old welding blanket is the best material of all because it won't melt or catch fire.

Dental Floss

Dental floss is the toughest "thread" you can buy. I use it to mend tears in packs, tarps and other heavy-duty camping items. *Tip*: You'll need a heavy-duty sewing needle with a *large eye* to accommodate the thick dental floss.

If you crack a canoe seat, thwart yoke or tool handle, try this: Apply instant epoxy to the crack then tightly and evenly wrap the crack with dental floss. Spread instant epoxy over the wrap and allow it to dry. Your repair will never let go!

Diapers and Diaper Pins

Diapers (cloth) make excellent camp towels. They're lightweight, compact and absorbent.

Diaper pins are much more rugged and visible in dim light (!) than other safety pins. Uses are endless and include: clothespins—pin *through* the line and wet clothes won't slide together; secure pockets in packs and clothes when zippers fail; pin money and credit cards inside pockets; attach a whistle to a life jacket; emergency replacement pin for eye glasses; hang a flashlight from a tent, etc. A dozen diaper pins are not too many to bring along on a camping trip.

Duct Tape

Duct tape is the most useful repair item you can have. The hard-to-find olive drab "army" tape sticks better than the common gray tape found in hardware stores. *3-M* brand silver duct tape is the best!

Be sure to include some nylon filament (strapping) tape in your repair kit: It beats duct tape for mending broken canoe paddles, boat seats and tool handles. *Tip*: Remove tape from its bulky roll and re-wind it on a short pencil. Now you can "write about what you fix." Everything should be multipurpose in a camping trip!

Ethics

The imperfect science of sanitation and ethical camping procedures

Background: It is no longer acceptable to build beds of green pine boughs (or dead ones, for that matter), lash log furniture, trench tents, hack green trees, and otherwise disturb the natural environment to suit our whims. There's just too little wilderness and too many of us. If we are to preserve the remaining backcountry for future generations, then each of us must adopt a solemn "I care" attitude. We must unfailingly practice ethical use of our natural resources, and we must teach—indeed, preach—ethics to all who will listen. And for those who turn the other ear, there must be laws . . . and penalties. The alternative is regulation upon regulation and a lessened quality of experience for everyone. Here are the recommended land and water use procedures:

Disposal of human and food wastes: Bury these wastes in mineral soil (if possible) 2–6 inches deep. The upper foot of soil contains the majority of decomposer organisms and so ensures the fastest rate of decay.

Toilet paper should be burned. Unburned tissue may take a season or more to degrade. Human waste will be gone in a matter of days if the weather is warm. When camping on the granite rock of the Canadian shield, or anywhere soil cover is at a premium, simply follow the recommended procedure for "shallow burial" and cover the waste with whatever soil cover is available.

Caution: Do not burn toilet paper unless you have a water bottle and can put your fire dead out! A number of forest fires have been caused by burning toilet paper!

Please do not leave leftover food around camp "for the animals"—this will upset their ecology and make them dependent on man, not to mention the aggravation they'll bestow on campers who will later occupy the site.

Fish entrails: It is illegal in most states to throw fish entrails into a lake or river, and for good reason. Bacteria consume the viscera and multiply, which raises germ levels to possibly dangerous proportions. Bacteria also use vast amounts of oxygen, which in turn robs fish and aquatic organisms of this essential element. Since food scraps react similarly, they too should never be tossed into a body of water.

Bury fish remains as you would food wastes—100 feet from water and well away from the campsite area. If you are camping in a very remote area where seagulls are common, you may leave viscera on a large rock—well away from human habitation—for the gulls. This procedure is not acceptable on heavily used lakes!

Cans and bottles should always be packed out of the wilderness. Tin cans should be burned out and crushed flat with the back of an axe or your boot, then packed out. The typical steel can requires about seventy-five years to decompose completely; aluminum cans may need five hundred years! A glass bottle could last a million years in the environment! We do not bury cans and bottles today. PACK THEM OUT!

Your garbage detail will be easier if you make a strong nylon bag, with drawstring, for this purpose.

Dish washing: Dishes should never be washed in a waterway. Food scraps encourage bacterial growth and even biodegradable detergents kill essential microorganisms. Dishes should be washed on land and in a large cooking pot. Dish water is best disposed of on mineral soil, 100 feet from a lake or river.

Swimming is fine, but "bathing" is not. If you use soap to wash your hair and body, please rinse on the shore (with a bucket of water), well away from the water's edge.

A word about biodegradable products: It's fashionable today to extol the virtues of biodegradable products over those which do not break down by bacterial action. Certainly, you should choose biodegradable detergents, tissues, and toilet paper whenever possible. Be aware, however, that even the best biodegradable products depend upon bacteria, moisture and time for decomposition. And this means increased germ counts, lowered levels of oxygen, and visual pollution for some time. There's no such thing as a free ride!

Bough beds: Cutting evergreen branches to make bough beds is illegal, immoral, and damaging to the trees. An air mattress or foam pad works better. The use of dead evergreen boughs or mosses should also be discouraged as this material provides a "surface cover" which blots out sunlight and consequently kills vegetation below. Campsites should always be left as natural as possible so that nature can effectively "do its thing."

Cutting green trees is, of course, illegal and damaging. Since green wood burns poorly, there's no sense cutting it for firewood. You'll find plenty of good dead firewood in the backcountry if you look for it (see *Fire Making*, page 77).

Graffiti: It's always shocking to see initials and names carved or painted on trees and rocks in the backcountry. But it does happen, even in the most remote wilderness. The rationale is certainly ignorance and insensitivity, neither of which can be tolerated by those of us who know and care.

Noise: Most people take to the backcountry to experience peace and quiet. Loud, man-made disturbances are obviously unwelcome, and in state and national parks, usually illegal. Please keep radios at home or use a personal Walkman.

Color: Some campers are offended by brightly colored camping gear and clothing. Consequently, the trend is toward gentle earth tones–greens, browns and grays. However, there's no denying the safety (and photographic) advantages of brightly colored tents, canoes and clothing in remote areas. Despite much hoopla, the color issue is exaggerated. There are more pressing environmental concerns in the backcountry.

Lugged hiking boots: Chunky-soled mountain boots churn up much more soil than non-aggressive footwear and are therefore discouraged in popular hiking areas. Primitive people got along quite nicely without Vibram lugs and you will too, not to mention the freedom of foot you'll enjoy by selecting lighter, more flexible shoes. Nonetheless, the damage that results from use of Rambo-style boots is probably over-rated. Like "color," there are more pressing concerns.

Fire site: Fire sites should always be left as natural as possible. In military terms, "everything that's not growing or nailed down" should be removed from the premises. Every scrap of paper, every shred of aluminum foil, down to the tiniest speck, should be picked out and hauled home. Ideally, there should be no partially burned wood left in the grate—absolutely everything should be consumed by flame before you pass on.

It is permissible, but no longer traditional (or even desirable) to leave cut firewood for those who will later occupy the site. Some modern campers consider the sight of a woodpile an "affront," one which detracts form the wildness of the area. So cut only the wood you need and put your fire dead out—check it with your hands to be sure it is DEAD OUT!—before you leave.

Education: Unfortunately, there are not yet enough of us who care who will carry the banner for ethical land use. We must spread the word as gospel, but quietly, sensibly and in a non-intimidating way, with full realization that you can always get more bears with honey than with guns. Studies show that the majority of campers mean well even though they often do what is improper. Most abuse occurs out of ignorance. The majority of people will willingly follow your lead if properly taught.

Fire-Making Procedures

Background: Anyone can start a fire on a bone-dry day, or when they're armed with dry newspaper, kerosene or charcoal lighter. But let the day deteriorate to persistent rain, and where there's smoke there won't be fire!

Here's how to make and maintain fire when foul weather comes to stay:

Tools: You'll need a sharp knife, hand axe, and a saw (folding saws are highly recommended). Contrary to the ravings of some "authorities," it is nearly impossible to make fire in prolonged rain without all these tools.

Procedure

1. In an evergreen forest: Collect several handfuls of the dead lower branches of evergreen trees. Wood should range in size from pencil-lead thickness to no bigger than your little finger, and it should break with a crisp, audible snap. If you don't hear the positive "snap," the wood is too wet, in which case proceed directly to Step 3.

   If the wood is suitably dry, it will burst into a bright flame the moment a match is applied. Use a small candle to provide sustained heat to your tinder ball if the bark of the wood is wet. From this point on, it's simply a matter of adding more wood and protecting the developing blaze from rain (*see *To maintain fire in a driving rain*).

2. Look for resin blisters on the outside bark of balsam fir trees. Break a few blisters with a sharp stick and collect the highly volatile resin. Use the resin as a "chemical fire-starter" to propel your tinder to flame.

3. Locate a dead, downed tree and saw off a portion which does not touch the ground. Grounded wood rots quickly, so is apt to be unsound. Especially

search for deadfalls which overhang into a sun-lit clearing or waterway. These are almost certain to be rot-free, as sunlight kills microorganisms which cause decay.

If you cannot find a dead downed tree to saw up, look for any floating log. If the log "floats," the center is dry. Splittings taken from the heart will burn.

4. When you have completed your first saw cut through the deadfall, check the center of the cut log with your hand. Is it bone dry? It should be. Even a month long rain will seldom soak through a 6 inch log!

5. Saw the deadfall into 12 inch sections then split each chunk with your hand axe by the method illustrated in Figure A-1. It should require only a few minutes to reduce each log chunk to half-inch diameter kindling by this procedure.

6. Cut wafer-thin tinder from a few splittings with your pocket knife. The key to producing long, thin shavings rather than little squiggly ones is to use a sawing, rather than a whittling action with your knife. Even a small, dull knife will produce nice shavings if you persistently saw the blade back and forth.

Figure F-0 shows a much more powerful way to cut long thin shavings. Simply *reverse* the knife edge and smartly pull the knife and stick apart, as illustrated. Before you "pull," be sure the stick is located *outside* of the knife (not in front of it) and the sharp edge has a good bite on the wood.

Tip: Stumps and roots are rich in volatile resins. Conifers, especially, have so much pitch that they will burn on their own for hours—a reason why fires in evergreen forests are so devastating. If you can find an old broken down stump, save some of the "fat wood" for starting fires.

7. Build a well-ventilated platform fire according to steps one, two, and three.

Step One

Establish a fire base of 1-inch diameter sticks as illus-

FIGURE F-0. An efficient way to cut shavings

trated. Place pencil-thin support sticks at right angles to the fire base.

Step Two
Meticulously stack wafer-thin shavings on top of the kindling to a height of about 1 inch. Place the shavings so that plenty of air can get between them. "Smoke" is nature's way of saying you're smothering the flame!

Next, put two ½-inch diameter "support" sticks at right angles to the fire base. These will support the heavier kindling you'll add over the tinder in step three.

Step Three
Now, pile on fine split kindling above the tinder box to lock the tinder in place. Again, leave space between the splittings so your fire can "breathe."

Your fire is now ready to light. Apply flame directly below the tinder (shavings). A small candle will furnish the sustained heat necessary to ignite damp wood.

Hand feed shavings (not kindling) one at a time into the developing flame. Don't heap kindling on until you have a bright reliable blaze.

Hints: Carry strike-anywhere matches in addition to a butane lighter and candle. Keep matches in a plastic jar with a cotton wad on top. A spent 16-gauge shotshell nested inside a 12-gauge case makes a tough watertight match safe.

Some campers waterproof matches by painting on nail polish, but this causes match heads to deteriorate. A waterproof match case is a better idea.

Step 1.

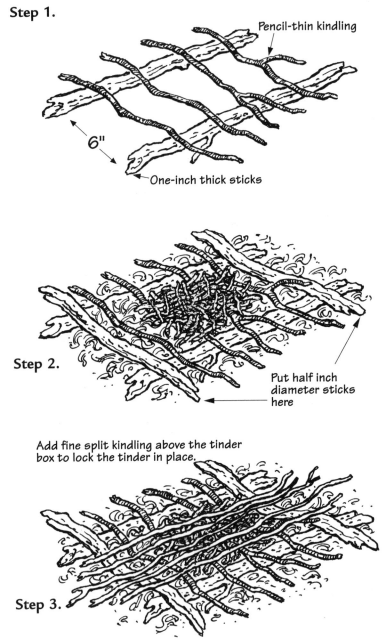

Pencil-thin kindling

6"

One-inch thick sticks

Step 2.

Put half inch
diameter sticks
here

Add fine split kindling above the tinder
box to lock the tinder in place.

Step 3.

FIGURE F-1. Fire building procedures.

An effective method of drying matches is to draw them briskly through your hair. Don't use your clothes; they are too abrasive.

"Fire-Ribbon"—a semi-liquid fire-starting paste is available at most camp stores. Just squeeze it on like toothpaste. A summer's supply will fit in a 35 mm film can.

You can make your own fire-starters by soaking miniature "logs" of rolled newspaper in paraffin.

Cotton balls dipped in Vaseline make wonderful fire-starters!

Emergency fire-making kits: You'll need a flattened half gallon milk carton, a handful of wood shavings (cedar is best), some splittings of scrap wood, fire-ribbon, and a small candle. Store everything in a Zip-loc bag. When emergency strikes, rip up the milk carton, splash tinder with Fire-Ribbon, and light your match. Materials will burn reliably for at least five minutes—enough time for you to search the woods for additional fuel.

Witch's broom is a blue-gray lichen which grows on the branches of some evergreen trees. It is extremely flammable when dry.

Paper is hydrophilic (loves water). It absorbs moisture on damp days. Don't depend on paper to start your fires!

In an emergency, you can always burn money!

One or two sticks robbed from a beaver's house makes good kindling and tinder. Beaver wood has been "debarked" so it is apt to be rot-free. For the sake of the beaver, please take only one or two sticks, then, only in an emergency.

Emergency ignitors: You can't beat a butane lighter and dry matches! The chemically impregnated magnesium rods sold as "survival tools" will ignite dry tinder, but are next to worthless when things are damp. And magnifying glasses must be very large (at least 2 inches in diameter) to reliably ignite tinder.

Steel wool makes excellent emergency tinder.

Flour (any kind) will burst into potent flames if sprinkled lightly over a blaze.

Cooking oil (vegetable oil) will enrich a flame only if the fire is already very hot.

Make a "tubular fire blower!" (Figure F-4). You'll need a six-inch long piece of narrow diameter copper or aluminum

FIGURE F-4. Tubular fire blower

tubing and eighteen inches of plastic or rubber "Bunsen-burner" hose. Most hardware stores have these materials.

Use your "blower" to nurse a fickle flame and whenever wood is too thick or damp to burn well. The concentrated air turbo-charges hot coals and turns them into willing flames.

An unused rain jacket or small square of plastic will provide all the overhead protection you need to start a fire in a driving rain. So will an overturned canoe, propped up by paddles shoved through the seat braces.

To maintain fire in a driving rain: Build a loose "log cabin" around your fire with whatever wood is available. Construct a two tier, flat "roof" for your cabin from newly cut kindling and fuel. The roof will deflect rain and the fire below will dry out the lower level of wood and bring it to flame. If you maintain a two-tier roof, you'll have a continuous supply of dry wood no matter how much it rains. *Note:* Since you're robbing the fire of oxygen, expect smoke . . . lots of it!

Banking the fire to preserve fuel: Use this procedure when you have a good hot fire but little wood to maintain it.

"Bank" your fire by setting small logs, parallel to one another, across the top. Rule of thumb for a smoke-free flame is to allow a radius width between parallel pieces of wood. Thus, a pair of 2-inch thick logs should be separated by a full inch to ensure adequate ventilation. Banking will reduce this distance to a mere (though identifiable) slit, which will naturally diminish use of oxygen and slow combustion. You should also eliminate any breeze coming into the fire. A large flat rock or a tier of logs will work fine.

Extinguishing the fire: Throwing water on a fire is not good enough. You must ascertain it is out by checking the fiery bed with your hands. If water is in short supply, use the "stir/sprinkle/stir" method outlined below.

1. Sprinkle a handful of water on the flames with your hands. Continue to sprinkle until the fire has gone out.
2. Stir the fire with a stick and sprinkle some more. Repeat as needed until the fire is DEAD OUT!

First Aid for the Common Ailments

The following tips and procedures are from the pen of my friend, Dr. Tom Schwinghamer. Tom is a family practitioner and a fellow of the American Board of Family Practice. He is also the Chief Operating Officer of the Allina Medical Group and continues to practice family medicine in Hastings, Minnesota. Before coming to Hastings, Tom practiced general medicine for 10 years in the U.S./Canadian border town of Ely, Minnesota. Here, he again and again came to grips with the injuries and ailments unique to the Boundary Waters Canoe Area wilderness environment.

I've had the good fortune to canoe many remote wilderness rivers with Tom Schwinghamer and to watch his expertise at work. His state-of-the-art methods and medications are uniquely tempered by the essential practicalities imposed by rugged, non-sterile wilderness settings and by the experience of one who has often treated life-threatening injuries alone without exotic hospital equipment.

(CJ).

Says Tom Schwinghamer: "Most of the wilderness accidents I encountered in Ely were self-inflicted—mostly drownings, frostbite and falls—that resulted from poor planning and careless behavior. Pre-trip planning that emphasizes caution is the best medical kit you can carry. There are no simple solutions for drownings, head injuries or multiple fractures. For starters, a medical history on everyone in your crew is a must. You must be aware of heart problems, insect sting and drug allergies, diabetes and asthma. There is simply no substitute for anticipating the unexpected. And, for being appropriately prepared!"

In preparing this section, I kept uppermost in mind that:

1. Most wilderness travelers have little, if any, in-depth first-aid knowledge and have neither the time nor inclination to make a study of the subject. Consequently, any formula for "wilderness medicine" must be brief, easy to administer, and correct.
2. Sanitary facilities are not available in the back-country. Nonetheless, sanitary procedures are often essential. Outdoors people need some "quick 'n dirty ways" to deal effectively with this problem.
3. Most outdoors men and women don't want to carry a sophisticated first-aid kit. Medications and materials should be few, and they should fit easily into a small nylon bag.
4. Most first-aid courses teach too much, in too much depth, too fast. And what is taught is seldom applicable to the wilderness environment. The majority of outdoor folk will do better to eliminate from concern heavy duty injuries and, to instead, concentrate on the most common disorders.

With this focus in mind, I offer these easy, practical methods for treating the most common wilderness ailments.

Building a simple, effective first aid kit

You need only four medications, so leave the aspirin, iodine, eye and ear drops and Epsom salts at home.

1. *CEFTIN antibiotic:* This is a broad-spectrum, 500 mg prescription drug that will kill most germs. Use it for an ear or eye infection, infected skin lac-

eration, inflamed fish hookfish-hook site, or sore throat. If it's hot, red and sore, it's probably infected, especially if there has been injury to the skin. Ceftin needs to be taken twice daily in the form of a 500 mg tablet, so a seven day supply will fit nicely into a 35 mm film can. Ceftin requires a prescription, something your family physician will surely write if he/she knows how you plan to use it.

Caution: Do not take ceftin if you are allergic to penicillin. Your family physician can recommend an alternate broad-spectrum antibiotic.

2. *TYLENOL #3:* This is a heavy-duty pain-reliever with codeine. Again, it's a prescription drug. It can sometimes produce nausea and vomiting, though this is rare. Tylenol #3 works well for nearly all forms of pain. Take one to three tablets every four to six hours as needed for pain.
2. *VOLTAREN-XR,* 100 mg: Voltaren-XR is an anti-inflammatory prescription drug that is excellent for all "over-use" symptoms (see *Over-use syndromes* on page 90). One tablet per day for swelling and pain is enough.
4. *BACTROBAN CREAM:* This is an excellent antibiotic cream that can be used for burns, abrasions and other minor skin injuries. It works best if applied early after the initial injury.

Equipment

XYLOCAINE (1 percent): It's almost impossible to remove a deeply imbedded fish hook without causing severe pain. Xylocaine is a safe, easy-to-use local anesthetic that will make the procedure virtually painless (see *Fish hook treatment* on page 87 for details). Ask your family physician to get you a 3 cc syringe loaded with 1 percent Xylocaine.

AIR CAST (ankle/foot): Here's a foolproof recipe for a sprained ankle, one that will be helpful if the sprain later turns out to be a nondisplaced fracture. Air casts are compact and require only a few minutes to apply. They can be purchased from your local clinic, hospital supply center or orthopedic house. This apparatus is a must for any serious backpacking or canoeing trip. Excellent instructions come with every air cast; you don't need a knowledge of splinting to apply it.

OVAL EYE PADS (sterile): Soft, contoured bandages used for corneal abrasions, blisters and any place you need lots of cushioning. Most drugstores carry them.

Tip: Eye pads work great for covering any wound. They're compact, soft and sterile.

MICROFOAM TAPE: Stretchy, foam-backed tape that stays put no matter how you move. Excellent for patching eyes, broken blisters, and most wounds. This is a standard item in all clinics and is occasionally found in drugstores.

IDOFORM SPONGE (a hospital supply center item): Technically called a "bactroscrub surgical sponge-brush," this iodine/detergent-loaded sponge is great for scrubbing away dirt without injuring tissue. The povidone/iodine solution kills germs. The idoform sponge is re-usable: Store it in a Zip-loc bag between uses.

NASAL STAT BALLOON: Optional, but possibly a life-saving item that will stop uncontrollable nose bleeds (see *Nose bleeds* on page 90). This product can be purchased from your local clinic or hospital supply center.

In addition to the above device, *POPE POSTERIOR NASAL PACKING* is a relatively recent development made by the Merocel Corporation. It is a simple packing that is easy to install into the nose, expands when inserted and is appreciably more comfortable than the nasal stat balloon.

EYE STREAM (sterile irrigating solution): You can buy a small bottle of sterile, normal saline solution at all pharmacies. Although completely sterile technique is impossible in the backcountry, having a small bottle of sterile solution for irrigating wounds, flushing foreign matter from eyes and clearing burns is extremely handy.

ANAKIT: Severe allergic reactions are extremely rare but when they do occur, they can present a life-threatening situation. Anakits—available by prescription at any drugstore—have specific directions on how to treat the individual who has become ill from a bee sting.

FOUR YARDS OF SIX-PLY GAUZE (need not be sterile).

Note: You can get prescriptions for all the suggested medications from your family physician. Other items mentioned here can be purchased through your local clinic or hospital supply center, or ordered by mail from *Chinook Medical Gear, Inc. P.O. Box 3300, Eagle, CO 81631, (970) 328–2100.*

The Mini-First-Aid Kit

If you're really going light and want the absolute minimum, assemble these items: twenty-four tablets of CEFTIN, four eye-patches, one roll of microfoam tape, one tube of BAC-TROBAN and a few bandaids. With these, and due caution, you can handle most of the common medical emergencies.

Ailments and Injuries
Skin Lacerations

Wound care: The initial treatment is the same whether the wound is a laceration, scrape or burn. You'll need sterile irrigation and an idoform sponge. Clean the skin injury with the idoform sponge and sterile water. Be sure you scrub out all the dirt and irrigate it away. Don't try to repair lacerations and don't terminate your trip because of them unless they are severe. Finish with a sterile dressing. One or two eye pads and microfoam tape will do the job on medium-size wounds.

If the wound becomes infected (hot, red and sore), start antibiotics. One tablet twice a day of ceftin will do the trick. Continue ceftin for seven days or until the soreness is gone.

Fish Hook

A hook in the cheek will kill the planned trip. You must be able to treat this injury if you have anglers along. A hook through the skin is one of the most common wilderness injuries.

Treatment: The common advice is to work the embedded barb through the skin, cut it off and extract the hook. But this won't work if the hook is embedded to the curve. You may have to back the hook out partially and re-set the angle so the tip will clear the skin rather than simply work deeper into it. In any case, you'll have a messy situation with lots of pain. Here's a painless way to extract the hook:

Start by injecting the entrance hole of the fish hook with 1–2 ml of Xylocaine from the pre-loaded Xylocaine syringe. Then, wait several minutes for the drug to take effect and proceed to work the hook back out slowly. If you're unsuccessful, turn it through the skin, cut off the barb with a small wire cutters and turn it back. Then, treat the wound as a skin laceration.

Note: Don't be scared off by the Xylocaine injection. There's no way you can mess up. The first time you extract a fish hook "cold turkey" you'll understand why a local anesthetic is so important! A less barbaric method of fish hook extraction without Xylocaine, as suggested by Dr. Bill Forgey in his book, *Wilderness Medicine*, is illustrated below. Use the "string-pull" method when the hook is embedded in insensitive regions like the shoulder, back of head and parts of the torso and extremities. Use the Xylocaine/ surgical procedure for sensitive areas, like those around the mouth and eye. If you are unsure of your extraction skills, tape the fish hook in place so it won't do further damage, and evacuate the victim to a hospital.

I've used the "string-pull" pull method on two occasions, and each time the victim said he felt no pain. In fact, the victim often doesn't realize when the hook is out! Here's the procedure (Figure F-5):

1. Loop light cord or heavy fishing line around the curve of the hook.
2. Push the eye of the hook firmly against the surface of the skin.
3. While holding the shank down, firmly jerk the cord.

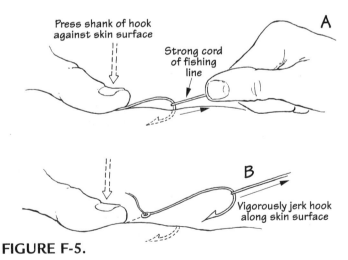

FIGURE F-5.

Burns

About the only way you can get badly burned in the back-country is to roll in the campfire while wearing polypropylene or nylon clothing. Or, to get struck by lightning. *Treatment:* Clean the burn with the idoform sponge and sterile water (see *Skin Lacerations,* page 87). Cover with Bactroban cream and clean gauze dressings and observe daily. Start oral antibiotics (one 500 mg ceftin tablet twice a day) at the first sign of infection.

Blisters

First line of defense is to keep the blister from breaking, which means isolating it from the abrasion of the shoe. "Standing operating procedure" (SOP) is to cover the cell with *moleskin,* an adhesive-backed flannel material available at drug stores. If you don't have moleskin, simply use a large bandage or an eye patch with microfoam tape.

If the blister breaks, treat it as a small burn (see *Burns* above). Two eye patches and microfoam tape will stabilize a broken blister well enough for the victim to resume walking in reasonable comfort.

Bee Sting

These usually produce just a sore red area but can be life-threatening to victims with bee-sting allergies. Following the directions in the Anakit can be lifesaving!

Frostbite

Treat these as burns and evacuate the victim if the frostbite is severe.

Eye Injuries

Most common is an invisible scratch to the "clear window" cornea. There is almost always a history of mild injury such as a tree branch scrape 12–24 hours before the onset of pain. *Treatment:* Patch the eye for just one day and administer Tylenol #3 pain medication. Patching is done not only to eliminate the irritating bright lights, but more importantly, to splint the eye and keep it from moving the injured part around under the lid. Use *two* oval eye pads plus 3M microfoam tape.

Ear Ailments
Ear pain is almost always an infection and it does not really matter whether it is a middle- or outer-ear infection. Start ceftin—500 mg twice a day—early. Administer Tylenol #3 if pain is severe.

Nose Ailments
Nose bleed is the only common problem. Treat by having the patient blow out all clots from the nose, then apply direct pressure to the nose by pinching it for approximately fifteen minutes just below the hard, bony part. If, after four attempts, the bleeding persists, you can use a nasal stat balloon, which is shoved into the nasal cavity and inflated, according to the enclosed directions. If you use the balloon, begin antibiotics to prevent infection. Don't forget the pope posterior packing. This is an extremely uncomplicated device and the ability to use it effectively in the backcountry is a good skill to have.

Note: I have never had to use a nasal stat balloon in the backcountry. However, it could be a lifesaving item in the event of an unstoppable nose bleed. Contrary to popular belief you *can* die from a nose bleed!

Throat Ailments
Don't sit around the campfire and debate when to start antibiotics for a sore throat, infected tooth or pus-filled wound. Start antibiotics at the first sign of these infections. Cough, fever and chest pain mean pulmonary infection. One 500 mg ceftin tablet twice a day will do the trick.

Back Ailments
Back pain is usually just muscular sprain from over-use. Treatment consists of rest and pain medication (Tylenol #3).

Over-use Syndromes
This is called many things and includes bursitis of the shoulder, tennis elbow, painful wrist syndrome and hands which "keep falling asleep" (a common canoeing malady). These problems all reflect soreness and swelling in an area that has been used a lot. Treatment is rest and an anti-inflammatory drug like Voltaren-XR (take one 100 mg tablet daily).

Ankle Sprains

Use the air cast. Soaking the limb in cold water initially for thirty minutes will retard swelling. A real advantage of the air cast is that you can wear your boot over it and resume near normal walking almost immediately.

About using the air cast, nasal stat balloon and other medical items: Excellent instructions come with all medical products. So don't be intimidated by your unfamiliarity with these products.

Dislocated Shoulder

A dislocated shoulder is one of the most common and painful ailments. Relocation is easy if you use the *Stimson* method illustrated in Figure F-6.

Procedure: Place the victim face down on a flat, elevated platform, like a rock face or over-turned boat. Place an approximate ten-pound weight inside a fabric stuff sack and tie the sack to the wrist of the fully extended arm with a soft handkerchief or padded belt. As the muscles tire, the victim will relax and the shoulder will relocate. The method is foolproof.

Warning: Don't assume you can handle all emergencies with the few items and skills suggested here. When serious injury threatens, your best bet is to evacuate the victim immediately. The items and methods outlined here are not a

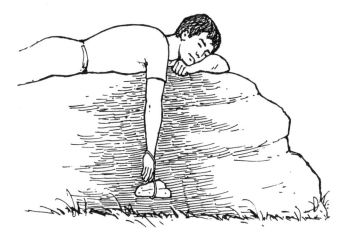

FIGURE F-6. Stimson manuever

substitute for the skills of a competent physician and the controlled environment of a hospital.

If you need more in-depth medical information than what's in these pages, see Dr. Bill Forgey's classic book, *Wilderness Medicine, 4th Edition*. You may also want to take some practical first-aid classes.

Flashlights and Camp Lighting Devices

Any light used for camping should be waterproof and have a lanyard ring so it can be hung in a tent. It should also have a positive rotary switch that won't accidentally turn on in your pack. Most popular flashlights are AA-cell models with alkaline batteries and high intensity bulbs. These tiny lights burn out batteries and bulbs quickly but are nice if you want maximum brightness and minimum size. Most practical—and still the best value for the dollar—is the old twin-C or D-cell standard flashlight, albeit with an angled head and high impact, waterproof case.

Head Lamps

Heavy-duty head lamps like the powerful "Justrite™ electric head lantern" (it runs on four D-cell batteries) really lights up the night. I like the Justrite™ for winter camping because its separate battery pack clips to my belt and stays warm inside my down parka.

For summer canoe trips, I prefer a tiny Maglite® or a lightweight AA head lamp like the PETZL EO3. These lights have a rotating lens that focuses the beam from flood to spot.

You can make a head lamp out of any small flashlight by tucking it inside—or Velcro-ing it to—a head band rolled from a cowboy neckerchief. There are some elastic head bands which convert AA Maglites to head lamps.

Bulb and battery basics

Battery features:
- Other things being equal, the bigger the battery, the longer it will last.
- Alkaline batteries cost much more than zinc-carbon bat-

teries but last about five times longer. Lithium batteries last longest (up to ten years!), but they're frightfully expensive. Anne Bancroft was the first woman to travel across the ice to both the North and South Poles. She carried an MSR head lamp and a small Tekna™ flashlight which she wore on a string around her neck. Both lamps were powered by lithium batteries—essential in the minus 70° Fahrenheit cold.

Rechargeable batteries:
• Zinc-carbon batteries can be recharged and used in any flashlight, but the charge won't last as long as expensive nickel-cadmium (NiCd) batteries. At this writing, Rayovac's Renewal® alkaline batteries, which last up to three times longer than NiCd's, are the only alkaline batteries which can be recharged.
• Gas-filled bulbs are much brighter and more expensive than vacuum bulbs but they don't last as long. Generally, the brighter a bulb, the faster it will burn out.

Candle lanterns are more "cutesy" than functional. Batteries burn for about the same length of time as quality candles of similar weight, and artificial light is much brighter than open flame. Nonetheless, candle lanterns are "fun toys," and they add some warmth to a tent on chilly nights. They are best at home for winter camping where every BTU of heat is appreciated.

Mantle lanterns: The mini-size Coleman Peak 1 lantern puts out nearly as much light (for half the size and weight) as its traditional big brother. Mantle lanterns are considered essential equipment for auto camping, but are viewed as *"gauche"* by the self-propelled camping crowd. However, they are strong enough to withstand the abuse of rugged canoe or horse packing trips if you pad the globes and pack them well. The new mantles are much stronger than those of decades ago.

Caution: Never inhale the fumes from a newly lit (previously unburned) mantle. The gasses which are released are highly poisonous!

If your lantern won't generate pressure, the leather pump gasket may be too dry (needs oil). Trail stoves also suffer from this malady. Most of the new pump gaskets are synthetic; the traditional leather models work better. Some leather stool washers (check the plumbing section of your hardware store) fit some lanterns and stoves perfectly!

Don't fill a mantle lantern more than three-fourths full of gas. You need air space to generate pressure.

GPS (Global Positioning System)

Hottest new navigational device is the hand-held GPS (Global Positioning System). With a GPS receiver, you can determine an accurate position anywhere on earth in a matter of minutes. Or, you can enter a set coordinates of a place you want to go and the GPS receiver will provide a compass bearing and distance that will be updated by satellite information as you progress. Press a button and you get a speed readout and an estimated time of arrival (ETA). You must be moving faster than about 11 miles per hour to get an accurate measure of your speed. Hikers and canoeists *should not* take GPS speed readings too seriously!

Without a map, a GPS can be used to track your location. Enter your starting position and save it as a *"way point."* Establish other way points as you proceed, then, like Hansel and Gretel, follow your electronic "bread crumbs" home.

When the military discovered that GPS receivers were more accurate than they expected, they became concerned that an enemy might use a GPS to target a missile. So they introduced a random error (there is talk of eliminating it) of 15–100 meters into the civilian GPS signal. To accomplish the error, the satellites slightly delay when they send their signals. This means that locating an obscure trail junction or campsite is not a sure thing. A GPS will get you in the ball park but you'll need a map to find the ball.

You must know how to read and interpret topographic maps in order to master GPS technology. You must also have—and know how to use—an accurate compass. The one built into a GPS has limited capabilities. Be aware that all hand-held GPS units operate on small batteries which could fail when you need them most. And few civilian GPS models are waterproof, which means you must be careful how you use them in rain.

It is not practical to leave a GPS on for continuous positioning unless you have battery recharging capabilities or an unlimited supply of batteries. The most useful GPS feature is its ability to verify your location on a map—possible *only* if your map has a reference system to which your GPS can relate. Not all maps have appropriate reference lines. Those that do include all U.S. and Canadian topographic maps which are marked with degrees of latitude and longitude. Canadian maps and U.S. military maps also provide decimal-based Universal Trans Mercator (UTM) coordinates which are much easier to use than latitude/longitude. Any GPS can be set to read Lat/Lon or UTM coordinates, as you prefer.

Maps that don't have a coordinate system to which the GPS can relate include nearly all public road maps, most state and national park hiking and boating maps and special purpose recreational maps, like those drawn for the Boundary Waters Canoe Area of Minnesota. If you use one of these special purpose maps, you'll also need to carry a GPS-compatible topographic map.

The bottom line: is that Your map must have integral GPS coordinates or you won't be able to plot the fix your GPS calculates! Topographic maps are hard to find in most towns, but you can mail order them from the government sources listed in the *Maps* section, page 116.

Hand Cream and Lip Balm

"Moisturizers" are among the most important—and forgotten—items on a camping trip. I double-up on tubes and keep them in different places in my pack. Warm Skin™, by

Aurora, is the best hand cream I've found. It acts like an extra pair of gloves and reduces wind-chapping. Its udder-balm and aloe formula doesn't make your hands or tools feel slimy. Anne Bancroft used it on her Antarctic adventure.

Honey—Good Medicine for Wounds!

Honey will sweeten your tea and heal your wounds. It is slightly acidic so it effectively kills micro-organisms. The University of South Florida in Tampa used honey on patients who were undergoing abdominal surgery. Doctors there found that the honey was more effective than some expensive antibiotics!

Dr. Avashalom Mirzrahi, a microbiology professor at Hebrew University in Israel, discovered that honey is also good medicine for treating burns and ulcers. Medical reports show that people who took 2–3 ounces of honey each day over several months cured their ulcer.

Hypothermia

Background: Hypothermia (commonly called "exposure sickness") is the most common and dangerous of outdoor ailments. No one is immune to its icy grip. You can suffer hypothermia while climbing a mountain in Tibet or biking across Chicago. Dozens of people die from it each year.

Hypothermia occurs when body temperature drops below about 95 degrees Fahrenheit. As blood is rushed to the vital organs, chilling spreads throughout the body. This is accompanied by clumsiness, slurred speech, and loss of judgment. Coma and death may result within a few hours if body temperature is not raised.

Hypothermics usually cannot identify their problem. They will maintain (often, until death!) that they are "okay." You must observe symptoms, diagnose correctly, and treat quickly. Your friend's life may depend on it. Check these symptoms:

1. Slurred speech, stiffness in limbs (difficulty in walking), an irrational view of reality. Victim acts

irresponsibly—loses hat, mittens, or other equipment along the trail. Loss of short term memory.
2. Victim can't walk a straight line.
3. Victim was shivering before, now shivering has stopped.

Note: Mild shivering is nature's way of re-warming the body. It does not indicate hypothermia. Hypothermia begins with violent shivering. Be aware, however, that some people—especially those who are over-tired—do not exhibit a shivering reflex. So do not rely on shivering to ascertain the onset of hypothermia!

Treatment:

1. Provide shelter at once! Any place out of the wind and wet is good enough.
2. Replace wet clothing with dry.
3. Apply moderate, even heat. If a fire is available, use it. If there are several people in your party, have them loosely "hug" the victim to keep him/her as warm as possible.

Be sure the victim's head and neck are covered with warm clothing (hat, scarf, etc.).

If the victim can swallow, hot soup (or water) will re-warm spirits and insides. Do not administer stimulants like alcohol, coffee, or tea.

For serious cases (where the victim is unable to walk, suffers amnesia, etc.) administer the "sandwich" treatment. This consists of stripping the victim's clothes and sandwiching him/her between two non-hypothermics. Cover the threesome with sleeping bags and clothing. Be sure to insulate everyone from the cold ground (use a foam trail pad, additional clothing, leaves, grass, branches, etc.).

Hypothermics must be handled gently: Rough-housing may initiate a heart attack!

4. Hypothermia drains both body and spirit. Considerable rest is warranted after the danger subsides.

Knives

The primary use for any camp knife is cooking and preparing foods. You'll slice vegetables, meat and cheese, spread jam and peanut butter, and cut your supper steak. Rambo survivalists will insist on a stiff-backed sheath knife with a blade at least 6 inches long, while more gentle souls will argue the merits of a pen knife. Between the two extremes are scores of expert campers who will agree that at least one knife in the camping party should meet these characteristics:

1. Enough length (4–5 inches) to slice meat and cheese and to reach deep into the peanut butter can without getting gunked up.
2. A thin, flat-ground blade for effortless slicing.

Nearly all knives sold for outdoor use have blades which are too thick. One-eighth of an inch across the spine is the maximum thickness permissible for a utility knife, no matter how delicate the edge. Try slicing a tomato with the typical "hunting" knife and you'll see why!

Your favorite kitchen knife would probably be perfect for camp use if it had a bit less length, more backbone, and better steel. In fact, the most popular knives on the frontier were the famous "Green River" models, which were nothing more than solidly built kitchen knives.

The primary camp knife may be a fixed blade or folding model. You'll pay much more for a good folder than for a sheath knife of similar length.

If your taste runs to folding knives, select a model with a 3–4 inch long, thin, preferably flat-ground blade. Despite advertising claims, knives with locking blades are no safer than those with traditional pressure springs. The only advantage of a lock-back is that it can be opened single-handedly while wearing mittens. Traditional folders require two hands to use.

Which knife for you? If you've read between the lines, you'll conclude that you need two knives for camping: a thin-ground, kitchen-style model for preparing foods, and a substantial multi-purpose folder of some sort. I carry a sheath knife with a 4⅓ inch blade, and a multipurpose Leatherman™ tool. There's also a Swiss Army knife hidden in my pack. The nail file and scissors are very useful.

Stainless or carbon steel? Stainless is much more difficult and expensive to "work" than carbon steel. It's also harder to sharpen, especially to the super-sharp shaving edge I prefer. My experience suggests that most people—particularly those who are not expert at sharpening knives—will be happier with a high grade carbon steel blade than a stainless one. Granted, carbon steel rusts, but so does a fine axe or gun. If you're serious about the outdoors—you'll take joy in maintaining your knife.

Steel hardness: The "Rockwell" (Rc) test is the standard by which the hardness of steel is measured. The higher the number, the harder the steel. Generally, hard steels take and retain a better edge than soft steels. There's a limit, of course—steel that is too hard may be too brittle for knives. There's a common agreement that a rating of Rc 56–59 is ideal for good edge holding with minimum brittleness (assuming that quality steel is used). Most cheap pocket knives run much less than Rc 56, while nearly all high quality knives fall into the 56–59 range. Some special steels, hardened to Rc 60 and beyond, are used on a limited basis for very expensive custom knives. Only diamonds are harder than zircon-oxide (ceramic) blades, whose Rc ratings approach 100(!). However, ceramic knives are much too brittle for serious outdoors use.

Smooth edge or serrated? A lion's share of today's outdoor knives have serrated edges which are great for cutting through wrist-thick rope and airplane doors. But how do they slice salami and pine? Not very well. And they are nearly impossible for the average person to sharpen! A folding saw, hand-axe and thin-bladed knife, in combination, will outperform *any* Rambo-style survival blade on the planet. Believe it!

Here are my preferences, along with some specific knives I can recommend:

Fixed-blade knives: In 1967 I purchased a fixed-blade Gerber Shorty. Its thin (.080"), flat-ground tool-steel blade had enough heft to split kindling, and sufficient flex to fillet fish. It applied peanut butter to pita bread with the efficiency of a professional spreader. I've resharpened the old Gerber till it can't be sharpened anymore, so in 1996, I set out to find a replacement. I began my search for a Shorty look-alike by studying every knife catalog in the land. I figured a knife as practical as the Shorty must have keen competition. Wrong! There wasn't a good "user" in the lot. Every blade I saw was either too short, too thick, hollow ground, too wide, or had dumb serrations. I wondered if the designers of these knives ever spent any time in the woods!

Ultimately, the choice came down to re-grinding an old carbon steel butcher knife or designing my own. I chose the latter option and asked Mike Mann—a full time custom knife-maker, living in a log cabin in the mountains of Idaho—to build my dream knife. Mann mostly forges award-winning blades for historical reenactments, but he also builds modern hunting, fishing and kitchen knives. He flat-grinds all his blades and he doesn't use stainless steel. I was thrilled to discover that his prices were well below his competitors.

I used the Gerber Shorty as a working pattern, added more belly and a sharp, dropped point. I specified a .078" thick blade and full-tang handle with polished wood (Mike used curly maple) scales. My new "Cliff" knife, as Mann calls it, is lighter, better balanced and much prettier than the old Gerber. You can get one outfitted to your tastes from *Idaho Knife Works and Crafts, P.O. Box 144, Spirit Lake, ID 83869. Shop phone, (208) 437–2086; cellular phone (509) 994–9394.* Write for a free catalog.

Note: I have no financial affiliation of any sort with Idaho Knife Works. I simply suggest the Cliff knife to you because it works so well for me.

I also like the new A.G. Russell *Deer Hunter* and *Bird & Trout* knives. The *Deer Hunter* has a thin (.080") 4-inch long blade; the *Bird & Trout* has a 3-inch long, .060" blade. Both knives are flat-ground from AUS8A stainless steel, hardened to 57–59 Rc. Admittedly, I would prefer carbon steel, but 8A takes an acceptable edge. The plastic molded handles on these knives are plain-looking but functional, and the positive locking sheath is brilliant. *A.G. Russell Fine Knives, 1705 North Thompson Street, Springdale, AK 72764-1248, (800) 255–9034.*

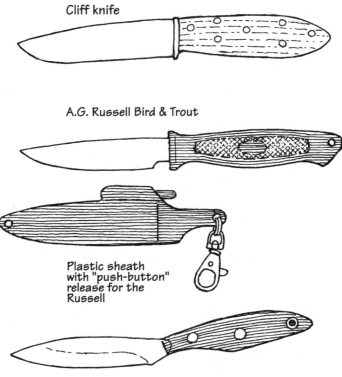

Cliff knife

A.G. Russell Bird & Trout

Plastic sheath
with "push-button"
release for the
Russell

Grohmann Trout & Bird

FIGURE K-A1.

I can also recommend the Grohmann #2 *Trout and Bird* knife, in *carbon steel* (don't get stainless!). The sabreground edge is somewhat severe for fine work, but the little Grohmann can be honed whisker sharp. *Grohmann Knives Ltd., P.O. Box 40, Pictou, Nova Scotia, Canada BOK 1HO, (902) 485–4224.*

Folding Knives: *Schrade* carbon-steel *Old Timer* knives are an outstanding buy. "Old Timers" come in a variety of styles from tiny pen knives to big twin-blade lock-backs.

Most discount stores have an assortment of these knives. There are also some practical sheath knives in the Old Timer line. I only wish Schrade would see fit to use thinner steel for the blades.

How to care for your edged tools: I occasionally spray working saws and axes with WD-40. I wipe kitchen knives with digestible canola oil or occasionally cut salami or cheese. **Caution:** *Do not* use petroleum oils on knives that will be used to cut food!

Flitz® and Wenol® are terrific metal polishes if you like a mirror-bright finish on your knives. RIG Universal®—a Vaseline-like product which is available at gun shops—provides superb long-term protection (even against salt water) for carbon-steel tools.

Sharpening: Don't ever sharpen a knife on an electric sharpener or one of those mechanical wheeled gadgets sold at supermarkets. You'll ruin the knife beyond repair!

Most sporting goods stores stock diamond stones (a first choice!) and medium grit soft Arkansas stones. If you want a razor edge, you'll need a hard Arkansas stone, as well.

Maintain a film of light oil on the natural stones (cutting oil, kerosene, or WD-40; use water on the diamond stones) to float away the steel particles which clog the pores of the stone and reduce its cutting efficiency. Clean the stone and blade frequently and apply new oil during the sharpening process.

Keep the back of the blade raised 15–20 degrees, and cut into the stone, while sharpening. A good way to maintain the proper angle is to adjust an overhead light so it casts a shadow along the back of the blade when the blade is laid flat on the stone. Raise the blade until the shadow just disappears and you'll have the recommended angle.

Exotic looking tools which clamp to the knife blade are sold for the purpose of maintaining the "proper sharpening angle." These tools work well but are nonetheless gimmicks for people who never learned to sharpen knives properly.

Take about four strokes per side before turning the knife over and use plenty of oil. If you can't maintain the proper sharpening angle, try using a circular motion (not recommended) of the blade instead.

If you want a fine razor edge, complete the sharpening process on a "fine" Arkansas stone. Finish by stropping the

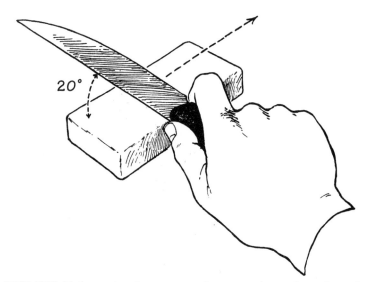

FIGURE K-1. Maintain a 15–20 degree angle, and cut into the stone. Use plenty of cutting oil and clean the stone (and blade) frequently.

sharpened blade on a piece of leather impregnated with jewelers rouge (draw the blade evenly across the leather, one stroke per side).

To check for blade sharpness: A knife is considered "sharp" if it will shave hair from the back of your hand. A less barbaric method is to shine a bright light on the sharpened edge. You should see no flat spots, no inconsistencies . . . nothing!

Sharpening (butcher's) steels do not sharpen a knife; they merely realign the microscopic teeth of the blade edge. A steel is handy for touching up a knife (it's simply a coarse version of a leather strop) but it can't take the place of a genuine whetstone.

Tip: If you dip the blade of your knife in boiling water for about thirty seconds, it will be much easier to sharpen.

Best way to carry a hefty folding knife is in a pocket sewn into the back of your field trousers. Sew a line of stitches through the pant leg and pocket as illustrated (Figure K-2) and attach a snap-flap or Velcro tab at the top.

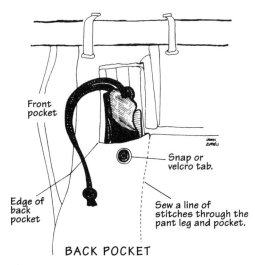

Front
pocket

Snap or
velcro tab.

Edge of
back
pocket

Sew a line of
stitches through the
pant leg and pocket.

BACK POCKET

FIGURE K-2. Carry large folding knives in a pocket sewn into the back pocket of your field trousers.

Equip your knife with a nylon lanyard so you can pull it out with one hand.

This system is more secure, less obtrusive, and more comfortable than a leather sheath worn on the belt.

To make a sheath for a fixed blade knife, you'll need: sole leather (the thicker the better), contact cement, two-piece rivets, paper, scissors, and a sharp utility knife. Leather and rivets may be ordered from any Tandy leather company store.

1. Make a pattern for your sheath from paper or thin, corrugated cardboard.
2. Transfer the paper pattern to the leather.
3. Soak the leather in lukewarm water until it is soft, then cut out the sheath pattern with a sharp knife.
4. Contact cement a ¼-inch wide "edge guard" of leather around the sheath perimeter.
5. Rivet a belt loop to the back of the sheath, then contact cement the sheath edges together.
6. Insert the knife into the glued sheath and painstakingly form the wet leather to fit. Work the hilt area carefully until you get a perfect fit.

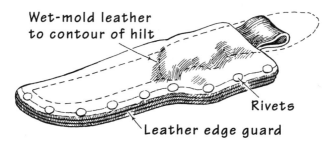

Wet-mold leather
to contour of hilt

Rivets

Leather edge guard

FIGURE K-A2.

7. Withdraw the knife from the sheath (the leather will remain formed) and rivet—or ask your shoemaker to sew—the sheath together.
8. When the sheath is dry, apply many coats of shoe polish. Do not use boot greases on sheaths; they will soften the leather.

Knots And Hitches/Lashings

While canoeing Manitoba's North Knife River in the summer of '91, my crew experienced three days of wind-driven, icy cold rain. Temperatures in the 30's and wind speeds of 30 miles an hour threatened to shred our paired (12' × 12') nylon rain tarps. I used every trick—and length of cord—to keep the shelter tight and well-drained.

When the skies cleared, we had one last admiring look at our storm-defying roof, before we began its disassembly. Resembling Charlotte's web, I'd used 200 feet of parachute cord, 100 feet of nylon rope, and two "Prussik's" to keep things taut. "Nice rig," remarked one man; "but how'll we ever get it down? Wet knots are murder to untie!"

"Just watch," I replied with a knowing grin. One pull of each "slippery" loop severed the lines in a matter of seconds. In all, barely five minutes were needed to coil ropes and cords and to stuff the flies into their awaiting sacks.

Fabric shelters must be tightly stressed to withstand high winds and prolonged rain. Guy and hem lines must be drum-tight, yet release easily (with a single pull!) when the storm subsides. The alternative to quick-release knots is to pick, swear, and cut them apart. Experienced outdoors people always end their knots with the "slippery" loops illustrated in this chapter. In Figure C-9, a quick-release knot is used to secure the mouth of a nylon stuff sack.

Outdoors handbooks define dozens of knots. But for camp use, the *half-hitch, power-cinch, sheet-bend* and *bowline* are enough. Occasionally, you may find use for the *Prussik loop* and the two common lashings illustrated here.

Use two half-hitches to anchor a rope or cord to an immovable object like a tree or rock. This is a good hitch to use when mooring a boat. You'll be able to untie the knot more easily if you end the second half-hitch with a quick-release loop as illustrated in Figure K-A3. Simply pull the line on through if you don't want the quick-release feature.

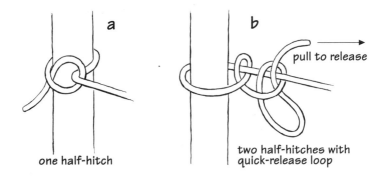

FIGURE K-A3. Two half-hitches

The *power-cinch* (a modification of the "trucker's knot") provides the block-and-tackle power you need to snug tent and tarp guy lines and keep them tight. The hitch ties and unties in a flash and is much more powerful, secure and versatile than the "tautline hitch" which is touted in old-time camping books. Use the power-cinch for rigging a clothes line, tying canoes on cars, securing a package on car-top carriers, and any place you need a tight lashing that

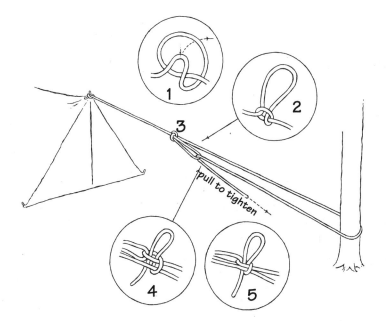

FIGURE K-A4. Power-cinch

won't slip. See my book, *The Basic Essential of Knots For the Outdoors,* for other practical uses of this ingenious hitch.

Begin the power-cinch by forming a simple overhand loop as shown in step 1. Pull the loop through as in step 2, forming the loop exactly as shown.

If the loop is formed as in step 2, a simple tug on the rope will eliminate it. This is preferable to the common practice of tying a knot in the loop, which after being exposed to a load is almost impossible to get out.

If you are tying a boat on top of a car, tie the long single line (shown attached to the tent) to the boat's bow or stern (use two half-hitches or a bowline) and run the double line through a steel S-hook on the car's bumper. Now, apply power, as illustrated. You have a tough pulley with a 2:1 mechanical advantage!

If you want a reliable knot, complete the hitch by tying a double half-hitch around the body of the rope. If you want the hitch to release with a single pull, end it with a single half-hitch and quick-release (slippery) loop as illustrated.

The *sheet-bend* is the knot of choice for tying two ropes together. Ropes tied with a *sheet-bend* won't slip under a load, and they come apart easily even after being pelted by heavy rain. When rope sizes are dissimilar, use the smaller diameter rope to make the bend and quick-release feature. If you want absolute security, as in rescue work, use the double sheet-bend!

Here's an absolutely secure knot that won't slip. Use it any place you need a non-slip loop at the end of a line. Mountain climbers use

Single sheet bend

Quick release (slippery) half-hitch
Pull to release

Double sheet bend

FIGURE K-A5. Sheet Bend

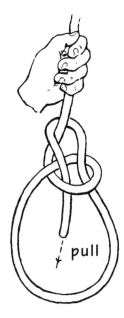

pull

FIGURE K-A6. Bowline

the bowline for securing their climbing ropes around their waists. If you require absolute security (especially with slippery polypropylene ropes), secure the tail of the finished knot around one arm of the loop with a couple of half-hitches.

Scenario: Rain is pooling on a portion of your

nylon cooking tarp. An aerial guy line would solve the problem but there is no place to anchor it. You could run a rope between two poorly situated trees then secure your guy line to it, but the pull would be parallel to the rope and the knot would slip down it. What to do? Why, rig a *Prussik* loop, of course! Use the Prussik whenever you want an absolutely secure loop that won't slip along a tight line. Mountaineers use this knot for footholds to climb a vertical rope. The Prussik loop slides easily along a tight rope, yet it jams solidly when a horizontal or vertical load is applied. Make the loop from an 18-inch length of parachute cord, completed with a sheet-bend.

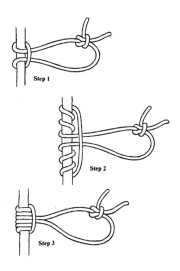

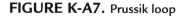

FIGURE K-A7. Prussik loop

Lashings

Use a "modified" *shear* lashing (Figure K-A8) to connect short spars together to achieve the pole length (around 6 feet) you need to heighten the roof of a rain tarp. A *diagonal* lashing (Figure K-A9) will connect spars in an "X" configuration and allow you to erect a tight ridge line when rope is in short supply.

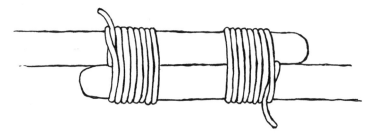

FIGURE K-A8. Modified shear lashing. Place the poles parallel to one another and tie a *clove hitch* around one pole. Then, wind your cord tightly around both poles several times and finish with a clove hitch.

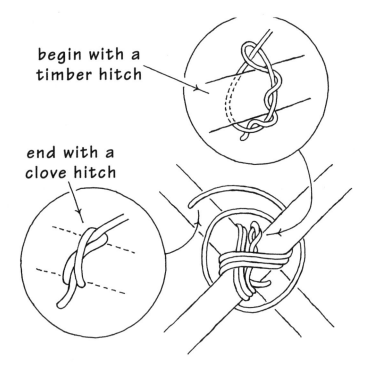

begin with a
timber hitch

end with a
clove hitch

FIGURE K-A9. Diagonal lashing. Begin with a very tight *timber hitch* around both poles. Take three or four turns side-by-side around one fork, and three or four more, side-by-side around the other. Then, tighten the lashing with two frapping turns and end it with a clove hitch around one of the poles.

L

Lightning

Background: Lightning is a more serious threat than most campers are willing to admit. Next to hypothermia, it is the most dangerous "thing" in the outdoors. Realities of back-country travel necessarily expose travelers to some risk of being struck by lightning, but this risk may be sharply reduced if you religiously follow these guidelines:

1. Lightning ordinarily strikes the highest object in its path, so if you pitch your tent in an open field or plateau, be certain there are trees or rock formations of significantly greater height nearby.
2. A cone of protection extends from the tallest trees or land mass (as the case may be) about 45 degrees outward. Pitch your tent, or walk, canoe, etc., within this cone of protection, but stay far enough from its source so that lightning can't jump from the object to you. Lightning may jump a dozen feet or more across water, so don't snug against the shoreline if you're canoeing or boating in an electrical storm. Instead, keep within the cone of protection offered by the shoreline trees.
3. Lightning may travel along the roots of trees, which may extend dozens of feet outward. If roots are close to the surface of the ground, as in rocky areas where there is little soil cover, sufficient energy may be transmitted along sub-surface roots to pose real danger to anyone standing on the ground above them. Keep this in mind when pitching your tent!
4. If you're caught outside the cone of protection and suddenly feel electrical energy building (dry hair will stand on end), immediately get as low as possible to reduce the human lightning rod effect.
5. The notion that non-metal boats are safer than metal ones in a lightning storm has no basis. A lightning strike generates millions of volts,

enough to fry anything in its path. Steel ships are occasionally struck by lightning, usually with no ill effects. This suggests that aluminum boats and canoes may in fact be safer than non-metal ones, simply because they more readily dissipate current around the hull into the surrounding water.

If lightning flashes all around, get down low in your boat (below the gunnels) to reduce the lightning rod effect. Again, try to maneuver into the cone of protection offered by the shoreline.

6. Always check your campsite for tall, leaning trees, especially dead ones, which may come crashing down on you in lightning or wind storms.

7. *If you're in a tent and lightning strikes all around:* Sit up immediately and draw your legs to your chest so that only your buttocks and feet contact the ground. A foam sleeping pad (preferably doubled) placed beneath you may provide enough insulation to keep you from being grounded. If you

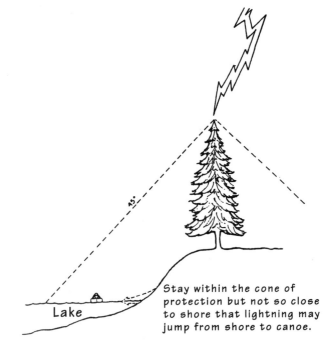

Lake

Stay within the cone of protection but not so close to shore that lightning may jump from shore to canoe.

FIGURE L-1.

have no foam rubber sleeping pad, substitute any material which will insulate you from the current.

It is absolutely essential that you maintain the recommended "sitting" position during an electrical storm. In the unlikely event you are struck by lightning while in this position, only your feet and buttocks are apt to burn. But if you're lying flat, electrical energy may pass through your heart and cause death.

Note: Use of a ground cloth inside your tent is highly recommended as it ensures you'll have a bone-dry tent. All your preventative efforts to outwit lightning will be dashed to the winds if your bedding gets wet. See, *Tents,* page 179 for a thorough discussion on the importance of an interior ground sheet.

After the Strike!

Lightning strikes a tree at the opposite end of your campsite. You run to your friends, one of whom is unresponsive and not breathing. One of his shoes is missing and there is a small deep burn on the sole of his foot. You check for a pulse; there is none.

Treatment: Lightning usually kills people by producing cardiac arrest. It may also paralyze the respiratory system. If your friend is alive, the burns are probably minor and you can attend to them later. Right now, you've got to get the heart and respiratory system working.

Begin CPR immediately! If you can restore heart rhythm and breathing, you can probably save your friend.

Keep the patient warm and send for help immediately. Electrocution may cause disorientation, coma, seizures and spinal cord injuries. It may also rupture the ear drums. All you can do till help arrives is to keep your friend immobilized and warm and convince him that he'll be okay.

Lyme Disease

According to wildlife experts, there are now more white-tailed deer in Minnesota, Michigan and Wisconsin than in the entire United States at the time of Columbus. Good news to hunters perhaps, but not to hikers who may contract debilitating Lyme disease which is carried by deer.

Over 20,000 cases of Lyme disease have been reported (in 43 states!) since 1980, and the number grows each year. Several species of *Ixodes* (deer/bear) ticks carry the disease. Ixodes ticks are very small, about the size of a sesame seed. Color is dark brown to black; the female often has a rusty brown appearance. You must be bitten by an infected tick to get Lyme disease. Other insects can carry the Lyme-producing bacteria, but they can't spread it to humans. Pregnant women *can* transmit the disease to their unborn infants. The disease has caused miscarriages, birth defects, and other health problems.

Symptoms: You won't feel the tick bite—it's painless. Symptoms may appear days (or years!) after being bitten. In the early stages, there's a red rash or lesion which can sometimes migrate to other areas of the body or spread in size. The lesion can be solid red or look like a "bulls-eye." The rash is usually about 4 inches across but can be much smaller or larger. You may experience fatigue, headache, fever, and muscle or joint aches. If Lyme disease goes untreated, it can cause arthritis, meningitis, and facial palsy.

Prevention

There's no vaccine for Lyme disease, so prevention is everything. Here are the most practical recommended field procedures:

1. Wear tightly woven long-sleeved shirts and long pants. Tuck your pants into high socks or rubberband or tape the cuffs to keep ticks from crawling up your legs. I prefer to tuck my pants into 12–16-inch high boots.

2. Ticks generally crawl upward, so a shirt collar may prevent ticks from crawling down your neck. Spray the collar of your shirt with insect repellent.

3. It's easier to see ticks on light-colored clothes than on dark-colored ones.

4. It's harder for ticks to hold on to tightly-woven fabrics than loosely-woven ones.

An Insecticide Plus Repellent is Your Best Protection
An insecticide which contains 0.5 percent *permethrin* will kill ticks on contact. Spray permethrin on your boots, pant cuffs and shirt sleeves, but *do not* get any on your skin! Permethrin should be sprayed on clothes and tent openings at least three hours before use, then allowed to dry in a well-ventilated area. Dried permethrin will kill ticks for up to two weeks and last through several rains and washings. Permethrin kills slowly; affected ticks may live an hour or more, which is not enough time for them to posture and dig into your skin! When used as directed, permethrin is safe and effective. Most sporting goods stores have it.

Use "skin-safe" repellents that have a high concentration of N-diethyl-meta-toluamide (DEET) on the exposed parts (avoid lips and eyes) of your body. Spread spray-on repellents *by hand* so you don't miss any spots. Treat arm and leg holes in clothing (tick "entry points") with both repellents *and* permethrin.

See page 30 for instructions on how to remove an embedded tick.

Maps and Map Tricks

Topographic maps, in the largest scale you can get, are best for finding your way in the backcountry. The smaller the denominator of the map scale fraction, the larger the scale and more useful the map. The numerator of the fraction indicates map units; the denominator equals ground units. Thus, a scale of 1/24,000 would be interpreted as "one unit of distance on the map equals 24,000 units of distance on the ground." Some representative comparisons are shown below:

1:24,000	1 inch on the map equals 2,000 feet on the ground.
1:50,000	1¼ inches equals one mile.
1:62,500	1 inch equals approximately one mile.
1:250,000	1 inch equals four miles.

For average field use, American maps in 1:62,500 scale, or Canadian maps in 1:50,000, scale are most versatile.

To order United States maps:
Branch of Distribution
U.S. Geological Survey
Box 25286, Federal Center
Denver, Colorado 80225

For charts and tide tables of U.S. coasts, the Great Lakes, sections of major rivers, and contoured fishing maps write:
National Oceanic and Atmospheric Administration/
National Ocean Survey (NOA/NOS)
Map & Chart Information, Distribution
Branch N/CG33
Riverdale, Maryland 20737

Until 1997, Canadian topographic maps could be purchased from:
The Canada Map Office
Department of Energy, Mines and Resources
615 Booth Street, Ottawa, Ontario
Canada K1A 0E9
Phone: (800) 465–6277

Now, Canadian maps must be ordered through U.S. or Canadian map distributors. Write or call the Canada Map Office for a list of distributors.

Map Index: Request a free index to topographic maps if you do not know precisely what to order. The index will tell you what maps are in print, in what scale, and at what cost. If you roughly define the area of your interest (to the nearest state or Canadian province), you'll receive the correct index from the U.S. Geological Survey or the Canadian map distributor.

Colored or monochrome maps? Some 1:50,000 scale

Canadian maps may be ordered as monochrome (black and white) editions. Monochrome maps are as accurate and easy to understand as colored versions but are less expensive. They also photocopy perfectly—something to consider if you want to provide low cost maps for a large number of people.

Aerial photos: All maps today are drawn from aerial photos. Photos are available for nearly every inch of land surface and are useful when you need the finest possible detail. Aerial photos are sometimes available as "stereo pairs." With them, you can accurately identify features as small as a boulder or tree. Inexpensive stereoscopes may be purchased from surveying companies and hobby shops.

The same agencies which supplied your maps can tell you how to get aerial photos. There are millions of photos on file, so be sure you accurately identify the location you need. Best way to get the right pictures is to box in the area of your interest on a large scale topo map. Send this map, with instructions, to the air photo library. They'll return your map with your order. You can also identify the photo location with precise latitude and longitude coordinates.

Land Use Information Series maps are available for some parts of Canada. They're standard 1:250,000 scale colored maps which have information about wildlife, fishing, geology, ecology, climate, places of interest, etc., overprinted on their surface. Land Use Information maps will tell you the precise location of lake trout, the migration route of caribou (and the time of migration), the nesting region for Peregrine falcons, etc. These maps are wonderful for planning trips or for dreaming! They cost no more than conventional topographic maps and they're available from the same place. Specify LAND USE INFORMATION SERIES maps when you order. A special index to these maps may be obtained free from any Canadian map distributor.

Provisional maps (white prints): Most topographic maps are old; some were last field checked decades ago. Topographic features won't change, of course, but man-made ones—roads, trails, buildings, powerlines, etc.—will. If, for example, you're going fishing in Canada, you'll want a map that indicates the location of recently built roads which service the area. Only the most recent topographic maps will indicate the features you want.

However, there may be provisional or white print maps available which have the information you need. Logging and mining companies and provincial Ministries of Natural Resources use provisional maps in their daily work. If these current, if unspectacular, maps are available, the MNR or the logging or mining company which services the area will know where to find them. The tourism office in the province of your interest will supply the addresses of MNR area offices. You may also call or write the Canadian Consulate for this information.

Contour lines: The light brown lines overprinted on topographic maps are called contour lines. They indicate the elevation (above sea level) of land features and thus permit you to view the topography in three dimensions rather than two. Entire books have been written about contour lines and their interpretation. However, you'll get along quite nicely if you master these basic rules:

1. Contour lines connect points of equal elevation. You will gain (or lose) elevation only when you travel from one contour line to another. If you walk along a contour line, you will "be on the level."
2. Closely spaced contour lines indicate lots of elevation change (drop) whereas wide-spaced lines show the opposite (Figures M-1,2).
3. The contour interval is the vertical distance between contour lines. Its value in feet or meters is stated in the map margin. If the "CI" is 50 feet, each successive contour line on the map increases or decreases (as the case may be) in elevation by exactly 50 feet.
4. The contour interval is not the same for all maps, so look closely. Convert meters (all the new Canadian maps are metric) to feet (one meter equals 3.3 feet) if you're confused by the metric system.
5. The larger the contour interval, the less clear are the characteristics of the area. In short, a map whose "CI" is 10 feet, gives a clearer picture of the topography than one whose "CI" is 100 feet.

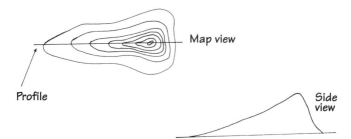

FIGURE M-1. Basic contour of a long sloping hill indicating the significant drop on the right side of the hill and the gentle slope at left.

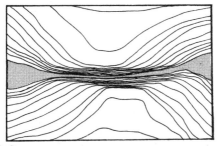

FIGURE M-2. Contour lines that run very close together and parallel to the banks of a waterway indicate canyons.

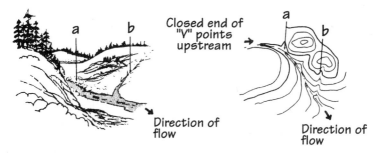

FIGURE M-3. Stream (b) flows into river (a).

6. Where contour lines cross or run very close together, you'll find an abrupt drop—a falls or canyon (Figures M-2, M-3).
7. The closed or V end of a contour line always points upstream (Figure M-3).

How to waterproof your maps:

1. Insert them in Zip-loc plastic bags. Giant 12½" × 16" Zip-locs are available from most office supply stores.
2. Cover them with clear contact paper—makes maps waterproof but you can't write on them.
3. Paint on *Stormproof*—a clear chemical that's especially formulated for use on maps and charges. Order by mail from the *Martensen Company, P.O. Box 261, Williamsburg, VA 23185.*
4. Apply *Thompson's Water Seal*—an industrial strength chemical that's used for sealing concrete block. "TWS" is available in hardware stores in aerosol cans and tins. Apply it with a foam varnish brush. TWS makes maps water repellent, not waterproof. You can write over it with pen or pencil.

Tip: Use a felt-tip "hi-liter" to mark your course of travel on your map. Hi-liter ink won't run or bleed and you can see topographic features through it.

To Determine the Drop of a River

For safety's sake, you should know the "drop per mile or kilometer" of any river you boat. "Drop" figures suggest the nature of rapids which lie ahead. By comparison, a drop of:

- 3–5 feet per mile is easy canoeing—suitable for novices.
- 6–10 feet per mile indicates easy rapids—some canoeing experience is desirable.
- 10–15 feet per mile is real whitewater—best know what you're doing!
- More than 15 feet per mile—watch out, big rapids! You may have to portage.

Caution: These are *rough* indicators only. Other factors, like the volume of water, exposed rocks, and how the drop occurs (whether gradually or all at once) determine whether you will paddle or portage a particular rapid!

To compute "drop":

1. Draw an arrow wherever a contour line crosses the river. Write the elevation in feet or meters

next to the contour line, as illustrated in Figure M4. Circle the number so you won't confuse it with other map data.

2. Determine the difference in elevation and the distance in miles or kilometers between the contour lines you've marked. Some canoeists prefer to make a table like the one illustrated.

3. Divide the difference in elevation (vertical distance) by the horizontal distance between points. In the example: From (a) to (b), the river drops 100 feet in 10 miles, or 10 feet per mile—"fun canoeing." From (b) to (c) the drop is 100 feet in 5 miles, or 20 feet per mile—a probable portage! My book, *Canoeing Wild Rivers,* provides more sophisticated examples for those who are canoeing in harm's way.

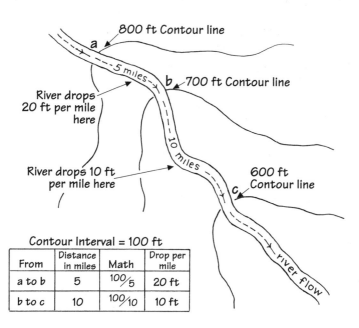

From	Distance in miles	Math	Drop per mile
a to b	5	$100/5$	20 ft
b to c	10	$100/10$	10 ft

Contour Interval = 100 ft

FIGURE M-4.

Monofilament Fishing Line

If you're camping out and lose the screw which holds the rim of your glasses to the bow, here's how to fix it. Tie a knot in a piece of monofilament fishing line and thread it through the screw hole. Knot the other end, then use a cigarette lighter to melt both knots to form a tight rivet. The repair will hold for quite some time.

Nalgene Bottle Trick

The plastic leash which secures the plastic cap to the bottle acts like a spring when the cap is open. You must hold the cap firmly away from the bottle when you take a drink or the tensioned leash will cause the cap to snap shut in your face. The solution is to remove the cap with its attached leash and reverse the leash on the mouth of the bottle. This twists the leash and holds the open cap away from the bottle, and your face!

Thanks to Pat Padden, of BP Associates in Minneapolis, for this clever tip.

Netted Bags

Strong, netted (mesh) nylon bags with draw cords are popular because you can see what's inside. Here are some other uses for these bags on a backwoods camping trip:
1. Put dirty clothes inside and "rinse-wash" (no soap) the bag in a nearby waterway. Or, loosely pack wet, newly washed and rinsed clothes in the mesh bag and tie the bag to your hiking pack. Clothes will dry in a few hours in the hot sun.
2. As an anchor for your boat or canoe: Put a rock inside the mesh bag and attach the bag to an anchor

rope. This is not as strong as a basketball net anchor.
3. To weight the end of a rope that will be tossed over a high tree limb.

P

Packs And Packing Methods

Care of packs: Abrasion (dirt!) is the major enemy of the polyurethane coatings used to waterproof packsacks, so wash your packs with a good detergent at least once each camping season. Tree sap (pitch) may be removed with a small amount of cleaning fluid or gasoline. Don't overdo it though; harsh chemicals may dissolve waterproof coatings!

Allow packs to dry thoroughly before you store them away. Wet canvas will mold and damp polyurethane coatings will mildew and peel.

Extending the closing flaps of packsacks: Some pack-sacks have closing flaps which are too short. The easiest way to extend them without cutting leather or nylon fittings is to sever the flap just behind the closing straps. Sew in a flap extension and re-attach the severed piece.

To improve the abrasion resistance of a soft pack, install a double bottom of the same or heavier fabric. An upholstery shop or shoe repair man can do this for you quickly and inexpensively.

The bottom corners of packs are subject to considerable abrasion. An early (and still excellent) solution was to crown them with glove leather. You can sew small pieces of lightweight leather to abrasion-prone spots or simply paint these areas with epoxy resin. Epoxy will stiffen the fabric and make it virtually tear-proof. Use epoxy to stabilize frayed threads and small holes which are awkward to patch with a sewing machine.

How to pack a soft pack: Now that nearly all packs have

internal or external frames, many campers discount the importance of "proper packing." This is unfortunate, for any pack—and your back— will benefit by "doing it right."

Procedure

1. Set the pack on its back and first insert along its length, all the soft items that won't gouge your back.
2. Weight should be kept as high as possible. Pack lightweight gear (except crushables) on the bottom, heavyweight items go on top.
3. For ease of identification and speed of packing, everything should be stored in nylon bags. For example, I commonly keep my extra clothing in a lobster red nylon stuff sack. My lightweight camp mocs go in an orange bag, the stove in a yellow bag, repair kit in a zippered canvas case, rain gear in a powder blue sack, etc. The nylon material of "stuff sacks" may be waterproof but the stitching and mouth of the bags are not. So don't depend on waterproof nylon bags to rain-proof your outfit. Instead, line your pack (in summer or winter) with a plastic bag and waterproof important items by the double-bag sandwich treatment outlined below under *Reliable Waterproofing*.
4. *Packing the tent:* Most tents have poles which are too long to fit the confines of a packsack. Consequently, tents and poles should be packed separately, as follows:
a) Stuff your tent (don't roll it—rolling takes too much time and identically creases the fabric) into its nylon tent bag. Pack poles and stakes into a special heavy-duty pole bag with drawstring closure. Sew a loop of nylon webbing to each end of the bag and attach lengths of parachute cord to the loops.
b) Place your stuffed tent inside your pack and set the pole bag horizontally under the pack flap. Snake the closing straps of the pack through loops in the cord end. Now your poles can't possibly fall out of your pack!

Reliable waterproofing: Most camping technique books recommend that you waterproof your gear by placing it inside a nylon stuff sack (or pack) that has been lined with one or two plastic garbage bags. If you've ever tried this procedure you know what happens—the thin plastic liner(s) destructs within a few uses. Of course, you can always carry along "a few" extra plastic bags. . . .

Here's a better way—one that won't fail three days into your camping trip:

FIGURE P-1. Tent pole bag secured beneath modern packsack flap.

1. Stuff your sleeping bag, clothing or other articles into a nylon sack (an abrasion liner) which need not be waterproof.
2. Place this sack inside an absolutely watertight plastic bag. Twist, fold over and secure the mouth of the plastic bag with a loop of shock-cord.
3. Set this unit inside a second nylon bag, which need not be watertight. Your articles are now completely protected against rain and a canoe capsize. Note that the delicate plastic liner is sandwiched between two layers of tough nylon, out of contact with abrasive materials. Use this "sandwich bag" method to pack everything you must keep dry. This is the best way to protect a sleeping bag that rides obtrusively on the outside frame of a back pack.

Hip belt and tumpline: Most backpackers know the advantages of a hip belt, but few appreciate the worth of a tumpline. A tumpline consists of a wide leather or fabric strap which is secured to the "ears" (sides of the pack at shoulder level) of a packsack. The packer places this strap just above his forehead, grabs the tumpline near his head, leans forward, and trucks confidently down the trail. The early voyageurs carried hundreds of pounds of furs by this method; packers in undeveloped countries still rely on this system.

Small pack

FIGURE P-2.

Tumplines are most useful when ascending steep hills, as they take considerable weight off the packstraps. To make a tumpstrap for your pack, simply sew a D-ring to each side of your pack at shoulder height, and mount the tumpline across them.

Tip: Place awkward bundles, like day packs, fishing rods and canoe paddles under the tump strap in the hollow of your back, as illustrated in Figure P-2. When your neck and head begin to ache, cast off the tumpline and shift the load to the shoulder straps. Change back to the head strap when the pain is gone.

Pack pockets: Sew up some small envelope-style pockets and attach them to the outside of your pack with heavy-duty glove snaps or Velcro strips. These "pack pockets" will add versatility to your hiking outfit. If you attach mating strips of Velcro to the inner walls of your tent, sidewalls or thwarts of your canoe or boat, etc., your pack pockets can be quickly re-mounted to provide added convenience.

Pillow

Everything should be multipurpose on a backcountry camping trip, even your pillow. A practical pillow case can be made from a lightweight terry cloth towel. Fold the towel lengthwise and sew up the two long sides. Set a Velcro tab or snap in the open end. Stuff your down or polyester vest into the pillow case. Add more clothes if you want more thickness. Terry cloth "breathes" and it won't slide on the slick floor of your tent. You can use your "pillow case" as an emergency sponge, bathing towel, dirty clothes bag or stuff sack. One friend made a luxurious polyester pile pillow case and sized it to fit his head so he would have an extra hat!

Rain Gear

Background: Rain gear has become quite stylish. Some parkas now feature hoods with integral bills that turn with your head, underarm zippers for better ventilation, drip-proof pockets, waist and hem cords, and much more. These niceties are nice, of course, but they won't keep you dry. What will, is a sensibly designed garment that is constructed of genuinely waterproof material.

Fabrics: There are those that work and those that don't. Some work "sometimes." And the difference between them is not necessarily a function of price. In fact, some of the best (most watertight, that is) rain wear costs less than some of the worst!

If you want reliable rain gear at a reasonable price, see what the professionals are wearing. Foresters, wildlife management people, and construction workers all require tough garments that are absolutely waterproof. Rain garments like these are available at every industrial supply store. The new industrial rain suits are constructed of fabrics which are similar, and often identical to, those used on the best foul weather sailing suits. But because there are no pockets, no underarm zippers, and often no hoods to boost the price, the cost is much less.

Camping stores also feature a wealth of different rain gear. Invariably, *el-cheapo* models are the best buy, that is if you're willing to seal the seams yourself with the special glue provided.

At the other extreme are PVC, neoprene, and hypaloncoated garments that will keep you dry no matter how long or hard it rains. And these suits are worth their high cost if you absolutely must stay dry in foul weather.

Gore-Tex™: Gore-Tex is relatively cool and comfortable (it "breathes"), even on hot, muggy days—something lesser rain garments can't match. I greatly criticized Gore-Tex at the start but it now appears that the bugs are out. I've been actively using an expensive double-ply Gore-Tex parka for three years now, and it hasn't leaked a drop. I think I'm ready to trust Gore-Tex at last.

Be aware that not all Gore-Tex garments are created equal. Those that have the "Rainwear Without Compromise" tag are *essential* if you want to stay dry. Pay particular attention to the closures at the wrist, neck and waist. Zippers should be covered with double-overlapping flaps to seal out blowing rain, and double-cuffs are essential to stop dribbles. Slash pockets *must* have protective rain flaps or they'll become ponds! Naturally, heavy-duty two-ply construction is more rugged, more reliable, and more expensive than lightweight single-ply construction. You can buy three professional-grade PVC-coated rain parkas for the price of a good Gore-Tex one. Keep this in mind if you're on a serious budget.

Style: Whether you hike, canoe, motorcycle, backpack or sail, you'll be happiest with a generously sized two-piece rain suit. Ponchos provide inadequate protection and may be dangerous in a boat upset. Below-the-knee rain shirts are ideal for casual fishing and auto camping but are otherwise impractical.

You'll put on and remove rain gear frequently between showers so select garments which are easy to slip on and off. Select jackets with zippered or snap fronts rather than anorak models which fit over the head. Pants which have an elastic or corded waistband are much more versatile than those with bibs.

Tip: Tear out the elastic waistband of rain pants and substitute a fabric cord and cord lock. Elastic loses its strength in time and rain pants will fall down. A cord provides quick, positive adjustments.

Avoid pants with snaps or Velcro tabs at the bottom. These restrict ventilation. Besides, primitive man learned long ago that water doesn't flow uphill! Ankle closures are only useful for mountaineering above the timberline. Pant legs should be oversized so you can easily slip them on over heavy trousers or boots. Some expensive rain pants feature baffled zippers at the ankles. Straight cut pant legs go over boots just as easily and are less costly to manufacture. Zippers eventually gum up with debris and fail—they're just another gimmick to drive up costs.

Tip: If you want to learn all there is to know about good rain gear, check out the best foul weather sailing suits. The only frills you'll see on these garments are ones that work. Now, compare your observations to rain garments in camping shops!

Jacket fit: Buy your rain parka a full size larger than you think you need, large enough so you can wear several layers of clothes beneath. Rain gear that looks trim in the store will be hot and restrictive in the field.

Color: Color is a personal choice, though navy blue garments outsell all others by a wide margin. And that's unfortunate, for this color attracts mosquitoes which invariably come out between showers!

Hoods: A traditionally styled sou'wester hat is much more functional than a restrictive hood. However, if you select a hooded parka, be sure the zipper comes right to your nose. Those which stop at the chin must have a throat strap to seal off the neck area or they'll admit cold air and rain.

Pockets, seams and zippers: Two covered pockets are more than enough in any rain jacket. Additional pockets add weight, bulk, and cost and threaten the integrity of the waterproof construction. The fewer the seams in any rain garment, the more watertight it will be. Except to close the front of a jacket, the value of zippers is over-rated. Underarm zippers (which are added for ventilation) keep out rain only if you don't raise your arms. And zippered flies in rain pants usually leak within a few seconds of instantly.

Waterproofing standards: The U.S. Army requires a garment to withstand a minimum of 25 pounds per square inch (PSI) water pressure in order to earn the title of "waterproof." At first thought, this industry-accepted minimum seems adequate, that is until you realize a person may exert that much pressure (or more!) simply by sitting on the edge of a boat seat. Kneel down or plant your elbows firmly in the duff and you may experience similar results. In all likelihood, minimally rated rain wear will not keep you dry! Good rain clothes will withstand two or three times the amount of water pressure specified by the military, but even this may not be enough for strenuous field use. Then, there's the matter of abrasion. Every time you put on or take off your rain parka, or move while wearing it, a micro-thin layer of waterproof chemical is scraped off the fabric. In time, leaks develop.

One answer to the abrasion problem is to sew a liner into the garment. But liners add weight, cost, and bulk. They also absorb sweat and are slow to dry. A better solution is to insist on a fabric with a minimum 100 PSI waterproof coating. And for really severe applications (like foul-weather sailing), you may want to consider the merits of a fabric which boasts a 150 PSI (or greater) rating.

Unfortunately, manufacturers of rain wear do not usually advertise the PSI ratings of their products. For comparison: A Kenyon Industries light polyurethane coating ("Light K-Kote," as specified on the garment label) will average 25–50 PSI on the Mullen hydrostatic test, which is used to determine waterproofness of fabrics. But a "Super (double) K-Kote" treatment will run 100 PSI or more, which makes it suitable for all but the meanest applications.

Tip: You'll increase the effectiveness of your rain gear if you double the thickness of abrasion prone areas—knees, elbows, and especially the seat. All you need is a sewing machine and some matching fabric. And don't forget to seal the seams you've sewn!

Rain gear for children: (see *Children,* page 46).

When not to wear rain gear: Some authorities suggest you eliminate a windbreaker from your clothing list and instead rely on you rain parka for wind protection. Frankly, I think this is bad advice. Every time you lean against a tree or scrape a rock, abrasion takes its toll. In no time leaks develop. If you want your rain gear to last more than a season or two, use it only for its intended purpose and switch to a wind shell when the need arises.

Tip: If you wear your rain coat over your nylon wind shell, you'll reduce abrasion to the waterproof inner coating (the shell acts as a liner). Twin jackets will also keep you warmer and drier than a single waterproof garment.

What to wear under rain gear: Don't wear cotton! It absorbs perspiration and super-cools the body. Since perspiration cannot escape through a waterproof covering, a wet, clammy feeling is guaranteed!

If you wear a pure wool or polyester pile shirt over a polypropylene undershirt, you'll stay dry and in command no matter how hard it rains. Moisture will pass harmlessly through the polypropylene weave into the wool or pile where it will be absorbed and wicked from fiber to fiber. It will take many hours to sufficiently load a wool or pile garment with enough moisture to cause concern. And if your rain clothes are at all ventilated (they should be), enough water vapor will be spilled to the environment to ensure your comfort no matter how hot or cold the rain.

Tip: Store rain clothes in a nylon stuff sack between uses. This will keep them clean and eliminate the abrasion which results from stuffing clothing into packs.

Care and repair of rain gear: Hand wash in detergent. Air dry thoroughly before storing. Store rain gear on hangers so air will circulate. Don't keep these items in confining stuff sacks—polyurethane coatings will mildew!

Patch holes and tears with matching material. Any portable sewing machine will work. Easiest way to get "matching fabric" is to cut up the stuff sack which came with all stitching with seam sealers, which you can buy at all camping shops.

Ropes

Background: To most campers, a rope is a rope, and they make no distinction between manila, polypropylene, Dacron, and nylon. That's too bad, because certain rope materials and weaves excel in different applications. What works best as waterski tow line is completely inappropriate for rigging a rain fly. Here are some differences and points to consider when choosing ropes:

1. *Flexibility:* Flexible ropes accept knots more willingly than stiffer weaves but are more likely to snag in their own coils. Choose flexible ropes for tying canoes on cars, and any place a proper lash-

ing is essential. Stiff ropes are best for throwing lines (lifesaving), boat mooring and tracking lines, and general use around water.

2. *Slipperiness:* A slippery rope is always a nuisance. Some ropes, notably those made from polypropylene, are so slippery that they will not retain knots.

3. *Diameter versus strength:* Modern synthetic lines are very strong. Even ⅛-inch diameter parachute cord has more breaking strength than you will probably ever need. However, large diameter ropes are much easier to handle, and less likely to snag, than small diameter ones. Quarter-inch diameter rope is about minimal for heavy-duty camping applications. One-eighth inch diameter parachute cords are the recommended camp utility cord.

Note: There are several grades of parachute cord. Avoid the cheap stuff that's commonly sold at hardware stores.

Types of rope

Nylon is the most popular fiber for utility rope, and for good reason. It's strong, light, immune to rot, and inexpensive. On the negative side, it stretches considerably when wet, shrinks when dry. This makes it a bad choice for mooring boats, for canoe tracking lines, and anywhere you need a rope that won't change dimensions. Nylon also degrades in the sun. A nylon rope may lose half or more of its strength in a single season if it's continually exposed to the weather.

The two most common weaves are the three-strand braided, and sheathed-core. Braided rope is very soft and flexible but it cannot be "flame-whipped" after it's cut. The ends of nylon and polypropylene ropes are usually sealed after cutting by melting them in the flame of a cigarette lighter. Three-strand braided rope simply unravels when heat is applied. It must be whipped the traditional Navy way by winding the ends with waxed string, or by dipping them in plastic whipping compound (available at marinas).

Sheathed nylon ropes (there are many variations) feature a central core surrounded by a woven nylon sheath.

This construction is slightly less flexible than the braided type but is pliant enough for camp use. Sheathed ropes flame-whip easily and do not unravel. Quarter-inch diameter stock is ideal for rigging clotheslines, tying gear on cars and trailers, and other utility applications.

Polypropylene: The choice lies between round, three-strand stiff-braided line and the cheap flat-woven stuff sold in hardware stores. It's no contest; the stiffer line excels in every category.

Polypropylene has two advantages over nylon: It does not degrade in sunlight, and it doesn't stretch when wet. These characteristics make it ideal for use around water.

Ropes for mountaineering: Some types of mountaineering rope make excellent utility line. The choice lies between three-strand hard lay construction, or the kermantle type (a core of braided or twisted strands, the kern, is covered by a protective braided sheath, the mantle). Three-strand rope is much cheaper than kermantle and it has a stiffer hand, which makes it ideal for lining canoes, mooring boats, and anywhere you need a snag-free rope that won't fail.

Dacron line is the material for sailboat sheet and mooring lines. It's wonderfully strong, beautifully soft, and frightfully expensive. If you're a sailor you know all about Dacron line. Advantages of Dacron over nylon include: 1) Very little wet-stretch/dry shrinkage; 2) It is immune to the degrading effects of sunlight—a feature which is very important on boats which are exposed to the weather.

Manila and hemp have almost gone the way of the passenger pigeon. These natural fiber ropes (manila is far superior to hemp!) have a nice hand; they coil beautifully, offer a textured grip, and they even smell nice, but they rot easily, and for their weight, aren't very strong. I can think of no reason to use natural fiber ropes when better synthetics are available for about the same price.

Tip: Abrasion is the major enemy of rope, so occasionally wash your ropes with detergent to remove ground-in grime. You'll prolong the life of your ropes considerably.

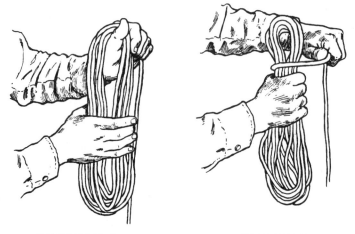

FIGURE R-1.   **FIGURE R-2.**

Rope Tricks

Nylon utility ropes are best coiled and bound by the old Navy method indicated below:

1. Coil the rope and put your thumb through the coils to hold them in place. Leave about 3 feet of rope uncoiled (Figure R-1).
2. Grasp the rope in one hand and pinch it at the waist to form an "eye." Coil the free end (tail) around the rope, upwards towards the eye. Overlap the first coil to lock it in place. Wind evenly and tightly (Figure R-2).
3. Form a loop near the end of the tail and pass it through the eye (Figure R-3).
4. Grasp the collar (wound coils) in one hand and the rope body in the other. Slide the collar up to the rope to lock the loop in place. (It may be easier to hold the collar firmly in one hand and pull downward on the body of the rope.) The rope is now secured; a pull on the tail will release it (Figure R-4).

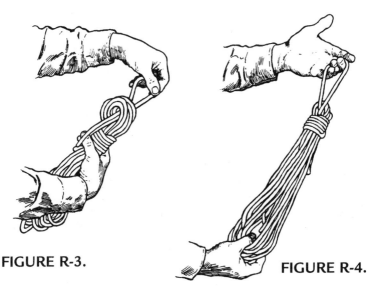

FIGURE R-3.

FIGURE R-4.

Throwing Coil

Use this method for large diameter ropes and throwing lines. The "old "sailing method" is faster to wind and release but the coils are more likely to snag when the line is tossed.

1. Coil the rope carefully, taking care to rotate your coiling hand downward so as to give each coil a half turn before you lay it in place. The "half-turn" keeps the strands of the rope aligned and prevents the coils from twisting. It is the secret to coiling a rope so it won't snag when you throw it.
2. Wind the tail tightly around the coiled rope. Overlap the first winding to lock it in place.
3. Make a loop near the tail and work it under your last winding. Pull the loop to tighten the winding. A pull on the tail will release the rope.

You can carry the coiled rope over your shoulder, hang it on nail or cleat, or secure it around a rod or canoe thwart as illustrated in Figure R-5d.

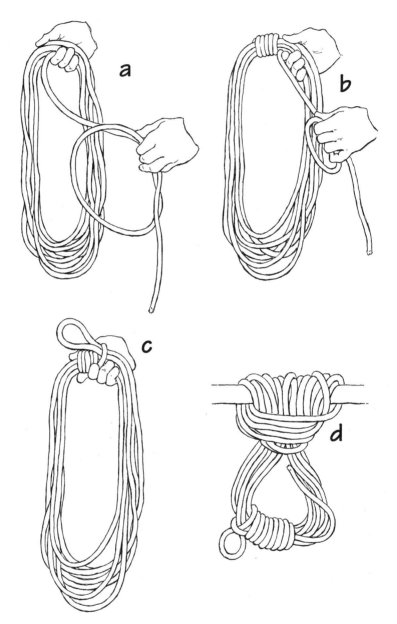

FIGURE R-5.

Saw (Folding)

A folding saw is one of your most useful camp tools. On a rainy day you may be unable to get a fire going without one! Triangular shaped metal saws are flimsy and they won't cut big logs. Best camp saw I've seen is a full-stroke rectangular model called the Fast Bucksaw. It's constructed of hard maple and has an easily replaceable 21-inch blade (refills are available from the manufacturer or at any hardware store). When assembled, it's so rigid you'd swear it was a one-piece model. These saws are available by mail from *Fast Bucksaw, Inc., 100 East Fifth Street, Hastings, MN 55033.*

Tips: Keep your disassembled folding saw in a nylon bag with drawstring closure. This will keep the parts cleaner and speed assembly time.

Occasionally wipe tree sap from saw blades with a rag dipped in gasoline or alcohol. This will improve cutting performance and slow rusting of the blade.

If you want to go light and can get by with a less efficient saw, I recommend the 10.5 ounce Sawvivor™. Its aluminum bucksaw frame assembles in seconds. A captive tensioning system ensures tight, positive lockup.

Shovel

A ¾ inch diameter, foot long aluminum tube, flattened at one end, makes an ideal camp shovel. Use it for burying fire remains, fish viscera, and human wastes where proper disposal facilities do not exist. (See *Ethics*, page 73, for the proper way to dispose of wastes in the backcountry.)

Shower

You can make an effective portable shower by attaching a light plastic hose and shower head to a folding plastic water jug. Use a long hose and drive the system with foot pressure. If stove fuel or wood (to heat water) is in short supply, consider bringing along a commercial *Sun Shower,* which is similar to the above system except for its special heat absorbing fabric. Sun Showers can be purchased at most camp shops and marinas. They are quite popular with yachtsmen.

Skis (Cross-country)

Under certain conditions, the surface of cross-country skis will load up with crusty snow and impede performance. To prevent this ice build-up, occasionally apply a paste wax to the top of your skis.

Sleeping Bags

Background: This is your most important item. With care, a good sleeping bag will last half a life-time, even with almost regular use. Serious backcountry travelers choose from these popular sleeping bag fills: goose and duck down, Polarguard®, Quallofil®, Hollofil®II, and Primaloft® (a "down-like" synthetic). Any of these products will serve you well if they're properly sewn into a well constructed bag.

Principles of sleeping bag design

1. The smaller the bag, the less area it will have to insulate. Translation: confining mummy bags are much warmer for their weight than roomy rectangular ones.
2. Most heat loss from a sleeping bag occurs through the open head end. It's nearly impossible to seal the open end of a rectangular style sleeping bag so that warm air won't escape. (One solution is to install a collar—see Figure C-6 for details.) For this reason integral hoods are mandatory on sleeping bags that will be used for cold weather camping.

   Tip: An effective makeshift collar can be tailored from a sweater or scarf. Drape the garment across your chest and bunch the fabric around your neck and shoulders, feathering it to the adjustment sleeping bag fabric. This will eliminate drafts and increase warmth.

3. Inexpensive mummy-style sleeping bags, and all rectangular models are built with a "flat" foot, which means the material is simply folded in half at the foot end, and a zipper is installed around the edge (as in a typical station-wagon sleeping bag). A "boxed" foot design, though more costly to manufacture, is much more comfortable. Here, a foot-high circular panel is sewn in at the bottom (like the end of a tin can) which allows you to maintain a comfortable "toes up" position without bearing against tight material.

4. A full-length zipper running from foot to chin is a must. Bags with half-length zippers become impossibly hot in warm weather.

Categories

Down and synthetic sleeping bags are generally categorized as:

a) *Summer weight*—comfortable in temperatures to freezing.

b) *Three-season*—warm to about 10–15 degrees Fahrenheit.

c) *Winter*—good to 20 below zero or more. There are some special Arctic bags which go much lower than that.

Note: "Comfort ratings" are speculative. Few sleeping bags are as warm as their manufacturers suggest.

Which sleeping bag for you?

Most people select three-season models thinking they represent the greatest value of the money. Wrong! The typical three-season sleeping bag becomes too warm when temperatures rise above 50 degrees Fahrenheit, which means they are next to worthless for average summer use.

Only if you do considerable primitive camping in the spring and fall, should you buy a three-season bag. Otherwise, a lighter, less costly summer bag will be a better buy. Tent temperatures commonly run about 10 degrees warmer than the outside environment, so a good summer bag will keep you toasty well below freezing. In really cold weather, you can mate your summer bag with an outer or inner liner, or a blanket.

Which is best, down or synthetics? Down bags are lighter, warmer, more compact, and have a more "gentle hand" than any of the synthetics. If you've ever slept under a down comforter, you know what I mean. Good down is also much more resilient and long lived than synthetics. For an equivalent weight of fill, down has a lower and wider temperature comfort range. This means down will keep you warmer when it's cold, and cooler when it's warm, than will a synthetic.

For example: Consider two three-season sleeping bags, one down, one Polar guard or Quallofil. Both bags are rated to 10 degrees Fahrenheit. Finished weight of the down bag will be at least a pound less than either synthetic and it will compact into a much smaller space. The synthetic bag will become too warm when the temperature reaches 50 degrees Fahrenheit, while the down bag will remain quite comfortable, even at 60 degrees.

However, good down sleeping bags are much more expensive than equivalently rated synthetic ones, and you can't beat them around as much. Wet down is almost impossible to dry under typical field conditions. Because down is a natural fiber, it absorbs body moisture, which in damp winter conditions can be serious.

For this reason, experienced winter hikers usually select "synthetic fill" sleeping bags.

Question: If down dries so slowly, shouldn't we eliminate it from consideration for summer use too? Absolutely not! If you "sandwich pack" your sleeping bag as I recommend in the packing section (page 123) and storm-proof your tent accordingly (see page 191), you will never get your bedding wet. I guarantee it! Only unskilled idiots get sleeping bags—or anything else—wet on camping trips. I've made some pretty substantial wilderness trips over the past thirty years and I've always managed to keep my down bag dry. If you follow the tips I've outlined, you will too.

Buy what you can afford; but whatever you buy, make

sure it has a hood to keep your head warm, a full-length two-way zipper to keep your feet cool, and a temperature range which matches the environment in which you'll camp. If you choose a "mummy bag"—and most experienced campers do—try it in the store before you buy it. Mummy bags come in different lengths and girths; some are quite restrictive while others are surprisingly roomy. If a bag feels tight in the store, you won't like it in the field.

Winter sleeping bags are more generously sized than summer ones to allow dressing space inside. Winter campers usually take their clothing and canteens to bed so they need space for all these "rummage sale" items. The typical polyester-filled winter bag weighs 5 pounds or more. Summer weight bags may weigh half that.

Packing the sleeping bag: Sleeping bags (discounting station-wagon types) should be stuffed not rolled. Zippers should be closed to prevent galling of the material. Just grab the foot end of the bag and stuff it, handful by handful into its nylon sack. This is easier on the fabric and fill than traditional rolling.

Do not store sleeping bags in stuff sacks; you'll wear out the filler in no time. Instead, keep sleeping bags in a breathable cotton sack (a pillowcase works fine), or store them flat or on hangers.

Cleaning your sleeping bag

Down bags and other down garments: Hand washing is the best way to clean any down-filled item. Nonetheless, manufacturers usually recommend drycleaning on down product labels simply because so many down items have been ruined by improper machine washing. Make no mistake: Drycleaning with powerful perchlorethylene solvents will reduce the loft and warmth of a down bag. But it will not destroy it. Improper washing will! Here's the recommended procedure for hand washing:

Directions

1. You'll need a huge basin to wash your sleeping bag. A bathtub is ideal.
2. Use lukewarm water and any mild soap. I've had good luck with Woolite, Ivory Snow, Ivory Liquid, Basic-H and other liquid dishwashing detergents.

There are also some special down soaps which may or may not be worth their high price.

3. Place the sleeping bag into the soap solution and sponge the shell thoroughly. Rub gently at stubborn spots. Do not use Spray and Wash or stain removers! The shells of sleeping bags are very tightly woven to contain the down, so it may require many hours for wash water to work through them.

   Allow the bag to soak in the wash water for an hour or so, then squish the bag gently with widespread hands. Carefully, work wash water well into the down. A couple hours of additional soaking and frequent "squishing" should remove most of the dirt.

4. *Rinsing the bag:* Drain the tub and gently press soapy water out of the article with both hands, fingers spread wide. Don't lift or wring out the article. A water-filled sleeping bag is very heavy and the delicate baffles may tear if you rough-house the project.

   A minimum of two rinse cycles is recommended. You absolutely must get all the soap out or the down will mat when it dries.

5. Gently place the thoroughly rinsed sleeping bag into a large plastic clothes basket for ease-of-handling. Now, it's off to your Laundromat with several dollars change in hand.

6. Place the incompletely rinsed bag into an "extractor" (a high speed centrifuge) and spin out the remaining water. If your laundromat does not have one of these machines, a large washing machine, set on spin-dry will work. One pass through the extractor machine or two passes through the washing machine will safely exhaust nearly all the water.

7. Next, place the bag in a large commercial clothes dryer set on very low heat. Be sure the dryer puts out low heat! If it does not, run it with the door ajar (jam a magazine through the door hinge over the safety button so the machine will continue to

run) to bleed heat. Check the progress of the bag every ten minutes. Some people place a terrycloth towel into the dryer to absorb the static electricity. This seems to speed drying.

It will take you a full day to wash your sleeping bag!

Warning: Do not attempt to dry a sleeping bag in family-sized clothes dryers. The heat is concentrated over too small an area. You may, however, safely spin-dry your sleeping bag in your home washing machine if a commercial extractor is not available.

When to clean your sleeping bag

Once every year or two is often enough, even if you use your bag a lot. A down bag will lose some loft and resiliency with the first washing. Additional washings seem to have no adverse effect.

Some campers never wash their sleeping bags; they believe that washing will ruin them. But body oils and dirt will accumulate and the insulative value of the bag will decrease accordingly. It's a catch 22. My advice? Keep your bag as clean as possible and wash it carefully when the occasion demands.

How to wash polyester-filled sleeping bags

Polyester-filled sleeping bags and garments cannot be drycleaned. The cleaning fluid will destroy the fill. These garments are best hand washed in the same manner as down bags. Yes, you can machine wash them successfully. However, most sleeping bags are too large to be safely washed in family-sized washing machines—some abrasion, stretching of stitches, etc., is sure to result. If you must machine wash your bag, use one of the large front loading commercial machines. Even then, my vote goes to hand washing.

Polyester-filled jackets, vests and other small items may be safely washed in most home machines (gentle cycle only). But, they must be dried with low (under 120 degrees Fahrenheit) heat—or better, no heat!

Dos and don'ts for sleeping bags

Don't roll sleeping bags; stuff them!
Don't yank sleeping bags out of stuff sacks; pull gently.
Don't leave sleeping bags stuffed for long periods of time.
Don't machine wash down sleeping bags.
Don't dryclean polyester-filled sleeping bags.
Don't wash down bags with harsh detergents.
Don't pick up a wet down product without adequately supporting it.
Do air and fluff sleeping bags after each use.
Do store sleeping bags flat, on hangers, or in large porous sacks.
Do sponge clean the shell of your sleeping bag occasionally.
Do wash your sleeping bag when it gets dirty.

Tip: You can get along surprisingly well in summer without a sleeping bag if you fold a blanket or two in the manner illustrated in Figure C-5. You an also increase the warmth of any station-wagon size sleeping bag by applying the procedures outlined in Figure C-6.

Sleeping Pads, Air Mattresses, and Sleeping Systems

Background: Toddlers and teenagers can get along quite nicely without a foam pad or air mattress, but these items are a must for most adults. In general, air mattresses are much more comfortable than foam pads, but they are cold to sleep on and they frequently fail. For this reason, most expert campers choose open- or closed-cell foam pads over more traditional air mattresses.

Air mattresses: Except for car camping, the traditional single-valved air mattress is extinct. Such mattresses require too much time to inflate and deflate to be practical on backwoods trips. The most popular system air mattress for self-propelled outdoors people is the type which features multiple, replaceable plastic tubes, each of which has its own inflation valve. These air pads are less comfortable than traditional types but are more easily repaired (you just remove the punctured vinyl tube and replace it with a new one).

Except in the heat of summer, air mattresses cannot be used with down sleeping bags. Body weight compresses down to near zero thickness and air mattresses do not have sufficient insulation to make up for this loss. In fact, the circulating air in an air mattress simply moves the cold from place to place. Even thick polyester-filled sleeping bags (polyester doesn't compress as much as down) may get cold when the temperature drops below freezing.

Tip: Place a thin closed-cell foam pad on top of an air mattress for the ultimate in warmth and comfort.

Closed-cell foam pads: You can choose PVC (poly-vinyl-chloride), polyethylene or EVA (ethyl-vinyl-acetate), or a number of "mix 'n match" types. EVA is so superior to other closed-cell foams that it defies comparison. EVA is unaffected by sunlight, heat and most solvents. It is almost immune to abrasion. It's expensive and worth it!

A ¼-inch thick closed cell foam pad will provide plenty of insulation for summer (but not much comfort). For winter, you'll need at least a ⅜-inch thickness, more for subzero temperatures. Closed-cell foam pads are immune to water and mild abrasion so it is not necessary to cover them with materials.

Open-cell foam pads: There are dozens of grades of open-cell polyurethane foam. Some foams are soft and cushy, others are highly supportive. There is a difference in price! Select the most supportive foam you can find (try pads in the store); avoid pads which bottom out when you roll over.

Open cell foam is delicate; it must be covered, preferably with a porous fabric which will pass insensible perspiration. Avoid covers made of waterproof nylon; you'll awaken in a pool of sweat!

Don't worry about getting your open-cell foam pad wet. If you storm-proof your tent, and pack as I suggest, you won't have problems with wet gear.

Air-filled foam pads: The Therma-Rest® began the revolution, now there's lots of competition. Basically, these units consist of a low density (soft and cushy) open-cell foam that's sealed in an envelope of vinyl and nylon. An oversized plastic valve controls the air flow. Open the valve and the pad inflates itself. Close the valve to lock in the air. The result is a very comfortable, incredibly warm (suitable for sub-zero use) and surprisingly reliable mattress. I've been using Therma-Rest mats for twenty-five years and have had few problems. My latest Therma-Rest is going on ten years old and there are no signs of a leak.

Tip: Make a tough cotton cover for your air-filled foam pad. This will protect it from punctures and keep it from sliding on the slippery nylon tent floor. The cotton cover will also be more comfortable to sleep on than the non-porous nylon shell of the air-pad. *Note:* Some air/foam pads have multiple air valves which control the inflation of different sections of the mattress. This feature supposedly makes for a more comfortable rest. You may need to customize your cover to permit use of the many different valves.

A crinkly "space blanket" (every discount store has them), silver side up under your foam pad will prevent it from slipping on your tent floor, and it will add considerable warmth to your sleeping system.

If you find yourself sleeping on an uncomfortable incline, level out your sleeping system by placing folded clothes beneath your air mat or foam pad. You can make an intolerable sleeping situation quite bearable by this method.

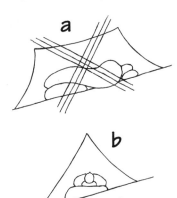

FIGURE S-1.

Tip: If you are stuck with an inclined site, pitch your tent *perpendicular* to the drop (one side lower than the other), rather than parallel to it with the entrance high, as suggested in most camping books. It's easier to level a "sunken side" than a "lowered end." Figure S-1 shows why.

Snow Glasses

Dark sunglasses are necessary to prevent snow blindness in dazzling white conditions. You can make an emergency pair by applying parallel strips of electrical or duct tape to the lenses of standard glasses. Leave a narrow horizontal slit to see through.

Snowshoes

For deep, open snow, select long slender snowshoes with high turned toes (the "Alaskan" or "Pickerel" style is best). Low toed models plow deep under fluffy snow and double your work output.

For crusty snow or wooded areas, a small maneuverable shoe is best. My favorite "woods shoe" is the narrow cross-country model, which is basically a miniature version of the old Alaskan, though with a lower toe. The "Sherpa" bearpaw with its ingenious binding and integral traction device may be the best deep woods/mountain trail shoe of all. The common Michigan/Maine pattern is a good compromise style, though its low toe makes it a poor choice for fluffy snow. No one snowshoe will do everything well!

Snowshoe bindings: Leather bindings get wet and stretch; neoprene is much better! The standard "Sherpa" binding is among the most comfortable, rigid and easiest to use of all bindings. The Sherpa features a thick neoprene toe cup with stainless steel hooks and wide nylon laces—and it goes on and off in seconds! All Sherpa brand shoes come standard with this unique binding, which can be purchased separately and installed on other shoes. You can even get special bindings that have quick-release straps and traction claws! Snowshoeing is catching on in a big way.

Snow Shelters

It's a well-kept secret that winter camping is a whopping good time. After all, when it's 20 below, only fools and "them's that knows what they're about," are apt to be out there. Along with predictable solitude comes exquisite beauty and awesome silence. Camped on a pristine blanket of white, there are no foot prints or garbage to muck up the view. Touch the crispness of dawn, hear the harsh stillness of night. Like those who lived here millennia ago, you are part of the land, not meaningless passersby. What was in summer is no more. Everything is covered by sterile white. Getting around in 4-foot snow drifts requires new technique. You shuffle along on snowshoes or glide on skis. Equipment is carried in special backpacks or on classic toboggans, polyethylene sleds, or fiberglass pulks. Fire building becomes an art, as well as a lesson in tedium. First, you establish a base of logs so flames won't sink into oblivion, then you split dry kindling from the heart of a snow-drenched log. A folding saw and axe, and a good sharp knife are essential tools in the winter woods.

And if you go above the tree line, there are new challenges and equipment. Instead of fires there are gasoline and butane stoves, low slung mountain tents with cookholes and tunnel doors; baffled parkas, balaclavas and face masks; vapor barrier liners, tinted goggles and frost cream. And when tents fail—or for those who just disdain them—there are snow caves and trenches, Quin-zees and igloos. To the uninitiated, "sleeping out" in the dead of winter flirts with death. To those of us who know and live by nature's rules, it's hyacinths for the soul.

Ask an experienced winter camper if he or she prefers unheated tents to snow houses and you'll get ten to one in favor of the huts. That's because unlike tents, snow structures are warm inside. Sometimes too warm. Everyone knows that snow is a great insulator, but you won't believe how good until you've crammed three people into a snow cave built for two. Add a candle or two for light and warmth and watch the thermometer rise. Keep a close eye on the mercury level, for when water starts dripping from the inner walls, you've got problems. Snow is porous but ice doesn't breathe. And if your home freezes solid inside, air won't get in. Overheating a snow house is a very real concern—one which newcomers to winter sport don't take seriously enough.

Warnings aside, snow huts are comfortable and eminently safe, and as every kid will attest, they are fun and easy to build. Here are some ideas to get you started:

Quin-Zee Hut

Background: A quin-zee is the white man's version of the traditional Eskimo igloo. It's made by piling up snow then digging out the center, rather than by carefully laying snow blocks. Quin-zees are as warm, as strong, and as spacious as igloos but they take much longer to build. Compared to igloos, they are terribly ugly. An Eskimo snow house is a work of art; a quin-zee retains the appearance of a shlocked-together snow pile (which is exactly what it is). Nonetheless, quin-zees are practical for base camp travel in winter and as emergency survival dwellings. Kids build them just for fun and occasionally someone makes news by carving a garage-size quin-zee from a giant snow bank. Quin-zees are similar to snow caves, which are also built from packed snow. Snow caves, however, are hollowed out from an existing packed drift, which is faster and simpler than piling snow. Both structures serve the same function— that of keeping you warm and dry regardless of the weather outside.

You don't need a thick layer of snow to build a quin-zee. You can simply haul in what you need or scrape a thin surface layer of snow to provide sufficient building material.

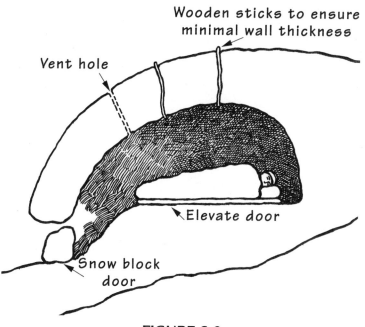

FIGURE S-2.

Building the Quin-Zee

1. First decide on the size. A 10–12 foot diameter is about right for two people. Most snow campers make their huts too small, so err on the large side. You can easily adjust the interior dimensions to a custom fit when you dig out the structure.
2. Pile up snow to a height of about 7 feet. This will provide comfortable sitting room inside for both occupants. You'll speed manufacture of the hut if you occasionally pack the snow pile with your shovel.
3. When the snow pile is complete, insert foot long sticks into the structure at approximate 18-inch intervals. "Porcupine" the hut with these sticks all around and on top. Don't stop until the quinzee resembles a medieval mace. These sticks provide a gauge by which you can judge the thickness of the walls when you dig out the center. It is essential to maintain a minimum 8-inch wall thickness. Without the "gauge," you'll shovel right through the side-walls, and once you've gone too far, repair is difficult.
4. If you want a tunnel entrance, now's the time to build it. Don't forget to porcupine the tunnel.
5. Now comes the hard part—finding something else to do for the next few hours. The structure needs time to settle, the snow must contract and harden. How long this takes depends on temperature, humidity, and age of the snow. If the snow is fresh and dry and it's very cold, the pile will take much longer to set. On warm days, the molecular change will occur much faster. Eight hours is usually enough time, regardless of the weather. Do not throw water on the hut to speed its cure; you'll wind up with an ice ball—one you can't dig out or breath inside of!
6. When the structure has hardened, prepare to dig. You'll need a small shovel and a friend. You'll get very wet from falling snow so wear rain gear or highly water repellent clothing. Dig out the tunnel entrance through to the center, passing carved

snow to your partner outside. Now, it's simply a matter of sculpting the interior to suit your fancy. Just remember to stop digging when you see the porcupine "hairs." You need to maintain an 8-inch minimum wall thickness! Do not remove the porcupine sticks from the structure; doing so will weaken the hut.

7. *Finishing the interior:* As everyone knows, warm air rises while cold air does the opposite. For this reason, you need to elevate the sleeping area a foot or so for additional warmth. While you're doing this you can also carve some "pockets" into the side-walls, in which to place small items. Make a small shelf for your candle—a single candle will light the entire structure and raise its temperature considerably.

8. *Vent hole:* It's not absolutely essential to cut a vent hole in the roof, but it will make for a better exchange of air if you do. Simply punch a ski pole through the roof or pull out one of the porcupine sticks. Don't panic if the hole eventually fills with snow and closes. You'll get plenty of fresh air through the doorway, and the quin-zee walls are porous.

9. *Doorway:* If you have a tunnel entrance to break the wind, you don't need a door. However, a snow block, angled across the entry way will reduce heat loss without significantly affecting ventilation. Just be sure you don't close the snow block door completely.

Tip: A length of nylon parachute cord makes an acceptable snow knife for cutting blocks. Just saw the cord back and forth through the snow until the block is free. This procedure will only work with "old snow," whose molecular structure has compacted.

Warning: The heat generated by two or three bodies in a small quin-zee will easily maintain an interior hut temperature of 20 or more degrees Fahrenheit. In fact, temperature may rise above freezing if you're not careful. The danger is not in being too cold; it is allowing the structure to overheat. If the temperature goes above freezing, the interior walls will melt and ice up, ventilation will cease, the structure will drip water and you'll have an intolerable mess. So watch your thermometer—and your hut temperature—carefully.

Sleeping Inside the Quin-Zee

As stated, interior temperatures are apt to maintain a balmy 20 degrees Fahrenheit even in sub-zero weather, so you don't need an Arctic sleeping bag for comfort. Any three-season bag will do, providing you have plenty of insulation beneath you. You're sleeping on ice, remember?

Your first sleeping layer is a waterproof plastic ground sheet. Atop this place foam pads, carpeting, cardboard—anything that will insulate your body from the cold ground. If you have an open-cell foam trail pad, a 2-inch thickness (or greater) will be required for comfort. A ⅝-inch thick closed-cell foam pad may provide enough warmth. You need much more insulation below than on top!

Common fears: There are two . . . 1) "I'll die from carbon-monoxide poisoning," and 2) "The hut will collapse and smother me." Both concerns are unfounded. You'll get plenty of air through the entry way and vent hole, even in the unlikely event the quin-zee freezes over. As to strength, there is no contest. Snow huts gain strength as they age. I doubt a polar bear could crush a week old quin-zee!

Tip: If you plan to use the shelter for several nights, chip away the ice build-up on the inner walls each day. This will maintain "breathability" of the structure.

Important: The entry way of a quin-zee or snow cave should always be placed on the windward side of the structure. If wind-driven snow begins while you sleep, sufficient snow could pile up on the leeward side of the hut to seal a leeward entrance. This could be quite serious (deadly!) in a snow cave, especially in a blizzard. It's always wise to keep a small shovel in a snow hut, just in case you need to dig out in the morning!

One person trench shelter

You can use a nylon tarp in a variety of creative ways to construct a trench shelter. One plan is illustrated in Figure S-3.

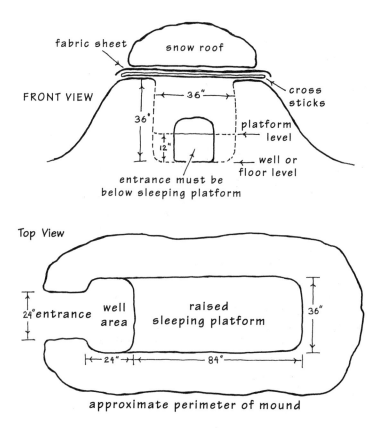

FIGURE S-3.

1. Make a snow pile 6 feet by 12 feet by 3 feet deep. Like the Quin-zee, let it set awhile before you begin the process of digging out. If you can find a snow drift of these dimensions, you may begin digging immediately.
2. Dig a trench 9 feet long, 3 feet wide, and 2 feet deep. Make the entrance a foot lower than the sleeping platform so cold air will be be drawn out of the structure.
3. Span the structure (side-to-side) with a couple dozen closely spaced sticks. Then set your tarp

over the cross-bars and cover it with an insulating layer of snow.

4. *Tip:* You won't need cross-sticks if you substitute two 7-foot-long aluminized space blankets for your nylon tarp. Merely overlap the cold-stiffened space blankets so they'll cover the 9-foot trench, then anchor the sides with snow. A real advantage of the space blankets over a conventional tarp is that they reflect much more warm rising air back to the sleeper below.

Retrieving your tarp: If you leave snow on your tarp overnight, the snow will compact and make the tarp difficult to remove in the morning. One solution is to allow the snow to set for a few hours, then pull out the sticks and remove the tarp from inside the trench (better have smooth sticks or you'll tear the tarp). Expect some falling snow, but the roof should hold. Like a Quin-zee, it will grow stronger with time.

Vaulted roof snow trench
If you have a snow knife (machine) and "old snow," you can build a vaulted roof like that shown in Figure S-4. Be sure to cut the blocks long enough so they'll butt at the peak. Fill cracks with loose snow.

FIGURE S-4. Trench shelter with vaulted roof

Sleeping On Snow

Sleeping on snow requires extra preparation. As mentioned, you need substantial insulation under your sleeping bag. Here are some other tricks that will add to your comfort:

- Place dry outer clothing in your sleeping bag before you retire. The clothes will absorb some of the bag's cold and reduce the size of the area your body must heat. Remove the clothing as the bag warms up.
- Wear long johns, balaclava, and down or Polarguard™ booties to bed for extra warmth. *Don't* bring down parkas into your bag with you; they will absorb insensible perspiration and become damp. Use the parka as a pillow or as extra insulation to cover your feet.
- If you eat some high energy food before you retire, your body will produce more heat as you sleep.
- Make a "draft collar" for your sleeping bag by placing a wool sweater or scarf across your chest and neck. Tuck the sweater sleeves around your shoulders to prevent air loss at the head of the bag.
- Don't cover your face with your sleeping bag if your nose gets cold. Your bag will not be able to eliminate the moisture from your breathing. It may even ice up on the outside—a dangerous situation! Instead, use a sweater or shirt as a face mask. You can easily breathe through this porous material.
- A midnight urination call at 20 below is no fun. Carry a special poly bottle for elimination. Women may want to try the proven "Sani-fem™" device.
- In winter, your sleeping bag cannot dissipate all the moisture your body produces, so air out your bag in the sunlight for several minutes each day.
- A candle will raise the temperature of your tent or snow shelter by 10 or 20 degrees. *Reminder:* Batteries don't work well when they're cold, so insulate them until they are needed.

Soaps

Backcountry soaps should be biodegradable and lather in cold water. They should also be highly concentrated for maximum efficiency. Bar soaps should not melt in the sun or crack in extreme cold. These are the traditional backwoods soaps:

- *Kirk's Coco Hardwater Castille:* Comes in bar form and lathers wonderfully in cold water. Very stable in heat and cold.
- *Dr. Bonner's Peppermint Soap.* The label provides hours of tireless entertainment. Surprisingly, a lot of it is true. Dr. Bonner's formula works well for everything from washing dishes to hair. I've even used it for shaving and to brush my teeth. The nice peppermint smell is compelling. Every "earth friendly" co-op and specialty store has it.
- There are a number of specialty liquid camp soaps which are similar to Dr. Bonner's. One of my favorites is *Huckleberry Finn's Peppermint Camp Soap*, made by Sawyer Products, Inc. Sawyer also makes a delightful travel soap that is formulated with citronella (*Citronella Travel Soap*). It keeps mosquitoes away. Barely.
- *N/R Laboratories No Rinse* shampoo and body bath are among the most interesting new products to come along in recent years. Just rub 'em in to create a rich lather then strip off the floating dirt and oil with paper or cloth towels. No water—or only a very small amount of water—is necessary. For example, one ounce of the body bath in a quart of water is enough for a full sponge bath! No water is needed when you shampoo. There is no residue, so no need to rinse. "No Rinse" cleaning products were first used on hospitalized patients who could not bathe normally. Now, NASA's astronauts have discovered their merits. "No Rinse" products are ideal for backpacking trips where clean water is hard to find. *N/R Laboratories: (800) 223–9348; fax (513) 433–0779.*

Sponge

A small sponge is one of the most useful and forgotten items on a camping trip. It will clean your tent floor, remove accumulated water from your canoe or boat, dissolve mud from your boots, mop up a tent leak and more. A natural sponge is much more absorbent than the best synthetic.

Stool (camp)

A camp stool is worth its weight and bulk on all but the lightest "go light" backpacking trips. Camp chores—cooking, washing dishes, sharpening edged tools, etc.—go easier when you don't sit on the ground. I most appreciate my stool when I must wait out a storm under my rain tarp or endure a long tour of kitchen duty.

Friends scoffed when I first began to bring a camp stool on my wilderness canoe trips. Now, they've all followed suit. I've tried all manner of stool designs and have ultimately settled upon a simple collapsible model like those used at competitive shooting events. Be sure you get a stool that sits on two parallel aluminum rails. Avoid individual pointed legs that can sink into soft ground. My favorite camp stool weighs ten ounces and has a canvas storage pouch beneath the seat. When not in use it folds flat and clips (with bungee cords) to my backpack.

Stoves

Camp stoves are pretty trouble-free. Most will give a lifetime of good service if properly maintained. Here are some troubleshooting hints and some dos and don'ts.

Troubleshooting
Problem: Flame sputters; stove won't reach normal operating temperatures.

a) Problem is likely due to *dirt in the mechanism.* Turn off the stove and pour about half the fuel out. Re-cap the tank and shake the stove vigorously for a few seconds (to dislodge the clogged dirt particle). Then pour out the gas and re-fill the stove with fresh fuel. If this doesn't work, drain the stove and force high pressure air (from an air-compressor) through the filler cap opening. If this fails, the stove must be disassembled and cleaned.

b) *The safety valve,* located in the filler cap, *is damaged.*

Squirt a small amount of liquid detergent on and around the cap and check for air bubbles. If the valve is blown, replace the filler cap.

c) *Stove needs more pressure.* If additional pumping doesn't do the trick, check the leather washer on the pump stem. Lubricate the washer with oil or grease. Most of the new stoves have synthetic (plastic) pump washers which don't work as well as the old leather ones. Check the plumbing section of your hardware store. Some leather stool washers fit some stoves perfectly. *Note:* Stoves must be insulated from the cold ground (in sub-freezing temperatures) in order to maintain operating pressure.

d) *Check for improper fuel.* You cannot use lead-free automotive gasoline in "white gas" stoves. Naphtha (Coleman fuel) is the cleanest burning of the stove fuels, and it is pre-filtered.

e) *For Optimus / Svea stoves* that don't have pumps: Nipple may have become enlarged by improper cleaning (a bent cleaning needle will do it). The nipple (a low cost item) must be replaced. Over-priming can burn the cotton wick and reduce its absorbent qualities. The remedy is to replace the wick—something that is best done by one who is familiar with the process.

Problem: Stove stays lit for about twenty seconds, then slowly goes out. Pumping it revives the flame.
Invariably, this is the result of a slow leak in the tank filler cap. Either the safety valve is blown or the silver solder around the filler neck has melted. Replace the pressure cap, or re-solder the neck.

Check the exact location of the pressure leak by squirting liquid detergent around the pressure cap. If the safety valve checks out okay, the gasket in the filler cap is probably at fault. Replace the age-hardened gasket with a new one.

Priming

Most white gas and kerosene stoves must be pre-heated or "primed" with gasoline or alcohol in order to bring them to sufficient temperature to vaporize raw fuel. You don't need much heat to prime a gasoline stove. On a hot day, the sun or heat from your hands may generate enough pressure to cause fuel to stream from the nipple.

Pumps do not vaporize fuel; they simply allow you to maintain greater pressure in the fuel tank, which makes the stove easier to start and maintain, especially in cold weather.

Procedure for priming pump-equipped stoves:
1. First, clean the nipple. Most stoves have a built-in cleaning needle which is activated by giving the adjuster knob a quarter turn counterclockwise.
2. Be sure the pressure cap is tight and the adjuster knob is closed. Then, pump the stove a half dozen times.
3. Crack the adjuster knob a quarter turn for about four seconds, and watch fuel stream into the spirit cup below the burner head. Do not fill the spirit cup more than one-third full of gas!
4. Close the adjuster knob and ignite the fuel in the spirit cup. While the fuel is burning, give the stove another dozen pumps. When the flame has nearly died, crack the adjuster knob to permit entrance of gas. An instant blue flame should result. Note: Over-priming (too much gas in the spirit cup) wastes gas, carbons up parts, and may overheat and damage stove parts. Under-priming makes stoves difficult to light. Learn to strike a compromise.

To prime stoves that don't have pumps:
1. Clean the nipple.
2. Remove the tank filler cap and withdraw an eyedropper full of gas from the tank. Replace the filler cap. Squirt the dropper-full of gas into the spirit cup.
3. Ignite the gas in the spirit cup. When the flame has nearly gone out, crack the adjuster knob one-fourth turn. You should see a bright blue flame.

Note: The Optimus mini-pump, which is sold for use in cold weather, is unnecessary if you follow the eye-dropper method of priming. Cupping stoves in hands, as is recommended by some stove makers, is slow, unreliable, and painfully cold in chilly weather.

Stoves: Dos and Don'ts

DO carry fuel only in recommended containers. Sigg aluminum liter bottles, or the original container, is recommended.

DO frequently check the temperature of your stove's fuel tank by feeling it with your hand. If the tank is too hot to hold, reduce pressure and/or pour water on the tank to cool it.

DO carry extra stove parts and tools. An extra pressure cap and leather pump washer is usually enough. Bring a small screwdriver and pliers.

DO empty the fuel in your stove after each trip. And burn the stove dry at the end of the camping season. Impurities in fuel left in stoves can cause malfunctions.

DO keep your stove protected in a rigid container when it's not in use.

DON'T loosen or remove the filler cap of a gasoline stove when the stove is burning. This could result in an explosion!

DON'T re-fuel a hot stove. There may be sufficient heat still available to ignite the fumes. Be especially careful in cold weather, as gasoline vaporizes much more slowly then.

DON'T set oversize pots on stoves. Large pots reflect excessive heat back to the fuel tank which may cause overheating of the stove. Run stove at three-fourths throttle if you use oversize pots.

DON'T start or run a stove inside a tent or confined area, or any place where there is insufficient ventilation.

DON'T poke wire cleaning tools into burner jets from the outside. This pushes foreign matter into the vaporization barrel and clogs the valve.

DON'T enclose a stove with aluminum foil to increase its heat output. The stove may overheat and explode!

DON'T fill gasoline or kerosene stoves more than three-fourths full. Fuel won't vaporize if there's insufficient room for it to expand. Some stoves erupt into a ball of fire when they're over-filled.

End-of-season stove maintenance

Once a year, fill the tank one-fourth full with fresh gas and add a cap-full (no more) of engine fuel-injector cleaner.

Burn the tank dry. The injector cleaner will remove harmful deposits which could cause clogging. Lubricate the pump washer with non-gumming high grade gun oil or synthetic motor oil. Spray exterior stove parts with WD-40 to prevent rust. Wipe the stove dry with paper toweling and store it in a dust-free environment.

Stuff Sacks

Nylon bags with drawstring closures are useful organizers for food, clothing and small items. Camping shops sell these bags in a variety of shapes and sizes. You can easily sew your own from nylon taffeta in a few minutes (see *Yard Goods*, page 217).

Note: Ordinary fabric shops usually don't stock waterproof nylon, but the best camping shops do.

Survival Shelters

Everyone who has spent much time in the woods has, at one time or another, become lost. In his memoirs, Daniel Boone tells how he once became "mightily confused" for three days. As a young forester, I once shared a similar experience while working in western Oregon for the Bureau of Land Management. I did an incredibly stupid thing—one which I am naturally embarrassed to share with readers. But I was barely twenty-one at the time, so I'll blame my incoherence on youth.

I'd just finished marking a timber sale near Coos Bay, when I was told the sale was cancelled. My instructions were to remove the yellow plastic ribbon from the trees which denoted the cutting line. Now, most people of normal intelligence would simply follow the flagging to the end, *then* remove it. Not me. I began picking ribbons off the trees the moment I entered the woods. I realized the folly of this almost immediately, but I continued on. After all, I'd established the cutting line, which for the most part, followed a ridge. Yeah, there were some crossovers, but these were "obvious." I was certain I wouldn't get lost.

By noon that day, I was "mightily confused." By dark, I

was hopelessly lost. Sure, I knew the rules: "Stay put, build a fire and someone will find you." But it was *Friday* and the government doesn't work on weekends. Monday was a holiday and I had Tuesday off for elk hunting. No one would even think of looking for me till Wednesday—five days from now! Besides, this was the Pacific Coast Range, where Douglas Fir trees grow tall as skyscrapers. Crown cover here was close to 100 percent. Even a combat chopper pilot couldn't spot me beneath all that foliage. And making a signal fire in the persistent December rain was out of the question. Suddenly, "survival" became a meaningful word.

Space does not permit sharing the details of my ordeal. Suffice it to say that I set my compass for due west—direction of the ocean and highway 101—and struck off into the rain-drenched forest. Clothed in woolens and waterproof rain gear, I also had a knife, cigarette lighter, Thermos of coffee, and my lunch. Water abounded everywhere.

Three days later I walked into the sunlight of an unimproved logging road, which I followed to the whistle-stop town of Remote, Oregon. From there, I hitched a ride back to my Jeep. I never told BLM about my adventure. Why? Because foresters *don't get lost!*

In this section, we'll examine some personal survival shelters and techniques for coping with a wilderness emergency. You'll find no energy-draining thatched roof lean-to's that take hours to build, for when you are lost, food is at a premium. Better to keep things simple by modifying natural shelters (caves, downed trees, brush piles, etc.) to meet your needs.

Frankly, a positive mental attitude (PMA) is your most important survival tool. I vividly remember praising my Silva compass at the end of my three day ordeal. Without it—and the knowledge to go west—I probably would have died in the Oregon woods, shelter or no. The "tools" of survival" are less important than believing you'll get out alive!

Shelters

Possibilities are endless if you have a tarp. If not, the rule is to modify an existing shelter. Can you remove the lower branches of a downed tree to create a small nest? Or burrow into the hollow at its base (Figure S-5). Perhaps you can stack some brush or logs along one side to block out the

FIGURE S-5.

wind. A tiny reflector fire will help you weather the storm.

Before you move in, check for potential dangers—dead trees that may blow down on you, loose rocks, dry wash, etc. Make your crawl space large enough to stretch out but small enough to conserve heat.

Next comes bark or boughs to insulate the floor and walls. If it's raining, divert the water with make-shift guttering. Otherwise, shingle fresh-cut browse. This is no time to think environmentally: Cutting vegetation and trenching your home are a tenet of survival.

Now, crawl inside and try the fit. If you're cold, use evergreen boughs or leaves for a blanket. Perhaps if you re-arrange the layering of your clothes you will add some warmth. For example, suppose you're wearing (from the skin out) a cotton T-shirt, cotton-polyester long-sleeved shirt, and wool sweater. Cotton wicks away body heat at a rapid pace, while wool does not. So wear your sweater next to the skin and the cotton garments over it. Don't overlook the value of non-traditional insulation like newspaper, leaves, life jacket, or your packsack. Rope, coiled about your body, will even provide warmth.

If you have a vehicle, you have lots of options. All you have to do is dissect the expensive upholstery and sew the pieces into clothing. Any sharp object will function as an awl. Fabric ravelings and electrical wire provide thread (have you tried dental floss?), sticks become buttons. No formulas; just ingenuity.

Survival Kit

Most commercial survival kits have cutesy items—like wire, fish hooks, bandaids, and safety pins—that you will never use. The result is a heavy, bulky unit that's more likely to be left at home than carried to the wilds. At the other extreme, are impractical belt-size kits whose miniaturized components defy productive use. For example, one enterprising company offers a wallet-sized "survival card" that comes with a magnetized disk (compass?) which points north when you float it in water. How absurd!

The kit illustrated in Figure S-6 is recommended by the Minnesota Department of Natural Resources. There is at least one documented case where quick thinking, and some of its components saved a life. Here's the story:

A Minneapolis teenager was snowmobiling when a blizzard created white-out conditions. Fortunately, the boy had recently completed an outdoor education class in high school, and he had a simple survival kit in his possession. When the young man could no longer see to drive, he used the coffee can to scoop snow from under the machine. Then he put on the plastic bag "rain suit," wrapped himself in the space blanket, and spent the night inside the hollow. His snowmobile suit kept him warm, the "rain suit" kept him dry, and the reflective space blanket helped retain body heat. Here are the contents of his survival kit, along with some proven extras.

Suggested survival kit contents

- Two large "leaf-and-lawn-size" plastic bags. Cut out the bottoms and duct tape them together to form a continuous tube which can double as a "tent" and "rain suit."
- Space blanket. Get one of the compact versions at any outdoor store. Don't open it; you'll never fit it back into the container! These space blankets are actually too small to cover an adult. Best use them to supplement your trash bags or to help warm a victim of hypothermia.
- Fifteen or twenty wooden stick matches, a large

small plastic
whistle

space
blanket

plumbers
candle

large
bandana

25 foot
nylon line

all go in
a two lb.
coffee can
container

15-20
matches

2 large
leaf-size
plastic bags

small
mirror

2 large
Zip-loc bags

pocket
knife

fire-starter

FIGURE S-6.

plumbers candle (which will burn for hours), and a solid fuel chemical fire-starter enable anyone to make a blaze in any weather.

- If space permits, add bouillon cubes, tea and sugar. Be aware, however, that food is a low priority item when you're lost. Your main concern is shelter, warmth, and *getting found.*
- A one-pound coffee can with a fitted plastic lid makes a handy pot, snow shovel, and container for everything.
- Carry a whistle (the new pea-less designs take up little space) and a small mirror for signaling.
- Two Zip-loc bags. Use them as a cold weather vapor barrier (wear them against the skin) on your feet or hands, and as a container for berries, minnows, tinder, etc.
- Twenty-five feet of strong nylon line suspends your "tube tent" from trees or becomes a belt to secure your "rain gear." **Warning**: *Never* seal the ends of a non-porous, plastic tube tent. Doing so, could cause suffocation!
- Large cotton bandanna. Doubles as a neck-warmer, sun and bug hat, cravat bandage, and spare sock. Use it to strain minnows and crawfish.
- Small, single-bladed knife. A razor blade is no substitute for a sharp knife. If you include a compass in your kit, make it a real one. The Silva Huntsman is the most compact, accurate instrument available.

Pack everything in the tin can and seal the lid with several feet of duct tape, which you can use to rig shelters and mend holes in plastic bags.

Tablecloth

Scenario: You are preparing lunch along the edge of a rain-soaked trail. Every depression is a pond, every leaf a pool.

You break out the crackers and slice the Swiss and salami. Where can you put them out of the muck?

On a tablecloth, of course! A small (2-foot-square) plastic tablecloth adds dignity to what might otherwise be a dirty free-for-all. My red-checkered tablecloth has painted "black ants" on top. It always draws a smile, even in rain.

Tarps (rain flies)

Background: Tarps are essential in a rainy day camp. Under them you'll comfortably prepare meals, make repairs and otherwise enjoy a day that might be soured by rain. The value of a "fly" is obvious, whether you're camped on a remote mountain vista or in the gentle confines of a state park. It requires skill and a bit of weather knowledge to pitch a drum-tight fly in a howling storm, yet anyone can learn how in less than an hour. A well-rigged rainfly exemplifies the experts' edge.

Materials: A 10 × 12 foot (or larger!) nylon tarp for every four people. I ordinarily rig a single fly in modified lean-to configuration, but for severe storms, I mate the pair into a giant open tent that everyone can crowd under. No need to purchase expensive tarps (I suggest you get two). Any waterproof nylon—ripstop or taffeta—is fine.

Customize your tarp(s) according to Figure T-1 and T-2. Two hours time and a light duty sewing machine are all you need.

Tips: Well sewn nylon loops (get inch-wide nylon webbing at any camping shop) are much more reliable than grommets. If you're a belt-and-suspenders person, you'll replace critically located corner grommets with well-reinforced nylon loops. Allow no more than 12 inches of space between loops or grommets. Be sure to back whatever you sew with heavy material.

Sew an 8-inch square "pole patch" of heavy material to the inside center (opposite the center guy line) of your fly, then sew on the two "butterfly pole" loops that are illustrated. Thread a 2-foot-long piece of parachute cord through the loops and secure the cords with a heavy-duty cord lock. This will allow you to use—and stabilize—an interior center pole when there are no trees to which you can attach an

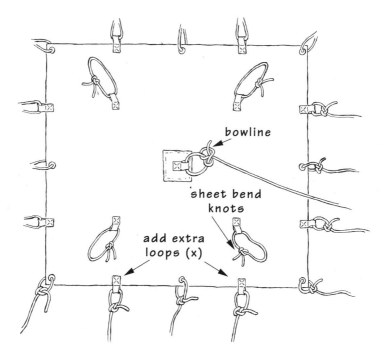

bowline

sheet bend
knots

add extra
loops (x)

FIGURE T-1.

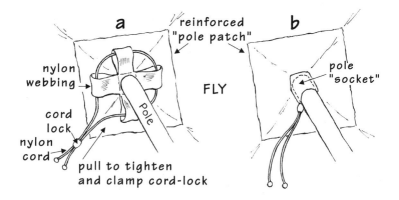

a
reinforced
"pole patch"

nylon
webbing

cord
lock

nylon
cord

pull to tighten
and clamp cord-lock

FLY

pole

b

pole
"socket"

FIGURE T-2.

outside guy line. Nylon stretches and abrades easily, so a reinforcing patch is essential if you plan to use a pole.

To use the "butterfly pole" loops: Center the pole in the "socket" and tighten the cord lock. The loops will wrap around the pole and hold it in place when the tarp is buffeted by wind. For extra security, wrap the cords around the pole a few times and tie them with a simple bow. In very high winds, you may need to stake the pole to the ground— simply run a guy line from the butterfly loops to a stake at the base of the pole.

Attach loops of parachute cord to each grommet or loop. Loops should be large enough to allow insertion of a wire stake. Leave at least 6 inches of "tie" hanging, as illustrated. *Tip:* Braided nylon cord holds knots better than the inexpensive sheathed parachute cord sold at hardware stores.

Attach generously sized chute cord loops to each of the five webbed loops on the face of the fly. Loops should be tied with a sheet-bend. One 20-foot-long cord should be permanently secured to the *center* face loop.

Tip: If you sew matching loops *inside* the tarp opposite those on the outside of the tarp, you'll have a handy place to hang flashlights, candle lanterns, stuff sacks etc.

Finally, waterproof all seams. I prefer *Thompson's Water Seal*—an industrial-strength compound used for sealing wood and concrete block. TWS won't crack and peel in winter or get sticky in July. Two applications, spaced an hour apart, provide life-long protection. Apply the product sparingly with a foam varnish brush. Use TWS on your tent seams, maps and journals too. Every hardware store has it.

Don't leave home without these items!

When suddenly the sky suddenly turns black and the wind grows deadly still, you generally have only a few moments to pitch tents and get everything and everybody under a storm-proof tarp. There's no time to cut hanks of line, fumble for tent stakes, poles or ground sheets, or wonder where you put your pocket knife. Suddenly, your worst foul weather concerns have materialized.

You'll avoid much embarrassment when the weather turns sour if you gather these materials before you take to the woods:

- One hundred feet of ⅛-inch diameter parachute cord for each tarp you plan to rig. Cut rope into 15–20 foot lengths and burn the ends so they won't unravel. Then, tightly coil each hank and secure it with the quick-release loop illustrated in Figure T-3.

Tip: Choose brightly colored cord that you won't trip over in failing light.

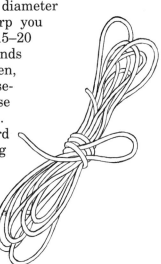

- Fifty feet of ¼- or ³⁄₁₆-inch diameter *braided* nylon rope (twisted rope unravels too easily) for each tarp. Singe the ends and coil the ropes by the method illustrated in Figure R3-1.

FIGURE T-3.

- A sharp knife. A hand axe and folding saw are useful when you need to cut extension poles from *dead, downed* timber.
- Inexpensive plastic sheeting can be substituted for nylon tarps (*please* don't leave plastic in the woods) if you have "Vis-clamps" (ball and garter devices) or small rubber balls or pebbles. Figure T-4 shows the attachment procedure.
- Waterproof tape for making repairs to nylon and plastic.

Pitching the fly

When thunderheads loom threateningly overhead and the wind builds to impressive speeds, you generally have only a few minutes to rig a storm-proof camp. So keep everything you need to rig your tarp—50 feet of rope, five 20-foot coils of parachute cord, and a dozen stakes, in a nylon stuff sack with cord lock closure.

Note: Military specification "kermantle style" parachute cord that has a lightly textured outer sheath is better than rough braided civilian cord that has no protective outer sheath. Rough cord holds knots well, but plant matter sticks to it. Get brightly colored cord so you can see it in dim light. You'll find the best cordage at mountaineering shops.

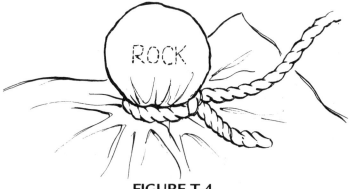

FIGURE T-4.

Tip: Stuff your fly, don't roll it. Stuffing is faster and easier on the waterproof coating. Be certain everything is bone dry before you pack it away. Dampness provides a media for microorganisms to attack the waterproof polyurethane coating on the fly. Microbes will not attack nylon, but they *will* devour the polyurethane coating on it! Ever see a tent floor whose waterproof coating has peeled? More than likely the tent was put away wet!

Rigs
Single Lean-To
This "meat-and-potatoes" configuration can be erected alone in about three minutes and will withstand winds of 30 miles an hour. The sloping design spills water effectively and conserves the warmth of a reflector fire.

Procedure:
1. Locate two trees about 15 feet apart and string a drum-tight line between them, about 5 feet off the ground. Use two quick-release *half-hitches* at one end, and a quick-release *power-cinch* at the other.
2. Take the pair of ties at one corner of the fly and tightly wind one tie of the set clockwise around the rope. Wind the other tie counter-clockwise. Take at least four turns around the rope, then secure the ties with an overhand bow.

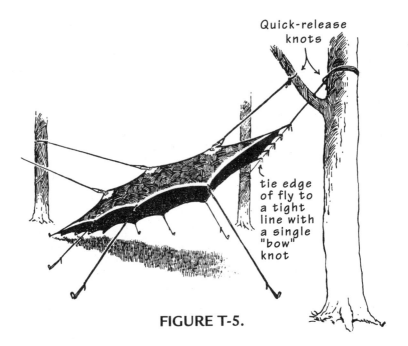

Quick-release knots

tie edge of fly to a tight line with a single "bow" knot

FIGURE T-5.

3. Pull the other corner of the open end of the fly tight along the rope and secure it with the ties, winding them around the rope, as above. The tie wrappings will provide tension to keep the corners of the tarp from slipping inward along the rope when the fly is buffeted by wind.
4. Secure all remaining ties to the rope with a simple overhand bow. Note that by securing the fly at several points along the length of its open end, rather than just at the corners, you distribute the strain across a wide area, thus increasing the strength of the fly. High wind will tear out the corner grommets or loops unless you distribute the load along a main hem line, as illustrated.
5. Pull the back of the fly out tight and stake it.
6. Run the center cord over a tree limb or a horizontal rope strung above and behind the fly. Snug the cord and secure it with a quick-release power-cinch. Use an interior center pole if trees are not

available. Connect additional lines (use a quick-release *sheet-bend*) to other face loops as needed to produce drum-tight geometry.

In ultra-high winds, guy or stake the side hems of the fly to the ground or adjacent trees.

Using Campfire and Single Fly Together

A fire built just under the open edge of the fly will provide substantial heat inside the lean-to. However, since the fly acts as a "wind eddy," you must backlog your fire (Figure T-6) or it will smoke you out. The bottom of an aluminum canoe works well, as does a large sheet of aluminum foil. You can even use several packs if you keep them well away from the flames. The real purpose of the backing is to draw smoke away from the enclosure, not reflect heat into it. Note that the fire must be completely *outside* the tarp. The backlogs have insufficient area to make up for the size of the wind eddy created by the huge tarp.

When rigging twin tarps, you can foil the smoke with the ingenious procedure illustrated in Figure T-7.

FIGURE T-6.

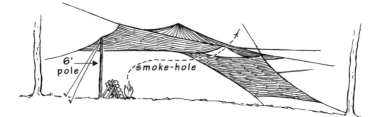

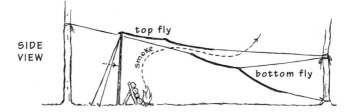

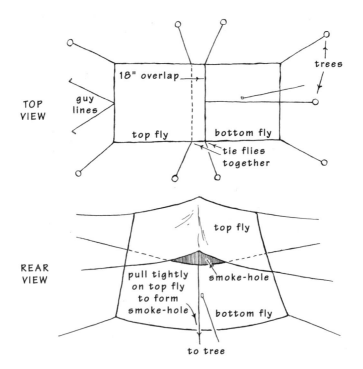

FIGURE T-7.

Twin Flies with Fire Slit

Here's a secure, airy shelter that will provide luxurious comfort for up to twelve people. Two people can rig it in about ten minutes, even in high winds. You'll need two 10' × 10' or larger "customized" flies and all your rope and cord.

The beauty of this arrangement is that you can build a rain-protected warming fire right underneath the fly. The combination back-log and overhead vent spills smoke through the opening on top. You can "float" the slanted roof, as illustrated, to provide more interior room, or stake it to the ground for protection from blowing wind.

Procedure:

1. Rig the single lean-to configuration shown in Figure T-5. In vertical rains, "float" the back as illustrated in Figure T-7. Remember to connect all lines to one another with a *quick-release sheetbend*.

2. Overlap to the second grommet, the hem of fly #2 over the hem of fly #1. This should provide an approximate 2-foot overlap. Then, secure the corner ties of fly #2 to the ties on the side hem of fly #1.

3. Attach a 20-foot length of chute cord to the center grommet of fly #2 (point "a" in Figure T-7) and secure this cord to a tree—or line strung between two trees—directly behind fly #1. If you won't build a fire under fly #2, you may guy this line to a stake at the base of fly #1.

4. Next, you'll need a six-foot-long aluminum or wooden pole. If you don't have a metal pole, cut one from dead, downed wood, or use a *shear lashing* to extend several short spars to this length. Tie the top of the pole to the center ties on fly #2. Run twin guy lines from the pole tip to the stakes below. Secure guy lines with a *power-cinch*. Stake or guy out the corners of fly #2.

5. Go to the back of fly #1 and tighten the overhead "vent" cord ("a") until the structure is tight. There should be an approximate 6-inch gap between the overlapped portions of the two flies. Last step is to add additional storm lines on the face and hem of both flies to produce a taut shape that won't

pool water. You now have a huge, sturdy shelter that won't pool water or flap in the wind.

Campfire Considerations

Build the fire just inside the hem of fly #2. Backlog it as explained. Smoke will follow the backlogged eddy line to the roof of fly #2 and be drawn out through the slit between the two flies. This works slick when there's no wind. You'll have to experiment here, as a good breeze may confuse the eddies and allow the shelter to fill with smoke. You will also discover that if you raise the back of fly #1 off the ground to provide more headroom, the bottom draft that results will pull smoke away from the vent and into the shelter. Ingenuity and strong backlogging will usually solve most smoke problems.

Special purpose rigs

Cliff 'N Dan Tundra Tarp

During the summer, I guide canoe trips in northern Canada for the Science Museum of Minnesota. I typically travel with a crew of ten, often in very rainy conditions. Rigging twin flies every night is time-consuming, so I leave the small tarps at home and instead carry a giant 15-foot square model that I designed with the help of Cooke Custom Sewing. This *tundra tarp*, as Dan calls it, has full bug netting sewn to all four sides. The netting rolls and ties out-of-the-way when it's not needed, yet it releases instantly. Surprisingly, there's no need to kill or shoo away insects that are trapped inside the enclosure. The bugs happily entertain themselves by crawling on the inside netting, away from you!

The tundra tarp is ingenious and expensive—and worth every penny when you need a bug-proof structure that stays up in high winds. I've used mine on the shores of Hudson Bay in sustained winds of 50 miles an hour! No problems. The outfit weighs about 14 pounds with (three) aluminum poles, stakes, lines and netting. Twelve people can crowd inside. Dan Cooke will build a tundra tarp to your specifications. *Address: Cooke Custom Sewing, 7290 Stagecoach Trail, Lino Lakes, MN 55014-1988; (651) 784–8777, fax (651) 784–4158.*

Quick Rig Tundra Tarp

Scenario: You're canoeing in the barren lands where no trees and high winds are the rule. Rig a "canoe prop," like that illustrated above, and it will go sailing off into the tundra before you can move in. What to do? Why, use your canoes to weight the tarp, of course. And, oh yes, you'll need one 5–7 foot aluminum pole.

Procedure:

1. Lay the tarp flat on the ground and weight two adjacent sides with over-turned canoes.
2. Hoist the apex of the shelter on a long pole then guy the pole and remaining loose fabric in place. Total rigging time? Less than three minutes!

Tips:

- You can construct a more spacious shelter by placing the canoes *inside* the fly, bellies facing the occupants. Drape the tarp partially over the canoes and tie it to them (you'll need several short lengths of cord).
- An overturned canoe blocked up on the sides makes a great table. Remove the side blocks and it becomes a windbreak for your stove.

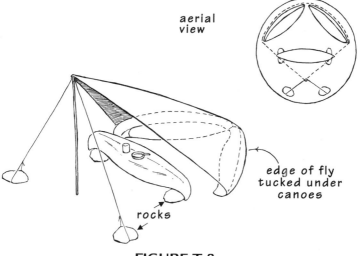

aerial
view

edge of fly
tucked under
canoes

rocks

FIGURE T-8.

Canoe Prop Method

Prop a canoe on paddles and cover it with your rain tarp, as shown in Figure T-9. If you have two canoes, prop them side-by-side about 6 feet apart, parallel to one another and cover them with a tarp. Stake and guy the tarp and push out the center with a paddle so it won't pool water. *Don't trust this set-up in a strong wind!*

If it's *perfectly calm,* you can prop up the back ends of the canoes, as well as the front, to produce a non-sloping shelter with more interior space.

I don't like the "canoe prop" method. It's hard on paddles and not very secure. But it is useful in light rain and handy when you need protection for a small fire.

Tip: A single "canoe prop" without fly makes a quick shelter for two in a light, vertical rain. I've used it many times to prepare lunch along a canoe portage on a rainy day.

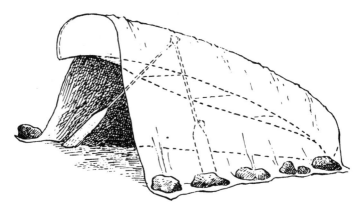

FIGURE T-9.

Single-walled Sun Teepee

Similar to the *quick-rig tundra tarp* illustrated in Figure T-8, the *sun teepee* requires one pole and one guy line. For a taut configuration you'll need to guy out the mid-point of the fly—impossible if there are no trees. However, stacking gear against the inside back-wall will stiffen the shelter considerably.

As you can see, there are dozens of ways to rig tarps. And that's the problem. Most people are so baffled by all the possible configurations that they never master a single design. My advice? Forget about the cute options suggested in survival texts and become expert at rigging the *single lean-to* (Figure T-5) and *twin flies with fire slit* (Figure T-7). For desert or barren land camping, the *quick-rig tundra tarp* or its derivative, the *single-walled sun teepee,* is most practical

Tents

And the night shall be filled with music
And the cares that infest the day,
Shall fold their tents like Arabs
And as silently steal away.

HENRY WADSWORTH LONGFELLOW
from *A Psalm of Life.*

It's been four hours now and still it continues. The water comes in sheets, cold and unrelenting. Everywhere, the ground is drenched with it; every rut holds a pool, every leaf a tiny pond. Contentedly, you peer through the mosquito net of your nylon tent at the vastness of the forest beyond. The sky, deep gray and foreboding, communicates that "more of the same" is on the way.

Overhead, a small aluminum candle lantern provides some warmth and enough light to permit reading a novel. You laze against the loosely rolled sleeping bag and momentarily stare into the dampness of the day. A smug smile flashes briefly: Granted, the 5' × 7' foot A-frame tent is a bit cramped for two. But no matter; it is warm and dry. Be it ever so humble, there is no place like home, even when it is a confining backpack tent pitched on a secluded ridge deep in the Adirondacks.

Five states to the west, a similar scenario is in progress. A man and woman, twelve-year-old-girl, and tow-headed boy of nine peer wistfully through the netted window of their spacious nine-foot-square umbrella tent. The walls of the 10-ounce canvas Eureka rustle contentedly to the rhythm of the wind-whipped rain. Outside, tiny icicles drip from the well bronzed canvas, but inside, warmed by the glow of a Coleman lantern, it is snug and dry. The six-foot peak provides plenty of room to stand and dress, and the spacious floor plan encourages games and socializing. This family has been confined for six hours but they are having a very good time. Yet, all around, far as the eye can see, the KOA campground is deserted. Where, earlier, dozens of tents had dotted the treeless field, now, there is only grass and rain. Everyone else has gone —casualties of the persistent precipitation.

At the top of the continent, just above the Arctic circle, two canoe campers ride out a polar gale in their low-slung geodesic dome. The state-of-the-art nylon igloo expands and contracts with every gust of the 50-mile-per-hour wind, but it holds firm. Thirty-six hours later, two smiling voyageurs emerge on to the still, sun-lit tundra, grateful that their tent had weathered the storm.

As you can see, there is no such thing as a perfect tent, or even an all-around one. What's best for car-camping is out-of-place in the tundra or on the hiking trail. Backpacking in the mountains is not like desert hiking or wilderness canoeing. And winter camping imposes new demands. Tents designed to withstand high winds may perform poorly in rain, and vice versa. Those built to withstand snow loads may be too heavy or difficult to pitch. Ones light enough to carry long distances may test your sanity on a rainy day, while larger models may strain the confines of your backpack. And so it goes. When you do find your dream tent it may simply cost too much.

But don't despair; there is order in the universe. The following principles of tent design and construction will help you separate the wheat from the chaff. Figure T-11 will help you with terminology.

Design and construction features

The construction features of most tents are vastly overrated. Commotion about thread count, number of stitches per inch, reinforcement of zipper ends and such, proudly touted by tent makers, takes a back seat to *good design*—a feature not always associated with quality construction or high price. In all my years of canoeing and camping, I've never seen a well-designed tent come apart at the seams or a zipper rip from its stitching. But I've experienced enough

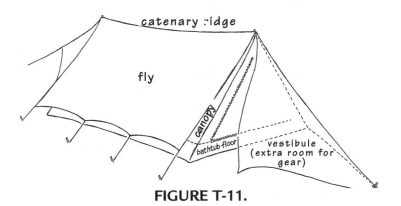

FIGURE T-11.

bent poles, torn flies, and broken zippers to know that fabrics and sloppy sewing are rarely the villains.

If you keep uppermost in your mind that good design, impeccable construction, and high price, don't always go hand-in-hand, you'll be on your way to finding the ideal tent for your purposes, and pocketbook.

Design Principles

If you asked a boating expert how to tell a seaworthy canoe from one that's not, he or she might use this analogy:

"Pretend your hands are water and place them on the keel-line of the canoe. Now, slide your hands up towards the rails. Is there substantial flare here? Good. Water will follow that flare away from the hull rather than into it. But if your hands "tumble home" (follow the inward curve of the canoe above the waterline), water will do the same. It's no mystery why flare-sided dories are more seaworthy than hard-chinned rowboats!

Now try this same test on your tent. Follow the fly to the ground, as if your hands were water. Do your hands fall on unprotected seams? If so, rain will pool here and seep into your tent. And seam-sealant (glue) won't keep you dry for very long. The most reliable way to keep seams from leaking is to cover them with waterproof material. A fly that stakes right to the ground will do the trick, but few tents come so equipped. To save weight, many tents have short "cap" flies which don't protect the canopy in wind-driven rain. Some sophisticated tents now feature machine sealed (heat tape) seams like those applied to the best rainwear. These seams won't leak in any weather. Exceptions aside, you are best advised to avoid any tent that has perimeter seams which are not fully covered by the fly. The floors of some tents, like the *Eureka Timberline*, are sewn to the canopy several inches above ground. This bathtub construction puts vulnerable seams under the protection of the fly where they belong. All the best rain tents have bathtub floors!

Now, check the tent corners where the floor seams and door zippers come together. Does the fly drip water onto any stitching? If so, find a way to fix it or keep shopping! Even the well-designed Eureka Timberline scores low in this category.

The entrance and window(s) are other critical components. Are there generously sized awnings over doors and vents to keep rain out? Are exterior zippers protected by weather flaps? Can you easily turn aside a weather flap with your hand? If so, wind will do the same. Many of the best tents use elastic or Velcro to keep weather flaps in place. Perhaps you can make modifications.

Vestibules are worth their weight in gold on a rainy day. They function as an extra room to store packs and wet gear. More importantly, they protect the entrance (all those exposed seams and zippers we are concerned about) against blowing wind and rain, and they provide a place to cook out-of-the-weather when you're too lazy to rig a rain tarp. Vestibules are generally add-on affairs which attach to the tent canopy with clips or shockcord. If you're serious about camping in rain, you'll *demand* a vestibule!

Geometry

There are A-frames, teepees, tunnels, domes, lean-tos and sophisticated geometric shapes that defy description.

Domes: Space-wise, domes are the most efficient of tent designs. The high, gradually sloping side-wall of a dome provide a pleasant spacious atmosphere, and the hexagon or octagon shaped floor permits occupants to sleep in any direction—a real advantage if the tent is pitched "wrong" or on a sloping site.

But domes have plenty of faults. Though they shed rain

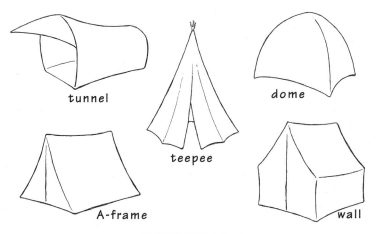

tunnel

dome

teepee

A-frame

wall

FIGURE T-12.

efficiently, they're poorly ventilated (the fly covers the windows and door) and not very wind-stable. *Geodesic* domes, which utilize a lattice of arrow-shaft aluminum poles, are the exception. However, serious geodesic designs are time-consuming to pitch and very expensive. All domes (geodesics included) crush in high winds unless they are well guyed and staked. This means running storm lines through slits in the fly to guy points on the poles. Rigging a dome for gale-force winds is quite a task, though once accomplished, the tent usually holds.

By design, domes cannot utilize bathtub floor construction. The many-faceted floor must be sewn to the canopy at ground level, which leaves plenty of seams for you to glue. Ironically, some of the best domes have short flies which leave perimeter floor seams exposed to the weather. Such construction guarantees a sponge party in prolonged rain.

Geodesic domes were designed as mountaineering tents. Since they're basically free-standing, can be shoved into small crevices, and don't need to be rotated to face into a changing wind, they are ideal for situations where creature comfort, light weight, small packed size, and wind-stability are important factors. Good geodesics are at best, mediocre rain tents. And conventional domes are worse. Inexpensive (cheap!) domes which have fiberglass poles and no awnings over the doors and windows are among the worst tents you can buy. Might as well get a play tent as one of these!

Teepees:

"You have noticed, " said Black Elk, "that everything an Indian does is in a circle and that is because the power of the world works in circles and everything tries to be round. The life of man is a circle from childhood to childhood. Our tipi's were round, like the nests of birds. But the white men have put us in square boxes. It is a bad way to live for there can be no power in a square."

John Neihardt, Black Elk Speaks
(from *The Tent Book,* by E.M. Hatton, 1979,
Houghton Mifflin Co.)

The teepee is perhaps the most efficient and ingenious of tent designs. No other tent of comparable size sheds wind and rain as well, is as cool in summer, as warm in winter, and as versatile. The American Indian knew what he was doing when he designed the teepee!

Indian teepees are actually egg-shaped, not round as is commonly believed. The long axis of the cone was placed windward to brace the structure against the harsh prairie winds. Ventilation was provided by the doorway and a clever system of flaps at the apex. In winter, fine brush (insulation) was stacked between the inner tent liner and outer wall. It was all very ingenious and difficult to improve upon.

The modern nylon teepee is a far cry from its skin-covered ancestor. Three aluminum poles provide support and a removable cap fly keeps out the weather. Entry is a zippered door or traditional hole.

Teepees light enough for backpacking share the same wet-weather inadequacies as domes but they're more rigid, and so remain rock-solid in winds that would flatten conventional tents of equal height. However, their flies are slow and awkward to install, have stakes and guy lines everywhere, and there is no awning over the doorway to keep rain out. Teepees are great for semi-permanent camps. Otherwise, forget 'em.

Tunnels are low-to-the-ground affairs which are supported by a network of semi-rigid aluminum hoops. Designed for severe service, tunnels are among the most wind-stable tents. Their small size makes them light and compact. Inside, they are cramped and dog-housy, but they're generally more rain-proof and better ventilated than domes. For high altitude work and where weight is critical, they have few peers.

A-frames are by far your best buy. These tents shed rain and wind effectively, allow construction of water-resistant bathtub floors and protective awnings, are well-ventilated and pest-proof, and are less costly to manufacture than other styles. In its most elementary form (a single I-pole at each end), the A-frame is the lightest, most compact, and strongest of all tents. The design is thousands of years old but it is still a good one.

Umbrella tents are traditional for family camping. And for good reason. They go up easily on any terrain and are almost entirely self-supporting. There's standing room inside and a generous awning out front under which to cook and relax. With full length flies, these tents are rain and windproof.

The umbrella design is not just for family tents. Some very sophisticated backpacking tents—like the Eureka *Equinox* are currently being built on this pattern.

Self-supporting tents: Any tent design can be made self-supporting if it's rigged with a tubular exoskeleton and shock-cord suspension system. Note that self-supporting tents remain "free-standing" only if there is no wind—a fierce storm will send any unanchored tent reeling across the countryside! The real advantage of self-supporting tents is that they require fewer stakes to erect than traditional U-stake 'em models. But these tents do require staking . . . nearly always!

Fabrics

Nylon is the most suitable fabric for lightweight backpacking tents. Cotton tents are too heavy and bulky for most forms of self-propelled travel. Nylon tents need a porous canopy to let body-produced moisture out, and a protective waterproof fly to prevent rain from getting in. Check the fit between fly and canopy: The two must not touch at any point (even when stressed by high wind) or condensation and dripping will result.

Poles and Stakes

Poles should be *aluminum*, no ands or ifs! There is no such thing as a good fiberglass or plastic composite pole! *Wands* (not supporting members) which are used to hold out awnings and vents are an exception, though even here, aluminum is better. It follows that large diameter aluminum poles of equivalent alloy are less apt to break than smaller poles. I prefer ¾-inch diameter, tempered poles if I can get them. Thin, arrow-shaft poles are fine, if there are enough of them. All poles should be shock-corded for easy assembly.

Tips:

• Tent poles are less apt to jam together if you polish the joints (a one time effort) with 400 grit *wet* sandpaper then wipe them with a cloth sprayed with liquid silicone.

• Remedy for stuck pole sections: Heat the joint lightly in the flame of your trail stove. The joint will expand and the poles will part easily.

• Aluminum poles will slide more easily through tight pole sleeves in nylon tents if, before your trip, you "squirt" talcum powder down the sleeves and lubricate the poles with liquid silicone. One application of silicone and talc lasts several weeks, even in rain. Gun shops sell special dry powdered lubricants which are used for resizing hand-loaded brass cartridge cases. These "cartridge case lubricants" work better than talcum powder, but they're much more expensive.

Tent stakes: Twelve-inch-long arrow-shaft aluminum stakes or "staples" (U-shaped stakes) hold best in sand; sharp aluminum skewers are good for compacted soil; narrow steel wire stakes are ideal for rocky ground, and so it goes. Ten-inch-long aluminum skewers may be the best all-around tent stake. Carry a *variety* of tent stakes so you'll always have what works best.

Tips:

• Eight-inch-long aluminum concrete nails make acceptable low cost tent stakes. The heavy steel and plastic "U-pound 'em" stakes sold at discount stores are useful only on big, semi-permanent canvas tents.

- Special stakes are unnecessary for camping on snow or sand. Conventional aluminum stakes can be buried, or guy lines wound about wooden sticks, then buried. Tin can lids (with the edges peened in for safety) make good snow stakes. Run the guy lines through holes in the center and bury the lids.

Features

Bug netting may be standard mosquito type or no-see-um-proof. I prefer the former as it is stronger, easier to see through, and allows free flow of air. Tightly woven no-see-um-proof netting can be stifling on hot nights. When the tiny gnats begin their act, simply spray your mosquito net with bug dope, or close the fabric door panel.

A well designed tent has the door panel *inside* the bug net so you can open the door to peek out without unzipping the screen!

Some tents have "niceties" like lantern loops and inside pockets for the storage of small items. These features—which require only a few minutes on a sewing machine to make—add considerable cost to a tent without significantly increasing its utility.

How to select a family tent

My family's first camping tent was a 9' × 9' umbrella model with a wet wax finish, a steel telescoping center pole, and two netted windows with flaps that tied shut. It weighed 52 pounds and when rolled, barely fit into the trunk of the car. In hot weather, it smelled like kerosene and paraffin, and in rain, it leaked profusely. But it was inexpensive and it enabled us to see a lot of country on not a lot of money.

Family tents, like the times, have changed. They've gotten more expensive, of course, but they're also lighter, stronger, roomier, and more weatherpoof than those of the sixties. And they're easier to pitch too. Guy lines are passé, as are obtrusive center poles and odors. Ties have been replaced by nylon zippers and Velcro, and shock-corded aluminum poles have succeeded steel ones. Even the largest family tents can be erected in less than fifteen minutes.

Your needs: For comfort, you need at least 21 square feet of floor space per person, more than that if you use cots. Tents with rectangular floors use space more efficiently than those with square or circular floors, which means more room between sleepers.

Weight: Three to four pounds per person is the rule for lightweight backpacking tents; five to six pounds for canoeing and high altitude expedition tents, and up to ten pounds for drag 'em out of the car family shelters. Many of the best tents weigh much less than this.

Height: Waiting out a rain in a tent you can't stand in is no fun. However, low profile tents with sloping sides spill wind better than high-sided umbrella and wall tents, so you may have to make some sacrifices if you camp where there are big winds.

Fabrics: Though nylon is the most popular and best fabric for the construction of small tents, lightweight cotton is still a good choice for family tents where weight is less of a concern. It's impractical to use double-walled (waterproof fly/porous canopy) construction in large tents, so one layer of waterproof nylon is usually used throughout—a design that encourages condensation inside. Big windows, and a porous cotton or nylon roof, help dispel some moisture, but not enough to prevent these tents from occasionally turning into saunas.

Nonetheless, if you confine your trips to areas where high humidity and rain are infrequent, then you may like an all-nylon tent. In any case, be sure the tent has at least two rain-protected windows. The best nylon family tents have four-way ventilation—three windows and a door.

Speed of pitching: A tent that requires ten minutes to pitch in dry, windless weather may require twice that long to erect in a rain storm. It's faster to assemble poles than to drive stakes and tie guy lines, so choose a tent that is supported mainly by poles.

Modesty curtains: Family tents are commonly used in areas where there are other campers, so they should be designed to provide privacy without sacrificing ventilation. Some tents have a "modesty curtain"—a short fabric panel that attaches behind the door—in addition to the regular entry flap. On hot days you can leave the door open for ventilation and close the modesty curtain for privacy.

Clothing loops: Convenience dictates plenty of D-rings, loops, or brass hooks at the ridge to hang wet towels, clothing, and your battery-powered lantern. **Warning:**

mantel lanterns put out enough heat to burn through the roof of flame-retardant tents. And they consume lots of precious oxygen as they produce poisonous carbon monoxide. For this reason, you should hang only *flameless* lanterns inside your tent. Heaters, except catalytic ones, are also unsafe in tents.

Winter tents

Most travelers use their three-season nylon tent for snow camping, which works well enough if they rig a *frost liner* inside. A piece of cotton sheeting, hung from the roof by ties or Velcro, absorbs exhaled moisture that might condense and freeze on the sleeping bags below.

A more gracious style of winter camping, which was popular a century ago, is again finding favor among those who spend long periods of time in the wilds. A 7' × 9' or larger canvas tent is rigged to accept a small sheet metal stove and pipe. A generously sized canvas fly defies blowing rain, increases interior temperatures, and protects the roof from sparks. The tent *must* be canvas. Hot sparks will melt nylon instantly and cause serious burns! Most winter campers use wall tents or vintage Eureka Drawtights. Authentic period canvas tents—some of which are wonderful for this sort of thing—are available from *Empire Canvas Works, P.O. Box 17, Solon Springs, WI 54873 (715-378-4216); TENTSMITHS, Box 496, North Conway, NH 03860, (603) 447-2344. Duluth Tent & Awning Co., 1610 W. Superior Street, Duluth, MN 55816-0024, (800) 777-4439,* also manufactures some wonderful canvas tents. Most notable is the "Campfire" tent recommended by artist/author/canoeist Bill Mason in his book, *Song of The Paddle.*

In summary, the best tents are largely self-supporting and have full-length flies and bathtub floors that wrap well up the side-wall. Protective awnings over doors and windows are a must, as are heat-treated aluminum poles and one or more vestibules.

Care and cleaning of tents

Canvas tents: Sweep 'em out, hose 'em down with water and let 'em sun dry until they are bone dry. Don't use soaps or detergents to clean cotton tents as these products will remove the waterproof compounds.

Tip: You can restore the water-repellency to small sections of cotton tents by rubbing a bar of paraffin across the fibers. Heat from the sun will melt the paraffin and the cotton fibers will absorb it.

Nylon tents should be thoroughly washed at the end of each camping season. Soak the tent for thirty minutes or so in a tub of lukewarm water and mild detergent. Tent manufacturers wisely suggest that you avoid use of detergents and chemical solvents as these products may dissolve waterproof coatings. However, sparing use of these products remove abrasive dirt, which is your tent's greatest enemy. Sponge troublesome spots with detergent. Tree sap may be removed with a *very small* amount of gasoline or alcohol. Don't overdo it though; gasoline is very hard on waterproof coatings.

Never roll and store a wet tent. Even rot-resistant nylon tents are sewn with cotton/Dacron™ thread which can mildew. As mentioned, damp polyurethane coatings provide food for microorganisms. Generally, it's better to "stuff" a nylon tent than to fold and roll it. Folding produces harsh creases which can damage waterproof coatings.

Caution: Tents like the Eureka! Timberline, with exposed metal hooks and pins which can puncture fabric when the tent is packed, should *always* be rolled, never stuffed!

Sustained exposure to ultraviolet light saps strength from nylon fabrics. A nylon tent may lose half or more of its strength in a single season if it's continually exposed to sunlight. Do sun-dry and air your tent regularly, but don't overdo it!

Nylon tent lines harden and lose strength. They should be replaced occasionally. Tent cords should be brightly colored for high visibility in failing light. I prefer bright yellow or hot pink!

Store tents in a porous cotton or nylon sack. Be sure the bag is large enough. A dry, properly rolled tent that "fills its sack" when dry, won't fit when it's soaked with rain! Never store a tent on a concrete floor or in a damp basement.

Waterproof the seams of a new tent. I prefer to use Thompson's Water Seal rather than glues which crack, peel, and absorb dirt. Apply TWS sparingly with a foam varnish brush. One application per seam side waterproofs seams forever. This product is also wonderful for waterproofing maps, journals, and hats.

A whisk broom and small sponge will keep your tent clean and neat.

Tips:

- Attach a tiny brass hook to the lanyard of your flashlight so you can clip it to a ridge loop or line inside your tent.
- Sew a D-ring or nylon loop inside your tent at each end of the ridge. A length of parachute cord strung between the D-rings makes a handy clothesline for light items like damp socks. Some campers sew up a miniature hammock of mosquito netting and suspend the hammock from the tent ridge. This "gear loft" will hold all manner of small items.
- It's worthwhile to repeat that a small candle lantern will raise interior tent temperatures by ten degrees or more and eliminate much dampness.

Storm-proofing your tent

A sewing machine and sixty minutes are all you need to turn your tent into a bomb-proof shelter!

You pitch your tent—a four person Eureka! Timberline—on a gentle knoll near a clump of youthful birch trees. There's a better spot 20 feet away—a well worn area where hundreds of tents have stood before. But there's a slight depression here; a good rain could flood you out. And nearby is a long dead spruce, its limbs poised menacingly overhead, waiting patiently for a high wind to send it crashing down.

Slowly it begins with the *tap, tap* of intermittent rain. Then it intensifies into unrelenting drizzle. For awhile, you stand complacently in the gentle shower and curiously watch the blackening clouds approach. Then you suddenly awaken to the realization that you have only a few minutes to get things under control before the storm unleashes its fury.

First, you string two parachute cord guy lines from each peak to stakes below (Figure T-13). Next, you weight the corner stakes with rocks then turn your attention to the right side-wall which is being crushed by the building wind. It would be nice if you could turn the tent into the storm, but the site won't cooperate. Besides, it's too late now; you'll

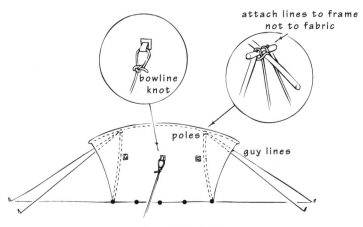

attach lines to frame
not to fabric

bowline
knot

poles

guy lines

FIGURE T-13.

have to make do by shoring up the windward side-wall and poles. You're glad now that you sewed storm-line pull-outs to the fly before you left home. As the wall firms under these tight guy lines, you wonder why they aren't standard equipment on every tent.

Satisfied now that everything's secure, you retire to the tent, confident you'll stay dry no matter how hard it rains.

Philosophy

Admittedly, staying dry in a deluge requires luck as well as skill. What would you have done if there had been no well-drained spot? Or if rocks or uncooperative ground kept you from placing your tent where you wanted? And don't forget that clump of birch you used for a windscreen.

Nonetheless, even a bad campsite can be made habitable if you correct the shortcomings of your tent and follow these rules.

1. *The right spot:* The following section, *Tent-Site: How To Cope With A Bad One,* reviews some things you can do to make a bad site habitable.

2. *Use a ground cloth inside your tent!* Even well-sealed seams will admit water in prolonged rain. And no tent floor will remain watertight forever. The solution is to always use a 4–6-mil-thick plas-

tic ground cloth inside your tent. Make the ground cloth large enough so it "flows" a few inches up the tent walls. If your tent springs a leak, water will be trapped under the ground sheet and you'll stay dry. *Do not* place the ground cloth outside the tent floor (exception—in winter to prevent the floor from freezing to the ground). Surface water may become trapped between the ground sheet and floor and be pressure wicked (from body weight) through the floor seams. You'll really have a sponge party if this happens!

Contrary to the claims of tent-makers, you don't need a ground cloth under your tent floor to protect it from abrasion. Holes in tent floors usually develop from the inside. If you don't believe this, begin a trip with a new plastic ground sheet inside your tent, then count the holes it accumulates with each day of use. Old beliefs die hard!

3. *Reinforce seams:* If a seam looks weak, it probably is. Reinforce stress points with heavy carpet thread and nylon webbing.

4. *Add extra stakes:* A-frame tents should have at least three stakes along each side to ensure adequate security in high winds. If the hem of your tent looks like it needs additional stake lines, add them!

5. *Double-stake or anchor guy lines in soft ground.* Two stakes per loop—each through a separate hole, and at a different angle—doubles the surface area and holding power in soft ground. In sand, use a "rock anchor" like the one illustrated in Figure T-14. *Tip:* Tie 3-foot lengths of parachute cord to each stake loop *before* your camping trip and you won't have to mess with cutting and tying these anchor lines in a rain storm.

6. Attach loops of shock-cord or bands cut from inner tubes to all stake points and guy lines (Figure T-15). Shock-cords take up the wind stress normally reserved for seams and fittings. Even a badly sewn, poorly reinforced tent can be used in severe weather if it's rigged with shock-cords.

7. Shock-cord your tent poles. Shock-cording kits are

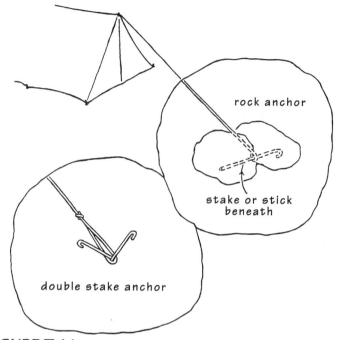

FIGURE T-14. Soft ground tent anchors

available at most camp shops. Color-code non-shock-corded pole sections and wands for easy assembly. It's frustrating to look for a "center ridge section" or "spreader bar" in failing light. Colored plastic tape sticks to poles better than paint.

Old tents reveal new secrets!

The best turn-of-the-century A-frame tents were better foul weather shelters than modern campers like to admit. Studying one reveals some interesting things about where to place seams, guy lines and stake points. Let's check out one of these canvas antiques:.

- There's a single vertical pole at each end. The poles are located at the apex of the triangular door and back wall. In essence, they form the "altitude" of each triangle.
- The tent has no floor, so there are no perimeter seams at ground level. A removable rubberized ground-sheet,

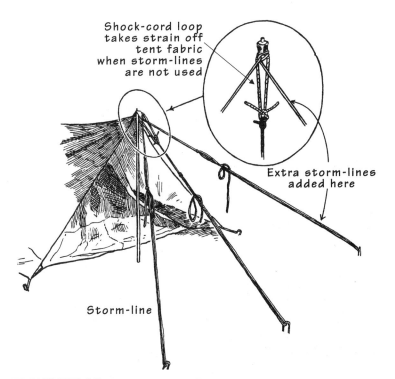

Shock-cord loop takes strain off tent fabric when storm-lines are not used

Extra storm-lines added here

Storm-line

FIGURE T-15. Stormproofing the tent

placed inside, protects occupants from flowing ground water and dampness.

• Including the corners, there are *five* stake points per side hem. A center stake halves the length of the sidewall material; the others split the distance between adjacent stakes. There's that "apex-of-the-triangle" relationship again.

• Guy lines at each end originate on the poles, or at heavily reinforced fabric very near the poles. The exoskeleton—not the fabric—absorbs most of the wind stress.

Rigging storm lines is largely a game of triangles. Locate an apex, put in a stake or guy line. This keeps fabric tight by equalizing strain. As any elk hunter will attest, a modern canvas wall tent will withstand quite a blow. That these tents perform much better than their simple geometry suggests is no mystery to those who use them.

Tuning the Eureka! Timberline and Similar Free-standing Tents

Let's use what we've learned to undress America's most popular tent, the Eureka! Timberline.

First, the "hem" test. Does the fly cover all exposed perimeter seams? You bet! At least along the side-walls. The Timberline has a full bathtub floor so fly coverage below the elevated bathtub seams isn't necessary, right? Wrong! Fabrics wear, and the floor side-wall are no exception. An extra waterproof layer here is always a plus. Seam coverage on the Timberline is adequate for vertical rain but not for wind-driven weather.

Rule: If your tent has exposed stitching, or a fly that can be blown aside by high winds, you may want to extend the fly by sewing on matching material. Make cuts above stake and guy line loops so you won't have to re-attach them to the new fabric. Matching (or contrasting) material can be obtained from the tent manufacturer and many outdoor stores (see section on *Yard Goods,* page 217). *"Thrifty Outfitters,"* a division of MIdwest Mountaineering in Minneapolis, is a complete source of tent fabrics, clothing and equipment repair materials. You may contact them at *(800) 866–3162; fax (651) 339–7249.*

Move to the corners where the toggle pins plug into the pole ends and note that some corner stitching is exposed to the weather. You'll have to rely on glue (seam-sealant) here—a bad idea. Or you can solve the problem instantly by attaching a vestibule to one or both ends of the tent.

Check out the hems along the side-wall. There are just two equidistant stake points, neither of which splits the distance between tent corners. The result is that a strong side wind can compress the center side-wall hem into the porous canopy. Correcting the problem is easy; just sew a third stake loop to the hem center at point "a" (see Figure T-13). Note how this one center stake firms the side-wall.

The Timberline is a comfortable, relatively high tent, with lots of side-wall exposed to the wind. Stiffen each wall by sewing a nylon storm loop to the center of the fly at point "b" of Figure T-13. Be sure to back with heavy fabric whatever you sew.

The aluminum A-frame is your final concern. Standard issue Timberline poles simply aren't designed for winds above 30 miles an hour. (The expedition poles are much sturdier.) Is there a way to stiffen the framework without adding weight or bulk?

You bet! Sew a nylon guy loop to the fly face at the midpoint of each pole which makes up the A-frame. Back the loop on the inside fly with a length of mating Velcro. When the weather gets nasty, secure the Velcro tabs to the poles and guy the outside loops. Since the Velcro tabs secure directly to the poles, there is no stress on the fly fabric—and no danger of tearing it.

Rule: Whenever possible, guy off the framework rather than the tent fabric!

Now, apply this philosophy to each end of the tent. The Timberline is effectively "freestanding;"; there are no forward and aft guy lines to provide stability in oncoming winds. To account for this, the manufacturer has provided a D-ring on the ridge at each end. You can attach guy lines directly to these, right?

Wrong! Re-read the rule above and you'll see why. The first good blast of air will tear the D-rings right off the tent. There's a better way.

1. Sew a Velcro tab to the underside of the fly, opposite the D-ring. Secure the tab to the plastic pole junction tube, *then* guy off the D-ring.
2. Or disregard the D-ring and secure your guy line(s) directly to the horizontal junction tubes. If possible, attach guy and stake lines to an immovable object like a tree or rock.

Waterproof Tent Seams

Earlier, I suggested that you waterproof tent seams with Thompson's Water Seal, or other commercial compound. Sealing seams helps, but frankly, it's mostly window dressing. If your tent fly covers every seam and zipper, you can eliminate this step. That's because rain which gets through stitching on the fly will, due to surface tension, slither harmlessly to the ground. There is no particular advantage in sealing floor seams if you use a ground cloth inside your tent.

Let's review the rules for storm-proofing tents:
• Perimeter floor seams (there should be none!) must be

fully covered by the tent fly. Check the tent corners. If there's a problem here, adding a vestibule may solve it. If not, sew on an extension of some sort.

• There should be enough stake points (you can never have too many) along the fly hem to prevent wind-whipped rain from getting under the fly and onto seams. If your tent needs more stake points, add them.

• High-walled tents can be stabilized by attaching a guy line to the center face of the fly. Back your sewing with extra material. Don't run a canopy "pull-out" cord from the inner fly face to the canopy to increase space inside the tent (Figure T-16). Rain will wick through the stitching on the fly face and slither down the side-pull into the sleeping compartment. If your tent already has a canopy side-pull, disconnect it the moment rain begins. If this is impractical, tie a cotton shoelace or handkerchief to the cord somewhere between the fly and canopy. Now, any water that wicks through will follow the hanky to the ground (at least for a while!) rather than into your tent.

• Whenever possible, guy directly off the framework of a tent. If you must attach lines to fabric, back what you sew with heavy material.

Now, stand back and take a long, proud look at your accomplishments. You have a tent that will keep you dry in any rain. Cost of materials? Under $10.00. Time involved? About three hours.

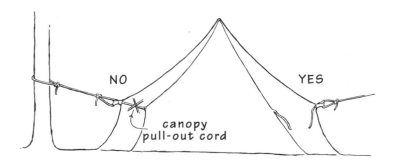

FIGURE T-16.

Tent-Site: How to Cope with a Bad One!

The camping literature is rich with advice on how to choose a good campsite. Requirements generally include high flat ground with good drainage, a south-facing slope (so you can enjoy the morning sun), and an open vista so a welcome breeze will blow away bothersome insects. In reality, a rank novice can tell a good tent spot when he or she sees one. Everyone knows enough not to pitch a tent on bumpy ground, on a rock face, or in a depression. However, most camping today is carefully regulated, and some programmed sites are downright awful. In most cases, you'll have to accept the inadequacies of the place and try to make the best of it. Here are some suggestions as to how to do just that:

1. Always use a ground cloth inside your tent. Storm-proof your tent as suggested in the previous section.

2. Know the shortcomings of your tent and correct them. For example, the most weather-vulnerable portion of any tent is the door end, where zippers and seams come together. A vestibule will solve this problem instantly; however, not all tents come so equipped. If the ground slopes, pitch the tent with the weather-vulnerable end downhill, so ground water will run away from the seams rather than on to them.

3. If the site drainage is bad, and there are a number of tents in your party, pitch each tent far enough away from its neighbor so that tent roofs won't funnel water onto nearby tents. Closely spaced tents act as gutters in a heavy rain!

4. Please do not "improve" the lay of the ground by attacking it with a hatchet and Rambo knife. Instead, use foam pads or air mattresses. Level your sleeping system by placing additional clothing beneath your trail bed.

5. There will not always be trees available from which to rig cooking flies. An extra set of collapsible tent poles will provide anchor points for tarps.

6. If, despite all your precautions, a heavy rain threatens to wipe you out, create water diversion

bars by placing logs alongside your tent's perimeter. The logs will function much like the erosion
control bars used for trail maintenance. After the
rain, return logs to the forest so you'll leave no
trace of your presence.
7. An anti-rain dance or thoughtful plea to the Great
Spirit will sometimes cause the brunt of a storm
to bypass a bad tent spot.

Tents: Classics You can Make

In the 1950s, when I was a boy scout, I owned a Spartan 5'
× 7' canvas "wedge" tent (Figure T-17). There were no zippers, bug nets, or windows, and no floor. A rubberized poncho doubled as a ground-cloth, and in buggy weather I wore
a head net. With two wooden poles and ten stakes, the little pup tent weighed exactly seven pounds—a respectable
weight for a hiking tent, even by today's standards.

I used the wedgie in all types of weather—backpacked
all over upper Michigan with it—and can recall only one
time when I was wet and cold. It was my "go light" philosophy and a cold, two-day rain that did me in. I got just what
I deserved when I placed my dry sleeping bag on top of my
wet poncho. From then on, I carried a special ground cloth
for use inside my tent.

In the '60s, I bought my first nylon backpacking tent—
a "three man" Gerry Fireside. More commodious and half
the weight of the wedge, it featured true double-walled
(waterproof fly over porous canopy) construction. The Gerry
had a window in back and an integral floor and bug net.
Man was I living! For more than a decade, the little tent
was a constant companion on canoe camping trips in Minnesota and Canada. It never failed me in any weather.

Though I now own more sophisticated tents, I continue
to use the Gerry for solo canoeing. Admittedly, my other
tents are "geometrically better," but none are lighter, more
compact, and faster to pitch. With its built-in (sewn to the
ridge) rain-fly and shock-corded I-poles, the Fireside goes
up in less than a minute. Few modern tents can do as well.

Admittedly, for high altitude and severe weather use,
state-of-the-art tents outshine the old-timers by a wide

margin. But for general camping in forested areas many turn-of-the-century tents are better. At any rate, the best of the nostalgic designs were lighter, better ventilated, and roomier than most people think.

Many of the old tents—like the "wall," "wedge," "baker," and "forester"—are still in production. Attempts to modernize these designs by substituting nylon for canvas has generally been unsuccessful. That's because "breathable" canvas still is the best material (and certainly the most durable) for large, airy tents. Though I spent considerable time "under canvas" when I was a kid, I now prefer nylon tents by a wide margin. Nonetheless, the traditional tents of the past have much to recommend them. Reproduced here, from the 1912 Abercrombie Camp catalog, are four of the most popular models for your interest and amusement. Study the specifications and you'll discover how light and versatile these shelters were. You may even want to build one yourself. Plans for the simplest models are included for your convenience.

Wedge Tent

Simplest of all designs, the wedge is versatile and cozy. When constructed with a doorway at each end, the structure can be opened to face a fire. Snap or Velcro a mosquito bar to the roof and you have a tent that is similar to the "convertible A-tent" recommended by the legendary outdoorsman, Calvin Rutstrum, in his book, *The New Way of the Wilderness.* The design is so simple you can easily draw your own plans from the specifications.

Note: A twin-door version of this classic tent is manufactured in mildew-resistant army duck by *TENTSMITHS, Box 496, North Conway, NH 03860.*

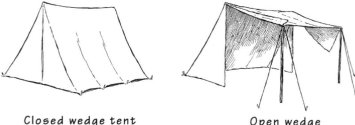

Closed wedge tent   Open wedge

FIGURE T-17.

Foresters' Tent

This ultralight tent was designed around 1910, by *Field & Stream's* editor, Warren Miller. Nothing more than a tapered tarp, the *Forester* goes up fast on any terrain and is very wind-resistant. The 1912 Abercrombie catalog lists a weight of just 2¾ pounds for the 8' × 8' version—this, in cotton canvas. Try finding a two person *nylon* tent that light today!

Build a campfire out front and you'll discover how well the cone-shaped entrance funnels heat to the occupants inside. The *Forester* was a standard offering in Boy Scout catalogs for nearly fifty years. David Abercrombie writes about the material used in this, and other Abercrombie manufactured tents:

> "The cloth is treated by a copper process which makes it waterproof, rot proof and vermin proof, and leaves it perfectly pliable and soft. Even the white ant will not attack it; neither does it burn as readily as unprocessed material and it is not affected by either tropic heat or Arctic cold, changes in temperature making little differences in its feeling.
>
> It is a non-conductor of heat, which makes it a cool summer and a warm winter tent. The color is a great advantage, the green being a shade that is easy for the eyes, and flies and gnats are not so troublesome in a green tent."

> from CAMP OUTFITS
> David T. Abercrombie Company,
> New York, NY, 1912

Baker Tent

Everyone who has camped out for very long eventually comes to know and love the baker tent. Guy out the fly and build a cheery fire beneath; gather the crew and deal the cards. There's room enough for all, even when heavy rain blows up. Add a sod cloth, bug net, side wings, and a privacy screen out front, and you have a snug four-season shelter that's as much at home in Patagonia as at a friendly KOA campground. Baker tents once were the backbone of every nineteenth century hunting camp, and in parts of the American west, they remain so today. Note that *CAMP OUTFITS*

| SIZE (k) | | HEIGHT (k) | | Weight |
Width	Height	Front	Back	Pounds
8 x 8		65	2	275
95 x 95		85	3	45

FIGURE T-18. Foresters' tent, from 1912 Abercrombie catalog

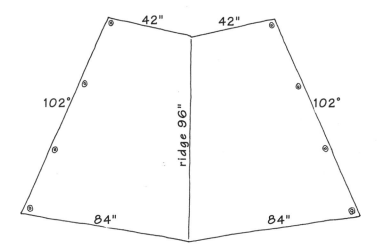

FIGURE T-19. Forester tent pattern

SIZE (k)		HEIGHT (k)	Weight
Width	Height		Pounds
8 x 8		6.5	5
95 x 95		7.5	675
95 x 95		8.5	975

FIGURE T-20. Baker tent, from 1912 Abercrombie catalog

lists the 8' × 6½' model at just nine pounds—lighter even than the popular nylon Eureka! Timberline.

You can buy a modern baker tent from TENTSMITHS, and many western outfitters.

Miners' Tent

When it comes to efficient utilization of space, the miners' tent is hard to beat. Four pegs and a tie at the top (or interior pole) stabilize this tent in winds that would flatten

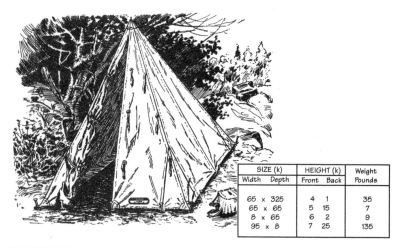

SIZE (k)		HEIGHT (k)		Weight
Width	Depth	Front	Back	Pounds
65 x 325		4	1	35
65 x 65		5	15	7
8 x 65		6	2	9
95 x 8		7	25	135

FIGURE T-21. Miners' tent, from 1912 Abercrombie catalog most conventional designs. Spread the door flaps and feel the heat of your campfire. Button up tight, and listen to the patter of rain while you stay dry inside. The miner is great for winter camping too: Just run the pipe of your sheet-metal stove through a thimble in the roof and watch things heat up fast inside.

Pyramid tents like these were popular in the cowboy days and well into this century. Journals of the early Arctic explorers praised the miner tent for its light weight, wind stability, and ease-of-pitching. Look around and you'll discover that this ancient design is still going strong. If you can draw a triangle, you can build this tent.

Whelen Lean-To

The Whelen Lean-to was designed by the famous outdoorsman, Colonel Townsend Whelen. A retired army officer, Colonel Whelen wrote prolifically about guns, hunting, and camping. Even when it was no longer fashionable, he preferred to base his hunts out of tents rather than RV's or motels. Whelen disliked the popular campfire tents of the day because their sloping back walls reflected campfire heat onto the floor rather than the occupants. And everyone had to sleep with their head or feet towards the fire, which cooked one end and froze the other. "Much smarter to sleep sideways, so all parts get done at once," snipped the Colonel.

FIGURE T-22. Whelen Lean-to

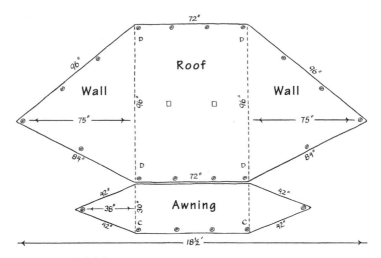

FIGURE T-22A. Whelen Lean-to plan

Whelen added a short vertical wall to the back of a conventional lean-to, then he sewed on a generous awning and side-flaps. Voila! The Whelen Lean-to was born. It's interesting to note that Eureka! offers a facsimile of this still popular 1926 design—in waterproof nylon, of course!

Towels

Cloth dish towels have no place on a wilderness trip. They trap and spread bacteria and absorb soot and dirt. Once soaked, they usually stay that way for days. Try these instead of towels on your next camp-out:

- A synthetic (cloth) chamois will absorb about ten times its weight in water. You'll find this product at kitchen supply and auto shops, and state and county fairs. Outdoor stores sell the highly absorbent PackTowl™, which comes in three sizes. A cloth chamois is my first line of defense against heavy spills. It works nearly as well as a sponge but it dries much faster.
- Absorbent paper toweling: Two sheets of paper toweling

per meal will dry dishes for four, if you first "chamois-dry" your cookware.

- The Boy Scouts consider toilet tissue so useful they call it "AP" (all purpose) paper. Use it to blow your nose, nurse a cut, clean a stove, etc. Uses are endless. *Tip:* To save weight and bulk, remove the cardboard tube and place the roll inside a Zip-loc bag. Pull the paper from the *center* of the roll (tube removed) and you'll have a steady stream of tissue that you won't have to unroll.

- A cotton bandanna, lightweight cotton dish towel, or cloth baby diaper is the only wash towel you need on a wilderness camping trip.

Ultraviolet Protection

If you want make your plastic canoe, polyethylene dry box, rubber moldings and dash board of your vehicle, carpeted car-top carriers and other sun-sensitive materials last almost forever, treat them regularly with *303 Protectant*. Many vinyl makers and vinyl accessory companies recommend 303 by name. Bell Canoeworks, in Zimmerman, Minnesota, says that 303 is the best UV protectant you can buy for use on their exquisite Kevlar/carbon-fiber composite canoes.

A 303 customer treated one panel of a nylon life vest with 303 Protectant and placed it on an aluminum roof in Portland, Oregon. He checked the vest four years later and discovered that the 303 treated panel looked fine, while the rest of the vest had completely disintegrated!

303 Protectant contains no petrochemicals, silicone oils or petroleum distillates. It's not greasy or oily and it repels dust, dirt and stains. I store my canoe trailer outside all year round and regularly use 303 to preserve the tires. It works!

W

Wanigans

Background: Wanigans are rigid boxes which are commonly used in the fur trade to carry hard goods like knives, guns and axes that would be uncomfortable in a standard soft pack. Modern campers can use wanigans for the same purpose. For auto camping, nothing beats a well organized "camp kitchen," which has compartments for tin cans, utensils and soft goods. Most commercial models have a plywood lid that doubles as both work area and cutting board. You can get detailed plans for making a camp kitchen from many scout and "Y" camps.

Smaller hard packs are handy for canoe camping, picnicking, berry picking, and anywhere you need a strong, rigid container. The traditional hard pack for canoeing is the Maine pack basket, which is available by mail from *L.L. Bean, Inc., (800) 221–4221,* and *Duluth Tent and Awning Co., (800) 777–4439.* If you place a woven ash basket into a waterproof sack (the army surplus waterproof clothes bag is just the right size), then set this unit into a tailored backpack, you'll have a strong, watertight container that's comfortable to carry.

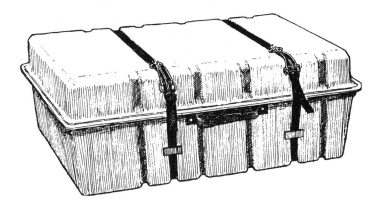

FIGURE W-1. The Stormy Bay Wanigan box

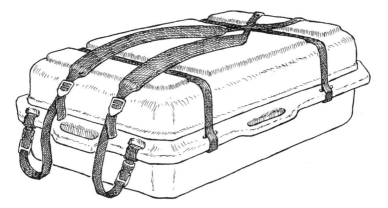

FIGURE W-2. The York Pack

Tip: Make a number of narrow fabric pockets and attach these to the inside rim of your packbasket. Store sunglasses, fillet knife, and other small items in these handy organizers.

A less expensive solution is to nest a cheap rectangular plastic trash container inside a soft pack. This outfit will protect all your breakables.

A medium sized plastic ice chest (cooler) can also be pressed into service as a wanigan. It will be easier to carry if you strap it to a tubular aluminum pack frame.

You'll find aluminum and plastic wanigans at some camping stores. Two that I can heartily recommend are the *Stormy Bay Wanigan* (formerly E.M. Wanigan) and the indestructible polyethylene *York Pack,* which comes in two sizes. Both wanigans have comfortable padded shoulder straps (an extra-cost option on the York pack) and attachment points for a hip belt and tumpline.

Addresses: Stormy Bay Enterprises, P.O. Box 345, Grand Rapids, MN 55744. Joel York & Associates, 15 West Main Street., Yarmouth, ME 04096, (800) 348–4923.

Water Treatment

There are few places in North America where you can safely drink water from a lake or stream. And conditions don't

seem to be improving. Water quality—and just plain avail-
ability of water—remains a major environmental concern.
Unless you always camp where the quality of drinking
water is guaranteed, you should carry your water or treat it
by one of these methods.

Field methods of water treatment

1. *Boiling* is the most reliable way to kill almost
everything. Even Cryptosporidium, which can
survive exposure to iodine, chlorine and bleach, is
killed by boiling. If you are uncertain about the
quality of your drinking water, boiling is the best
way to make it safe. Simply bring your water to a
rolling boil then shut off your stove. There's no
need to adjust boiling times for altitude.

2. *Filtration:* Mechanical filters have improved
steadily since the first edition of *Camping Secrets.*
There are a lot more options than a decade ago. If
you opt for mechanical filtration, choose a large
capacity unit whose pores will remove the smallest infectious agents you are likely to encounter.
By comparison, a filter with a four micron "absolute" pore size will stop *Giardia;* A one micron
filter will halt *Cryptosporidium.* "Absolute" pore
size means that no hole in the filter is smaller
than the diameter indicated. Generally, large
pores mean fast delivery while small pores slow
the flow. The industry standard for removing bacteria has been 0.45 microns (absolute) but new research is pushing for a 0.2 micron size. Science
aside, a 0.4 micron filter is a pretty safe bet in
most wilderness areas. Be sure you can easily replace or clean the filter. Naturally, it's wise to
carry a spare.
    My favorite field units are the high speed PUR
Explorer, which filters one liter of water per
minute and cleans in seconds with a twist of the
pump handle, and the PUR Hiker which pumps
more slowly but is lighter, smaller, and much less
expensive. I also like the archaic Katadyn Pocket
Filter which is beautifully machined from aluminum. The Katadyn is terribly slow and fright-

fully expensive but it is very easy to maintain and so reliable that you don't need to carry a second filter. And its ceramic filter leaves no bitter aftertaste. **Note:** Some filters "purify" the water as well as filter it. For example, the PUR and SweetWater Guardian models contain iodine which *kills* microorganisms on contact—any harmful microbe that sneaks through the pores is killed by the iodine. The drawback is that the iodine imparts a slight aftertaste which some people find objectionable. An optional carbon cartridge removes most—if not all—of the bad taste.

3. *Chemical treatment:* Halazone tablets are an old standby, available in corner drugstores for years. If you use Halazone, take an unopened bottle on each trip. The product loses considerable strength when exposed to air and heat. Halazone tablets release chlorine, which is carcinogenic.

   Chlorine: Liquid chlorine bleach with 4–6 percent available chlorine may be used to purify water. Use two drops of bleach per quart of clear water and four drops per quart of cold or cloudy water. Let treated water stand for thirty minutes before using. You should be able to smell the chlorine gas. If not, repeat the dosage and let it stand another fifteen minutes before using. If the water is very cold or cloudy, let it stand overnight before using.

   Note: None of the chemicals work very well in cold, cloudy water. Under these conditions, your best bet is to boil your water!

   Tip: You can sterilize your camp dishes by simply adding a splash of chlorine bleach to the final rinse water. Or, add a convenient Effersan® tablet. Effersan tablets have thirty percent available chlorine in a handy, dry form. Address: *Effercept Products, Division of Micrel Ltd., Inc., P.O. Box 1248, Laramie, WY 82070, (800) 841-0410.*

   Iodine: Place 6 grams of iodine (your pharmacist will weigh it out for you) in a 1-ounce amber bottle. Fill the bottle with water. The iodine crystals will dissolve until a saturated solution results, then no more crystals will dissolve.

Sterilize a quarter canteen of water by pouring about half (the amount isn't critical) the iodine solution into the canteen. Let the canteen stand at least thirty minutes before drinking. Allow additional time for cold or cloudy water.

Recharge the iodine bottle with fresh water after each use. Only a small amount of iodine will dissolve from the crystals each time, so you may continue to use the "iodine decant bottle" dozens of times until no more crystals are visible.

Caution: Do not allow any iodine crystals to enter your canteen. Large doses of iodine can be fatal! (Iodine is a rather heavy metal and is quite visible in solution, so you'll have no trouble seeing the crystals or containing them in your bottle.)

You may also treat your water with a commercial tablet that releases iodine. Potable Aqua (sold nearly everywhere) is highly recommended.

A 2 percent tincture of iodine solution may also be used to purify water. Use six to eight drops of iodine per quart of drinking water. Let the chemical work for at least thirty minutes before you drink the water. Double the dosage and working time if the water is cold or cloudy.

Note: Products which release chlorine will not destroy Giardia cysts under all conditions, and they won't destroy Cryptosporidium cysts under any conditions! If you suspect contamination by these parasites, boil your water or use a water filter with an absolute pore size of one to two microns or less. Authorities generally agree that compounds which release iodine are more reliable than those which emit chlorine.

Where not to get your drinking water

1. Go well away from the shoreline to get drinking water. If you're camping at a spot frequented by man or animals, go upstream of the source to get water. On lakes, go a minimum of 150 feet from shore, and the farther (and deeper) the better.

   Tip: Place a rock in your largest cooking pot

and lower it deep into the lake with a long rope. Work the bucket up and down like a yo-yo to guarantee good exchange of water. Water taken 20 feet or more below the lake surface is apt to be most trustworthy.

2. Avoid water which has a greenish color. The green tinge indicates the presence of algae, which attracts microorganisms. Tan-colored water, however, is usually safe. Invariably, this color suggests natural run-off of tannic acid from adjacent conifer stands (quite common throughout the upper midwest).

3. Take your drinking water from fast moving areas; avoid backwaters, stagnant areas, and eddies which are breeding places for microorganisms.

4. Never drink any water which has been contaminated by wastes from a paper mill. Instead, secure your water from incoming streams or springs.

5. Don't take water near beaver dams or lodges. Beaver are the favored hosts of Giardia lamblia, a small protozoan that may cause severe discomfort. Giardia enters a water supply through the feces of the host. Its cyst can survive up to two months in 46 degree Fahrenheit water, and up to one month in 70 degree water!

   The infection carried by the organism is called "giardiasis," characterized by severe diarrhea, cramps, nausea and vomiting. Incubation time is one to two weeks, though some people have gone as long as two months without getting sick. If untreated, the disease may go on for years!

   Giardiasis is usually diagnosed by stool examination, which is not always reliable. Most physicians just haven't had enough experience with the disease to correctly diagnose it. As a result, many victims suffer for months before they get the help they need. Not everyone who is exposed to the Giardia parasite comes down with the disease. Indeed, most people are simply carriers.

6. Contrary to popular belief, clear water tumbling over sunny rocks *may not* be safe to drink. While ultraviolet light does kill microorganisms, flowing

water mixes them and increases the chance they'll get in your drinking water. Better to take your drinking water from the deep sun-lit pool nearby.

Treatment for Giardiasis and Cryptosporodiosis: Metronidazole (Flagyl) and furazolidone (Furoxone) are the recommended prescription drugs for treating Giardiasis. It's a good idea to carry a supply on long trips. There is no treatment for Cryptosporodiosis, whose symptoms are similar to Giardiasis. Cryptosporodiosis usually runs its course in one to two weeks.

Weather Forecasting

Background: Every outdoors person should have a basic understanding of weather phenomena and be able to make reasonably accurate short term weather predictions. Some campers take forecasting quite seriously; they arm themselves with min/max thermometers, barometers, cloud charts, and weather tables. Whether or not this paraphernalia will improve your short range forecasts is debatable. After all, primitive man is right on target more than 80 of the time, simply by looking at the sky, sensing the wind, and "feeling" the weather. You can approximate this enviable success rate by applying these time-proven principles:

1. "Red sky at night, sailor's delight; red sky in the morning, sailor take warning." Translation: A red morning sky indicates possible rain that day; a red evening sky suggests the next day will be clear. The color difference relates to the reflective value of the low lying cloud cover.
2. Check the grass, tent, canoe bottom, or whatever, for the presence of dew in late evening or early morning. A heavy dew at either of these times usually suggests eight to twelve hours of good weather.
3. Watch the smoke from your campfire. If it hangs low (a function of low pressure) to the ground, rain is on the way. If it rises high into a nice ver-

tical column (high pressure), count on good weather.

4. Check out the air bubbles in your coffee cup. They'll ring the edges of the cup when a low pressure (rain) system sets in.

5. You can sometimes smell a coming storm, as the low pressure allows methane (swamp gas) to rise and drift with the current. In boggy areas, the odor is quite pronounced.

6. "When the peacock loudly bawls, they'll be both rain and squalls." Translation: Birds sing loudly just before a storm.

7. Geese and seagulls won't usually fly just before a storm. Low pressure air is thin and it's hard for them to get airborne.

8. The ears of many animals are sensitive to low pressure. Wolves will howl before a storm. Dogs will become nervous and emit howls or howl-like sounds.

9. To determine the distance of a lightning strike, count the seconds between the flash and the thunder boom. Divide by five and you'll have your answer in miles.

10. Noises all become louder and more vibrant just before a rain, because the sound is reflected and magnified by the low clouds. The croaking of frogs, yodel of loons, etc., will echo loudly if rain is imminent.

11. Be alert for changes in wind direction. Storms are whirlpools of wind that rotate counterclockwise in the northern hemisphere (remember high school science?). The adage, "Wind from the south, brings rain in its mouth," is the keystone here, as the wind which proceeds a storm usually blows from the south. Counterclockwise wind shifts therefore usually bring rain, while clockwise movements indicate fair weather. You can keep these directional changes straight by remembering the rhymes . . .

"Wind from the east brings weather that's a beast." (Suggests a counterclockwise wind shift from south to east, east to north, etc.)

"Wind from the west brings weather that's best." (Suggests a clockwise wind shift from south to west, north to east, etc.)

12. Most everyone knows that frogs emerge from the water just before a storm and croak their fool heads off. Frogs breathe partly through their skin (which must be kept moist), so when the humidity rises just before a storm, they climb ashore and sing happily.

13. If you're a canoeist you know that about eight to twelve hours before a storm, mosquitoes and black flies begin to swarm and bite more than usual. Up to two hours before the storm they quit biting altogether.

14. Check out the rainbow: A heavy red may mean more rain; vibrant rich blue suggests clear skies ahead.

15. Here's an old "down east" proverb: "Filly tails make lofty ships wear low sails." Translation: Thin, hair-like clouds forecast rain within the day. These "filly tails" are really streaks of ice thrown skyward by the rising air of a coming storm.

16. "A mackerel sky (tiny scale-like clouds that resemble a mackerel's back), just twenty-four hours dry." Translation: Expect rain within the next day!

17. Any fireflies around? When rain approaches, these little insects light up the woods, according to the rhyme: "When the little glow bug lights his lamp, the air around is surely damp."

18. Listen for the rustle of leaves as the wind precedes the storm.

19. If you can't see the sharp points on a half moon, rain may be on its way. Translation: Low clouds and haze distort sharp images.

20. Bright, twinkling stars usually indicate high altitude winds which may be bringing in a storm.

21. There's a good chance that foul weather (rain or snow) will fall within three days of a new moon phase.

22. "The weather out west had best be best, for tomorrow will bring it to you to test!" This means

that in all likelihood, the weather system to your west will be at your location tomorrow.

23. In summer, a "sun-dog" or halo around the sun, generally predicts the coming of rain. Sun-dogs are caused by sunlight streaming through the ice particles of high cirrostratus clouds. A halo around the moon may also indicate rain.

24. "Evening fog will not burn soon, but morning fog will burn before high noon." Invariably, a fog-borne day will become perfectly clear (an ideal day) by noon. Fog forms when water vapor reaches the dew point and condenses on dust particles near the ground. When the day heats up the fog evaporates and turns to invisible water vapor.

25. "Short notice, soon it will pass. Long notice, expect it to last." Watch the clouds. If they take several days to build, a warm front—and prolonged rain—is usually in the offing. If the storm system builds suddenly, it will probably pass quickly.

26. And, of course, everyone knows: "Rain before seven, dry by eleven."

Yard Goods And Repair Materials

Tools you need to make repairs

Sewing machine: From time to time you'll have to mend tears in tents, sleeping bags, tarps and clothing. Of course, you can send things out for repair, but it's less expensive—and frankly, more fun—to do it yourself. By and large, you'll be sewing lightweight fabrics, so any light duty sewing machine will do. Many years ago, I purchased a coal black, 1958 model Singer. It sews forward and back, that's all. I've used the old Singer to patch countless packs and tarps and to build more than twenty nylon splash covers for canoes. I

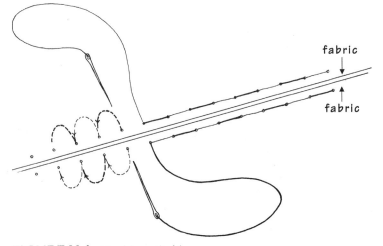

FIGURE Y-1. Machine stitching

paid $75.00 for the Singer, complete with maple cabinet. Good buys on old machines are still available.

Sail-maker's needles and waxed thread: Sail-maker's needles are available from Tandy Leather Company and others who sell leather supply products. Half a dozen heavy duty needles and a bobbin of waxed thread should last for years. Use *two* needles when you sew. Figure Y-1 shows how to make a strong machine-like stitch that will never let go. *Tip:* This "double-needle machine stitch" is the one to use when sewing a knife or axe sheath. At home, use an electric drill to make the needle holes in thick leather. In the field, a thin awl will do.

Sewing awl: The awls which come on Swiss Army knives and multipurpose tools are too coarse for fine work. Get a small, sharp awl at your local fabrics store.

Speedy Stitcher/Repair sewing Awl: The "Speedy Stitcher" has been around for decades. It has a self-contained bobbin and a strong, replaceable needle. A heavy wooden handle allows you bore through thick material. In all, the Speedy Stitcher is a solid and practical little machine, though it's a bit cumbersome for go-light trips. Two sail-maker's needles and a sharp awl are slower to use, but produce results as good as the "Speeder Stitcher."

Don't forget to include in your repair kit: Swatches of

material to match your equipment, buckles, 1-inch wide nylon webbing, two-piece, solid brass snaps (a Tandy Leather Co. item), instant epoxy, nylon filament tape, gray duct tape, tweezers, long nose pliers, scissors, safety pins. *Where to get repair materials:* Two good mail order sources of fabrics, hardware and repair materials are: *CAMPMOR, Inc., P.O. Box 999, Paramus, NJ 07653-0999, (800) 226–7667,* and *Thrifty Outfitters Inc., 309 Cedar Avenue South, Minneapolis, MN 55454, (651) 339–6290.* As mentioned, Thrifty Outfitters is the midwest's only authorized repair center for Gore-Tex™ items.

Here's the low down on all the modern "yard goods:"

Cotton

Cotton is a marvelous material for large, semi-permanent tents and for any application that requires breathability and durability. Military tents are still constructed from cotton canvas duck, as are most of the high grade wall tents you see in western hunting camps.

Canvas breathes as it sheds water, which means that tents made of this fabric are wonderfully comfortable (no condensation) in wet weather. Worn canvas is easily restored to "waterproof condition" by painting on chemicals which can be purchased in most hardware stores. Mending the damaged polyurethane coatings on nylon fabrics is at best difficult.

Cotton has a non-skid surface, a nice soft "hand," and it feels good against the skin. It's ideal as a covering for foam sleeping pads and seat and boat cushions, for tent and tool bags, and hats. A cotton-poplin parka is luxurious and will ward off quite a shower if treated with water repellent chemicals. Cotton fabrics retain water-repellents much more willingly than do nylon materials. Note that nylon *stretches* when it gets wet, whereas canvas *shrinks.*

Being a natural fiber, cotton also has considerable flex. Haul a heavy nylon pack across sharp granite and the nylon fibers won't give much. Do the same with a canvas pack and the cotton fibers will stretch and return to shape. The result is that canvas packs often outlive nylon ones, even though they are "technically" less strong. Some of my canvas duluth packs are thirty years old and are still serviceable.

Army duck is the strongest and heaviest (and most expensive!) of the cotton fabrics. It is woven so that each warp yarn passes over (or under) a single filling yarn (similar to those loop pot holders you made as a child). "Duck" is available in weights from 7–15 ounces per square yard. The army prefers 12–15 ounce fabrics for their heavy truck tarps and bivouac tents, but 7–8 ounce weights are better for family campers. Army duck is the king of cotton tent fabrics.

Twill is woven so that each warp yarn passes over two or more filling yarns. It's less strong than duck and is used mostly to make military uniforms. It's tough stuff and it weighs about 8 ounces per square yard.

Drill is a three-leaf twill made from fairly coarse yarns. It's more loosely woven than duck and less expensive. The cheapest canvas tents are often made from drill.

Cotton-poplin is a tightly woven fabric that's produced by using yarns which are heavier and more coarse than the warp yarns. Poplin comes in weights of 4–11 ounces per square yard. Some family-sized wall tents are woven from 5½-ounce fabric.

Egyptian, Pima, and Supima cotton: Egyptian cotton has the longest fibers of all cottons and it makes into the strongest and silkiest yarn. It is by far the most luxurious fabric for the interior shells of sleeping bags; no other material feels better against the skin. "Pima" cotton was developed by U.S. growers to compete with the Egyptian product, and it is nearly as good. "Supima" is the top of the Pima crop. Tightly woven high grade cotton isn't used much in its pure form anymore (it's very expensive). However, it is a marvelous material for sleeping bags, windshells and summer shirts.

Cotton ventile was originally developed by the British to keep downed RAF fliers from freezing in the North Sea. It is so tightly woven that it will repel a shower for twenty minutes or more without the aid of chemical water repellents. Until the advent of Gore-Tex™, all the best parkas in the world were made from ventile. Unfortunately, this fabric is heavy when dry, heavier when wet, very expensive and difficult to find. It is a wonderfully luxurious and long-lived material.

Waxed cotton: Wax or oil is applied to densely woven cotton duck—a method of waterproofing that dates back to the days of iron men and wooden ships. Now, scores of fashionable parkas—notably, Australian "outback" riding garments—are waterproofed by this method. Pluses include a soft, draping "hand" and luxurious texture, good breathability and durability, an attractive natural odor and a techy but traditional look. Waxed cotton garments must be periodically maintained by rubbing in more oil. These garments work well in moderate rains but not in bad storms. They are no match for today's best rain gear. Waxed cotton parkas have become a cult thing among outdoor enthusiasts: They are quite expensive.

Nylon fabrics
Nylon is used for everything from tents to boots. Nylon is strong, light and relatively inexpensive. On the negative side, it degrades badly in ultra-violet light and it stretches considerably when wet. It also shrinks over the years.

Taffeta is a flat woven fabric that weighs between 2.5- and 3.5 ounces per square yard. Taffeta is more prone to tear than rip-stop, but it has greater resistance to abrasion, the reason why most tent flies and floors are made of this material.

Polyurethane-coated nylon taffeta is the fabric of choice for lightweight rain gear, stuff sacks and backpack tarps. Uncoated (porous) taffeta is a popular fabric for garments. Uncoated taffeta has no water repellency. Waterproof coatings last for years, not decades. Best to toss your rain gear at the first sign of a leak then to attempt repairs with the expensive "paint-on" chemicals sold which are available at camping stores.

Rip-stop has a gridwork of heavy threads woven in at quarter-inch intervals to increase fabric strength. It weighs 1.5–2.0 ounces per square yard. Rip-stop is widely used for lightweight tent canopies, sleeping bag shells and wind garments. Coated rip-stop makes a nice lightweight rain tarp.

Vinyl-coated-nylon is a heavyweight plastic-coated nylon used largely for heavy-duty tent floors and tarps. It's much stronger and more resistant to abrasion than coated taffeta but its vinyl coating may soften or peel if it is exposed to heavy doses of harsh solvents, such as those used in some insecticides.

Cordura is the toughest nylon of all. It resists abrasion and puncture far better than any other fabric of equal weight. Many of the best backpacks are made from it and it's widely used in the manufacturing of lightweight hiking boots. However, heavy-weight cordura does not accept waterproofing compounds very well. Invariably, tiny pinholes (which you can see when the fabric is held to a strong light) of untreated material remain which will admit some water.

Packcloth is a medium-weight nylon weave with a heavy polyurethane coating. Packcloth is lighter, less abrasion-resistant, and more waterproof than cordura. It also costs less than cordura.

Coated oxford cloth[1] (which weighs about 6 ounces per square yard) is a strong, absolutely watertight fabric used in the manufacture of lightweight backpacks. This is the same stuff that Eureka! uses for flooring in their outfitter Timberline tents. It is the best material I've found for making fabric splash covers for canoes.

Taslan nylon: Nylon yarn is textured with jets of air to make it feel soft and cottony. Taslan nylon fabrics are lightweight, durable and very resistant to abrasion. Taslan nylon is much less "slippery" than regular nylon.

Ballistics cloth is a 1050+ denier nylon. The yarn was originally developed as a tire cord then later refined into cloth for military flak vests. Ballistics cloth is exceptionally strong and abrasion-resistant. It is less flexible than Cordura or cotton-canvas. Like all synthetic fibers, ballistics cloth must be coated with polyurethane to make it waterproof.

Polyethylene and polypropylene

Polyethylene-coated-polyethylene is a tough polyethylene fabric with a polyethylene plastic coating on both sides. The material is mildew-proof and is commonly used for heavy-duty tent floors and tarps. Both vinyl-coated nylon and polyethylene-coated polyethylene are much more dimensionally stable (less wet-stretch/dry-shrinkage) than polyurethane-coated nylon.

Propex (Condessa™) is a woven polypropylene that is designed for use in luggage. It resists solvents, stains, molds, abrasion and tears. The (coated) material weighs about 12 ounces per square yard and looks and feels almost

---

All these nylon fabrics can be had with or without waterproof casings. Weight and cost of the fabrics will vary depending upon type and amount of coating applied.

exactly like 18-ounce canvas. Tough stuff . . . and very beautiful. *CLG Enterprises, 3838 Dight Avenue, South, Minneapolis, MN 55406, (800) 328–5215,* makes beautiful packs from this material.

Blends

Sixty/forty cloth (60 percent cotton/40 percent nylon) is woven with nylon threads in one direction and cotton in the other. The nylon supplies strength, the cotton provides water repellency and a luxurious feel. A lot of great mountain parkas are built from 60/40 cloth.

Sixty-five/thirty-five cloth: Cotton and polyester yarns are blended together then woven into the garment. Threads of each yarn run in both directions. This fabric is supposed to be more water-repellent and have greater strength than 60/40 cloth.

There are also a number of exotic blends which feature cotton, polyester and nylon in varying weaves and amounts. Generally, the higher the nylon content, the stronger, lighter and less water-repellent the garment. More cotton and polyester mean a softer "hand," higher water repellency and heavier weight. In practice, the differences between these similar fabrics are relatively insignificant.

Here are some other common fabric terms you may encounter:

Acrylic: The generic name for fibers which are made from polyacrylonitrile. Acrylics are soft, washable, non-allergenic and they dry very quickly. In the days before fleece, acrylics were *the* substitute for wool. They are still a good choice for growing kids and those on a budget.

Olefin (polypropylene): A paraffin-based fiber that doesn't absorb water. See the discussion of polypropylene long underwear on page 51.

Spandex (Dupont calls it "Lycra") is very stretchy but has a good memory for shape. It's always used in combination with other fibers like cotton or nylon.

Tri-blend: Three different fibers woven together—like cotton/nylon/polyester. Each fiber contributes something special to the blend.

Tricot: A strong "double-thread" weave that doesn't easily tear or fray.

Appendix A

Glossary of common camping terms

agonic line: a line of zero compass declination, along which the compass needle points to both true and magnetic north.

A-frame tent: an inverted V-shaped tent with one or two poles at each end.

anorak: a shell parka that goes on over the head. Anoraks have chest-length zipper or snaps. They conserve heat better than a full-zip parka.

Arkansas stone: a medium-hard mineral stone used for putting a fine edge on knives.

azimuth: commonly used to indicate a directional bearing in degrees or mils. Technically, *azimuth* relates direction to one (or a fraction of one) of the 360 degrees of the compass rose. A *bearing* (often used synonymously with azimuth) relates direction to the north or south cardinal point. Example: an azimuth of 330 degrees equals a bearing of N 30 degrees W. An azimuth of 160 degrees equals a bearing of S 20 degrees E, etc.

baffle: fabric panels sewn to the inner and outer shell of a sleeping bag. Baffles keep the insulation in place. Down bags must be baffled. Most synthetic bags feature quilted insulation.

bannock: the traditional trail bread. Usually made in a skillet by a combination of frying and reflective baking.

bathtub floor: a tent floor which wraps 6 inches or more up side-walls of the tent before it is sewn in. This construction eliminates perimeter seams at ground level which can leak.

Bean boots: slang for *Maine hunting shoe.* The leather-top/rubber-bottom boots invented by Leon Bean.

bearing: a compass direction (see *azimuth*).

billy can: a straight-sided cooking pot with a wire bail.

bivouac: technically, a temporary encampment. Modern usage connotes an emergency or bush camp made where no other camp has stood.

blousing bands: elastic bands used by the military to secure pant leg bottoms around boots. Blousing bands are useful for sealing trouser legs against mosquitoes and black flies.

breathable: refers to the porosity of fabrics. Breathable materials are not waterproof.

bug jacket: a fabric mesh jacket impregnated with insect repellent.

cagoule: a waterproof, ankle-length, over-the-head parka used by mountaineers for bivouacking. Cagoules have tailored hoods and drawstring hems. The wearer pulls his legs inside, draws the hem tight, and "outlasts" the elements.

canopy: the (usually porous) roof of a tent. Not to be confused with the waterproof tent fly.

cap fly: three-quarter length tent fly. Tents with cap flies are not as weather-proof as those with full-length flies.

catenary cut: the natural curve formed by a rope tightly strung between two trees. A tent which has a catenary cut rigs tighter (less side-wall sag) than one without catenary cut. Catenary cut is a feature of the best tents.

chute cord: slang for parachute cord.

contour lines: thin brown lines on maps connecting points of equal elevation.

cord lock: spring-loaded nylon clamp used to secure the drawstring closures of stuff sacks.

crash out: to bushwhack out of a forested area to a trail, road, or meadow.

cruiser compass: a needle compass which has the numbers on the dial reversed (running counterclockwise rather than clockwise) to permit reading bearings in the same plane as the observer's eye. Cruiser compasses are still used by some professionals, but there are better choices for campers. The outdated design of these instruments originated in the nineteenth century.

Cryptosporidium: a protozoan you won't want in your drinking water! Causes symptoms similar to Giardiasis. Cryptosporidium cysts may be killed by boiling or removed by filtering. They resist most chemicals. The parasite made headlines in 1993 when 400,000 people in Milwaukee, Wisconsin, got cryptosporidiosis, and thirty died from drinking city water.

declination: the difference between true or geographic north and magnetic north. Declination (also called *variation* by mariners) is expressed in degrees east or west of the agonic line.

DEET: slang for diethyl-meta-toluamide, the active ingredient in most insect repellents.

diamond stone: a type of man-made sharpening stone which contains powdered diamonds. Diamond stones are lubricated with water (not cutting oil). They remove metal much faster than traditional oil stones.

differential cut: the inner shell of a sleeping bag is cut smaller than the outer shell to produce a Thermos-bottle effect. The merits of this construction are still being argued by equipment freaks.

dining fly: an overhead tarp (fly) used for protection from rain. Usually erected just before meals, hence the descriptive name.

double-wall tent: a tent with a double-layered wall. All modern nylon tents are built this way, featuring a breathable taffeta canopy (inner wall) and a watertight rip-stop fly (outer wall). Double-wall canvas tents are sometimes used in winter (with a sheepherder stove) to conserve heat.

draft tube: a down-filled tube that runs the length of a sleeping bag zipper—prevents cold air from filtering through the zipper teeth.

dropped-point knife: the favored style for hunting knives. The point is centered (similar to a spear-point) on the blade. Dropped-point knives are ideal for skinning game animals but are not the most suitable style for camp knives.

Duluth pack: a voluminous envelope-style pack (usually, canvas), popular with canoeists.

Dutch oven: a unique oven consisting of a heavy-walled pot and cover with a large retaining rim. Coals from the fire are placed on top of the pot lid and the affair is set into the hot ashes. Heat from the top does most of the baking.

EVA (ethyl-vinyl-acetate): strongest, most resilient, and most expensive of the closed-cell foams. *EVA* makes an excellent trail mattress.

fanny pack: small, zippered nylon pack that's attached to a waist belt.

ferrule: the metal sleeve attached to fiberglass tent poles. *Ferrules* form a joint between pole sections.

filling power (of down): same as *loft.* It's the thickness of a sleeping bag lying flat and fluffed. Generally speaking, the greater the loft of a sleeping bag, the warmer it will be.

fisherman's shirt: Same as a *cagoule,* only calf-length and without a drawstring hem.

flat-fell seam: overlapping construction. The seam goes through four layers of material.

floating dial compass: the compass needle is part of the numbered compass dial, which rotates as a unit. This allows the instrument to be read in the same plane as the eye of the user. Some styles are very accurate.

foam pad: a sleeping mattress made of either open- or closed-cell foam.

frame pack: a pack with an exterior aluminum or fiber framework.

frost liner: a detachable inner roof for a tent. Absorbs moisture which could otherwise condense, freeze, and drop on sleeping occupants. Frost liners are made from cotton or cotton/polyester fabric and are needed only in below-freezing conditions.

fuel bottle: traditionally refers to Sigg aluminum bottles, which are used for the storage of gasoline and kerosene.

gators: nylon anklets (usually with side zippers) used by skiers and mountaineers. Gators prevent snow from getting in your boot tops, and they add extra warmth.

Giardia: the causative pathogen of Giardiasis.

giardiasis: a waterborne disease carried by the protozoan Giardia. Giardia is commonly carried by beaver. Incubation time is one to two weeks. The pathogen is very hard.

geodesic dome: a dome-shaped tent with a strong faceted framework of tubular aluminum. Geodesic domes are the Cadillac of domes!

GPS: An electronic unit that receives positioning information from twenty-four orbiting satellites. With a civilian model GPS, you can locate your position anywhere on earth in a matter of minutes. Accuracy is 100 meters or less! Most units run on small batteries.

hip belt: a padded waist belt that secures to a backpack—makes carrying the pack much more comfortable.

hollow-ground (knife): the edge is ground to a concave bevel which produces a thin, razor-sharp edge and a stiff spine.

hood closure: the tie cord and fastener which secures the hood of a sleeping bag around the sleeper's face.

hypothermia: a potentially lethal physical state caused by lowering of the body's core temperature, due to exposure to cold, wet weather. Also called *exposure sickness.*

internal frame pack: a hiking pack with internal stays. The stays give the pack shape and make it more comfortable to carry than a traditional soft pack.

I-pole tent: a tent with a single vertical pole at each end.

Jello-mold oven: an oven made from a large ring aluminum Jello mold.

kindling: pencil-thin pieces of wood used to nurture a fire to a reliable blaze.

layering: wearing several thin layers of clothes, one over the other. Layering is the most efficient clothing system for cold weather.

lensatic compass: a compass which features a built-in magnifying lens for ease of reading directions. The old army lensatic compass (no longer used) is the best example of this type of instrument. Lensatic compasses are impractical for camping (they don't have built-in protractors), slow to use, and no more accurate than modern orienteering instruments.

lock-back knife: a folding knife that has an integral lock which secures the blade when open. Some modern lockbacks are really side-locks or front-locks. Lock-back knives do not have pressure springs like ordinary jack knives, so they can be opened easily with one handle while wearing mittens.

loft: thickness of a sleeping bag while laying flat and fluffed. Generally speaking, the higher the loft, the warmer the bag.

map index: a specially gridded small-scale map which lists *maps in print,* how and where to get them, and their cost.

millar mitts: fingerless gloves used by mountaineers for technical climbing. Millar mitts are great for fishing, canoeing and general hiking.

mocha: a popular camp drink of hot chocolate and coffee.

Moleskin: brand name of soft-surfaced bandaging material used to protect blisters. The sticky side of Moleskin is placed over the unbroken blister; the cushioned surface absorbs the friction from socks and boots.

mountain parka: a generic name for full-zipper, thigh-length parkas. Mountain parkas usually have lots of pockets. They're traditionally constructed from 60/40 (60 percent nylon, 40 percent cotton) cloth, which is doubled for added warmth. The U.S. Army field jacket is a true mountain parka.

Orienteering: an international sport which combines the skills of map and compass reading with cross-country running.

Orienteering compass: a compass with a built-in protractor which allows you to determine directions from a map without orienting the map to north. This is the most practical compass style for outdoor use.

overlapping V-tube construction (sleeping bags): a type of baffle construction in which down is secured into V-shaped tubes which overlap one another. Some very warm winter sleeping bags are built this way.

pack basket: a basket pack traditionally woven from splints of black ash. This original Indian-made item is still going strong in the New England area and is available from L.L. Bean. Pack baskets are ideal for berry picking, picnicking, canoe trips, and auto camping. They will protect all your breakables. Compared to fabric packs, they are quite inexpensive.

parka: a thigh-length shell garment with integral hood. Parkas may be lined or filled with down, polyester or other insulation for use in cold weather.

Pelican case: hard plastic, absolutely waterproof case that comes in many shapes and sizes—the Cadillac of waterproof cases.

pile: a luxuriously soft fabric made from polyester. Pile absorbs little water and it dries quickly. Pile has almost replaced wool as the material for cold weather camping.

Polarguard: a synthetic polyester material widely used in sleeping bags and parkas. Polarguard is considered one of the best synthetic insulators.

poly-bottle: short for polyethylene bottle.

poncho: a rectangular, hooded rain garment. Ponchos provide good ventilation and can be worn over a hiking pack. They do not supply reliable protection from rain.

prime: (as in *priming* a gasoline or kerosene stove.) Stoves are usually primed by filling an integral spirit cup with gasoline or alcohol, then setting the fuel aflame. Stoves can be over-primed. If too much gasoline is forced into the spirit cup, the unit may ignite into a ball of uncontrollable flames.

prismatic compass: a compass with a built-in sighting prism. Prismatic compasses are a step up from lensatic types. They're expensive but not very versatile.

Quallofil: a synthetic material developed by Dupont for use in sleeping bags and parkas. Each filament has four longitudinal holes which trap air and add warmth. Quallofil is one of the best synthetic insulators.

quilt construction: a type of sleeping bag construction in which the insulation is sewn (quilt-like) in place. This is an inexpensive way to make a summer weight sleeping bag. This construction is suitable for winter use if the bag is double-quilted.

quick-release knot: a knot which can be removed by a simple pull of the tail. The most common quick-release knot is the *bow* used for tying your shoes.

reflector oven: an aluminum sheet-metal oven which bakes by means of reflected heat. Reflector ovens are hard to keep clean and they are very cumbersome. They require an open flame for baking and cannot be used on stoves or over charcoal. They are very efficient if you have a nice bright fire.

ridge vent: the triangular window at the ridge of A-frame tents.

rip-stop nylon: a lightweight nylon fabric that has heavier threads sewn in at approximate ¼-inch intervals. Rip-stop is less likely to tear than taffeta but it has less resistance to abrasion.

seam-sealer: a special glue, available at all camping shops, used to waterproof the stitching on tents and rain gear.

Sixty/forty parka: a parka made from fabric which consists of 60 percent nylon and 40 percent cotton. The term 60/40 is now generic; it defines any mountain-style parka, regardless of the fabric composition. See *mountain parka.*

shell (garments): refers to unlined garments, or the interior or exterior wall of a sleeping bag.

self-supporting tent: theoretically, a tent which needs no staking. However, all self-supporting tents must be staked or they'll blow away in the wind.

semi-mummy bag: a sleeping bag with a barrel-shape and no hood. A good choice for those who feel confined by the mummy shape but want lighter weight and more warmth than that supplied by standard rectangular sleeping bags.

sewn-through construction: same as quilt construction.

side-wall baffle: a baffle that is opposite the zipper on a sleeping bag; it keeps the down from shifting along the length of the bag.

siwash: a turn-of-the-century term that means to live off the land with a bare minimum of essentials. Modern campers do not *siwash!*

snow-flaps: ear-like flaps which are sewn to the perimeter of a tent floor. Snow-flaps are folded outward then piled with snow eliminating the need for staking the tent. Snow-flaps are an extra-cost feature of special purpose winter tents.

sou'wester: the traditional rain hat of sailors and commercial fishermen. The sou'wester was developed centuries ago and it is still the best of all foul weather hats. The best sou'westers have ear flaps, chin strap, and a flannel lining.

space-filler cut: where the inner and outer shells of a sleeping bag are cut the same size. This construction allows the inner liner and fill to better conform to the curves of your body than the Thermos-bottle shape of the differential cut. The merits/demerits of space-filler versus differential cut are still being argued by sleeping bag manufacturers.

space blanket: a mylar-coated "blanket" used in survival kits. Space-blankets are waterproof and are very warm for their size and weight. Every camping shop has them.

spreader bar: same as a *wand.* Used for spreading out a portion of a tent.

sternum strap: a short nylon strap which connects the shoulder straps of a hiking pack. A properly adjusted sternum strap transfers some of the pack load to the chest.

storm flap: a panel of material which backs the zipper of a parka and prevents the storm from getting in.

stuff sack: traditionally a nylon sack in which a sleeping bag is stored. The term now defines any nylon bag with drawstring closure.

Swiss Army knife: originally the issue knife of the Swiss Army. Now, generic for any scout-style multi-tool pocket knife.

Svea: brand name of the venerable Svea stove.

tinder: ultra-fine dry material used for starting a fire.

Tingleys: Tingley® brand rubber boots slip on over street shoes. They grip like iron, even on wet rocks, wear like steel, weigh almost nothing and are very inexpensive. Most construction supply stores have them.

topo map: a "topographic" map which shows the lay of the land by means of contour lines.

toque: a jaunty wool stocking cap traditionally worn by the Voyageurs.

trenching (also called "ditching"): digging a trench around a tent to carry away ground water which accumulates during a heavy rain. This form of guttering is illegal in all wilderness areas. Ground cloths and tent floors have eliminated the need to trench tents.

tumpline: a head strap used to carry heavy loads. Voyageurs carried hundreds of pounds of furs with only a tumpline. Today this feature is found only on traditional canvas duluth packs which are used for wilderness canoeing.

twist-on-a-stick: baking powder bread made by twisting dough on a stick and baking it over the fire.

UTM (Universal Transverse Mercator): a metric coordinate map grid that is universally used by the U.S. and Canadian military. UTM grid lines are always 1 km (0.62 miles) apart. UTM coordinates are easier to use than latitude/longitude grids because their "easting" and "northing" values are decimal based.

vestibule: an alcove or extension which secures to one or both ends of a tent. Vestibules provide a place to store gear out of the weather.

Wachita stone: a medium-hard mineral oil stone used for sharpening knives.

Wellies: short for "Green Wellies"—the traditional knee-high (green) British rubber boot used by gardeners, hunters and just about everyone else—a cult boot.

wind shirt: differs from a wind parka in that the shirt is cut to waist length and does not have a hood. Wind pants are made of breathable fabric and are popular for winter camping.

white-print map: a provisional map that's similar to a blueprint. White-prints are up-to-date maps which show the location of logging and mining roads and man-made structures. These maps are designed for professional use; they are not listed in standard map indexes.

Appendix B

Sources of recommended products

A.G. Russell Fine Knives
1705 North Thompson Street
Springdale, AK 72764-1294s
(800) 255–9034, fax (501) 751–4520
http://agrussell.com

Complete catalog of knives, including the recommended
Russell *Deer Hunter* and *Bird & Trout* knives.

Cabela's, Inc.
812-13th Avenue
Sidney, NE 69160
(800) 237–4444

Huge assortment of outdoor gear, including wonderful
Thermax®/Thermastat® long underwear.

Caldwell Enterprises
1335 West 11th
Port Angeles, WA 98363
(360) 457–3009

Source of *Counter Assault*®—a potent form of bear mace.

CAMPMOR, Inc.
P.O. Box 999
Paramus, NJ 07653-0999
(800) 226–7667

Complete mail order source of camping gear.

Cascade Designs, Inc.
4000 First Avenue South
Seattle, WA 98134
(800) 531–9531

Reliable waterproof bags and the original "Therm-a-Rest"
foam sleeping pad.

CLG Enterprises/Superior Packs
3838 Dight Avenue South
Minneapolis, MN 55406
(800) 328–5215, fax: (651) 721–1835

Superior packs and rodeo accessories.

Cooke Custom Sewing
7290 Stagecoach Trail
Lino Lakes, MN 55014-1988
(651) 784–8777

Superb packs for canoeing, winter mukluks, "Cliff 'n Dan tundra tarp" and "Susie bug-net."

Duluth Tent & Awning Co.
1610 W. Superior Street
Duluth, MN 55816-0024
(800) 777–4439
Fax: 218–722–9575

Superior canvas packs and luggage. Home of the original duluth pack.

Effercept Products
P.O. Box 1248
Laramie, WY 82070
(800) 841–0410

Effersan® dry chlorine tablets. Great for sterilizing camp dishes.

Empire Canvas Works
P.O. Box 17
Solon Springs, WI 54873
(715) 378–4216

Expedition-quality canvas products—tents, winter mittens, wind parkas and more. They make the best canoe portage pads around.

Grohmann Knives, Ltd.
P.O. Box 40
Pictou, Nova Scotia, Canada BOK 1HO
(902) 485–4224

Outstanding fixed blade "working knives." Specify *carbon steel* blades.

Idaho Knife Works and Crafts
P.O. Box 144
Spirit Lake, ID 83869
(509) 994–9394, Cellular (509) 994–1633

Wonderful *carbon steel* fixed blade knives. Offers the Cliff knife, which I designed.

Joel York & Associates
15 West Main Street
Yarmouth, ME 04096
(800) 348–4923

Toughest, most waterproof wanigan around.

L.L. Bean, Inc.
Freeport, ME 04033
(800) 221–4221

Is there anyone who hasn't heard of L.L. Bean?

Nationwide Marketing, Inc.
1550 Bryant Street, Suite 850
San Francisco, CA 94103
(800) 777–5452

Distributes the excellent FOODSAVER, vacuum-sealing machine.

N/R Laboratories, Inc.
900 E. Franklin Street
Centerville, OH 45459
(800) 223–9348, fax (513) 433–0779

No rinse body bath and shampoo.

Sawyer Products, Inc.
P.O. Box 7036
Long Beach, CA 90807
(213) 423–0405
Superior insect repellents, high lather camp soap, the "Extractor" and "tick pliers."

Steger Mukluks
125 North Central
Ely, MN 55731
(800) MUKLUKS
Wonderfully warm and comfortable winter and summer mukluks, made in traditional Native American styles.

Stormy Bay Wanigan (formerly, E.M. Wanigan)
P.O. Box 345
Grand Rapids, MN 55744
(218) 326-5105
Well designed, practical plastic wanigan box.

TENTSMITHS
Box 496
North Conway, NH 03860
(603) 447–2344, fax (603) 447–1777
Old-time tents made from genuine canvas.

Thrifty Outfitters
A Division of Midwest Mountaineering, Inc.
309 Cedar Avenue South
Minneapolis, MN 55454
(800) 866–3162, fax (651) 339–7249
All sorts of fabrics and repair materials. The midwest's only authorized Gore-Tex® repair center.

303 PRODUCTS, Inc.
P.O. Box 966
Palo Cedro, CA 96073-0966
Superior ultraviolet protection in a can.

Index

A

a-frame tents, 185
air cast, 85–86
air mattresses, 144–46
Anakit, 86
anchor, 1
animals, 1–7
    protecting food from, 1–3
axe, 8–14
    sharpening, 9–10
    splitting logs and kindling
      with, 8–9, 14

B

baker tent, making, 202, 204
baking, 15–17
    Jello mold oven, 15–16
    triple pan method of, 16–17
bannock, 17–19
    easy scratch, 18
    serious sourdough, 18–19
batteries, 92–93
bears, 3–7
    "bear mace," 6–7
    black, 3–4
    grizzly, 4
    polar, 5–6
    protecting food from, 1–3
bee stings, treatment, 89
binoculars, 19–20
blisters, treatment, 89
boots, 20–26
    breaking in, 21–22
    care of, 22–23
    improving warmth of, 23
    selecting, 20–21
    winter, 23–24
bottles, 26–28

bowline knot, 108
bugs, 28–34
    effect of colors on, 28
    repellents, 31
burns, treatment, 89

C

camera, waterproof protection
    for, 34–35
camp lighting devices, 92–94
    types, 93
canteens, 35–37
car-top carriers (canoe racks),
    37–40
    tie–down procedures, 39
canoe and boat rigging, tips
    for, 40–46
    canoe pockets, 41
    making a belly cover, 43–45
children, camping with, 46–49
    clothing, 47
    rain gear, 46–47
    sleeping gear, 47–48
clothing, 49–52
    care and cleaning, 50–52
    fit, 49
compass, 52–54
adjusting for declination,
    52–53
    using a watch as, 54
contact cement, 54
contour lines, 118–19
cooking, 54–68
    cold weather tips, 67–68
    cookware, 54–58
    food ideas, 58–66
    See also baking.
cord, 69–70

cord locks, 69–70
  See also rope.
cozies, 70–72
  suggested fabrics for, 72

D
DEET, 31–33, 115
dental floss, 72
diapers and diaper pins, 72–73
dislocation, shoulder, 91
dome tents, 182–84
duct tape, 73

E
ethics, wilderness, 73–76
  bathing, 75
  color of equipment, 76
  education, 76
  fires/fire sites, 76
  graffiti, 75
  noise, 75
  waste disposal, 74
eye injuries, treatment, 89

F
fabric, 219–23
  for cozies, 72
  for rain gear, 127–28
  for tents, 185
fire, 77–83
  banking to preserve fuel,
  82–83
  emergency kits, 81
  extinguishing, 83
  procedures for making,
  77–83
  tools, 77
first aid, 83–92
  building a simple kit, 84–85
  injuries and ailments,
  87–92
  other equipment, 85–87

flashlights, 92–94
  bulbs and batteries, 92–93
flies, 29
food ideas, 58–66
footwraps, 24–26
foresters' tent, making, 202,
203
frostbite, treatment, 89

G
gauze, 86
GPS (Global Positioning System), 94–95

H
half hitch knot, 106
hand cream, 95–96
honey
  as medicine, 96
hypothermia, 96–97
  symptoms, 96–97
  treatment, 97

I
insects
  See bugs.

K
kindling, how to cut, 9
knives, 98–105
  carrying, 103–04
  making a sheath for, 104–05
  selecting, 98–102
  sharpening, 102–03
knots and hitches, 105–09
  bowline, 108
  half hitch, 106
  lashings, 109–10
  power cinch, 106–08
  sheet bend, 108

L

lightning, 111–13
    treatment for strike by, 113
lip balm, 95–96
Lyme disease, 113–15
    symptoms, 114
    prevention, 114–15

M

maps, 115–21
    charts and tide tables, 116
    ordering United States, 116
    reading, 118–19
    using to determine drop of
    river, 120–21
    waterproofing, 120
miners' tent, making, 204–05
moisturizers
    See hand cream.
monofilament fishing line, 122
mosquitoes, 28–29

N

Nalgene™ bottle trick, 122
netted bags, 122–23
no-see-ums, 29–30

O

one person trench shelter,
    152–54

P

packs, 123–26
    care of, 123
    packing methods, 124–26
    waterproofing, 125
pillow, 126–27
plastic food tubes, 28
power cinch knot, 106–08

Q

quin-zee hut, 148–52

building a, 150–51
sleeping inside a, 152

R

rain gear, 127–31
    care and repair of, 131
    fabrics for, 127–28
    features of, 129
    fit of, 129
    for children, 46–47
    what to wear beneath, 131
repairs
    tools needed for, 217–19
rigs, 171–79
    special purpose, 176–79
ropes, 131–136
    choosing, 131–32
    rope tricks, 134–36
    types of, 132–33

S

saw (folding), 137
sheet bend knot, 108
shovel, 137
shower, 137–38
single lean-to, 171–74
skis (cross-country), 138
sleeping bags, 138–44
    cleaning, 141–43
    principles of design, 138–39
    selecting, 139–41
sleeping pads, 144–46
sleeping systems, 144–46
snow glasses, 146–47
snowshoes, 147
    bindings, 147
snow shelters, 147–54
    one person trench shelter,
    152–54
    quin-zee hut, 148–52
    vaulted roof snow trench,
    154

sleeping on snow, 155
soaps, 156
sponge, 156–57
sprains, 91
stool (camp), 157
stoves, 157–61
  maintenance, 160–61
  priming, 158–59
  troubleshooting, 157–58
stuff sacks, 161
survival kit
  suggested contents of,
164–66
survival shelters, 161–164

T
tablecloth, 166–67
tarps (rain flies), 167–79
  materials of, 167
  pitching the fly, 170–71
  rigs, 171–79
teepees, 184
tents, 179–98, 200–206
  care and cleaning, 189–91
  design principles of, 181–85
  fabrics for, 185
  features, 187
  making, 200–206
  poles and stakes, 186–87
  selection, 187–89
  storm proofing, 191–92
tent site, 199–200
ticks, 30–31
  See also Lyme disease.
tools
  for fire making, 77
  for repairs, 217–19
towels, 206–07
  diapers as, 72, 207
tundra tarp, 176–79
  canoe prop method, 178
  "Cliff 'n Dan," 176

  quick rig, 177
  single walled sun teepee,
  178–79
tunnels, 184–85
twin flies with fire slit, 175–76
U
ultraviolet protection, 207
umbrella tents, 185

V
vaulted roof snow trench, 154

W
wanigans, 208–09
waterproofing
  cameras, 34–35
  maps, 120
  packs, 125
  tents, 190–91, 197–98
water
  treatment 209–12
  where not to get, 212–14
weather forecasting, 214–17
wedge tent, making, 201
whelen lean-to, making,
205–06

X
xylocaine, 85, 87–88

Y
yard goods, 219–23
  blends, 223
  cotton, 219–21
  nylon, 221–22
  polyethylene, 222–23